RAINBOW DREAMS

35 Years of Empowering Children with Autism
and Other Developmental Challenges

RAINBOW DREAMS

35 Years of Empowering Children with Autism
and Other Developmental Challenges

Editors

Kenneth Poon
National Technological University, Singapore

Sze Wee Tan
Rainbow Centre, Singapore

Faridah Ali Chang
Rainbow Centre, Singapore

Manoj Pathnapuram
Rainbow Centre, Singapore

Kenneth Lyen
Founder of the Rainbow Centre, Singapore

World Scientific

NEW JERSEY · LONDON · SINGAPORE · BEIJING · SHANGHAI · HONG KONG · TAIPEI · CHENNAI · TOKYO

Published by

World Scientific Publishing Co. Pte. Ltd.

5 Toh Tuck Link, Singapore 596224

USA office: 27 Warren Street, Suite 401-402, Hackensack, NJ 07601

UK office: 57 Shelton Street, Covent Garden, London WC2H 9HE

British Library Cataloguing-in-Publication Data
A catalogue record for this book is available from the British Library.

RAINBOW DREAMS
35 Years of Empowering Children with Autism and Other Developmental Challenges

ISBN 978-981-126-487-0 (hardcover)
ISBN 978-981-126-588-4 (paperback)
ISBN 978-981-126-488-7 (ebook for institutions)
ISBN 978-981-126-489-4 (ebook for individuals)

For any available supplementary material, please visit
https://www.worldscientific.com/worldscibooks/10.1142/13101#t=suppl

Typeset by Stallion Press
Email: enquiries@stallionpress.com

Foreword by President Halimah Yacob for Rainbow Dreams

The inclusion of children with autism and developmental disabilities in our community requires a person-centred approach that involves putting the child first. With quality and timely intervention and strong support from others, we can enable them to maximise their fullest potential at each stage of their life.

Rainbow Dreams brings together insights and perspectives from medical professionals, allied professionals, social service professionals, and educators associated with Rainbow Centre. It was developed as a resource to avail information about care for the children, focussing on a person-centred, multi-disciplinary, and quality-of-life approach. This has been the core of Rainbow Centre's work.

This publication is a special one as it coincides with Rainbow Centre's 35th anniversary since its inception in 1987 as Singapore's first school to educate children with multiple disabilities. It also established Singapore's first programme for children with autism in 1989. Today, it has taken the leap through bold community-based services for young persons with disabilities.

I congratulate the management and staff for their dedication, work, and effort to distil their community's practice into this publication, ensuring its relevance to evolving needs on the ground. Their efforts must be supported by a whole-of-society endeavour to build bridges for the children and youth to participate in communities which are authentic, supportive, and inclusive, so that they can have a good quality of life.

On behalf of the children, youth, and caregivers who have benefitted from Rainbow Centre's care and education, I thank Rainbow Centre for its service.

Halimah Yacob
President of the Republic of Singapore

Preface

This book celebrates Rainbow Centre which was established to care for children with disabilities 35 years ago.

In *Rainbow Dreams*, we address issues that are relevant and useful to parents, caregivers, and professionals alike.

The first section introduces the reader to the history of special education in Singapore. The next section looks at how developmentally challenged individuals are supported across the lifespan. Following that we follow how the medical professionals approach these children. We look at how children with developmental disabilities are supported in school, home, and in the community. Detailed and practical steps on helping children and adults through the removal of barriers, working together in teams, and forging strong partnerships are shared. The book concludes by looking at the future and how society can integrate and include challenged individuals into society.

The book is written for parents, teachers, therapists, social workers, caregivers, psychologists, developmentalists, general practitioners, medical students, and everyone interested in the care of children on the autism spectrum and other developmental challenges. Resources for further study are also given at the end of each chapter.

We are grateful to President Halimah Yacob for writing the Foreword. We also appreciate the contributions from all our authors who have shared their extensive personal experiences and knowledge in the care of children with special needs. We believe that this book provides an invaluable source of information to help everyone involved in the management of developmentally challenged children.

Established in 1987, Rainbow Centre is a registered charity and Institution of a Public Character. Rainbow Centre envisions a world where persons with disabilities are empowered and thriving in inclusive communities. We work with their partners to create opportunities for persons with disabilities to make the most of their abilities and participate meaningfully in society. Through practical education, meaningful support and effective training programmes, they strive to increase the quality of life for them and their families.

All proceeds from the sale of this book will support Rainbow Centre's work.

Kenneth Poon
Manoj Pathnapuram
Tan Sze Wee
Faridah Ali Chang
Kenneth Lyen

Editors
Authors

List of Editors

Name of Editor	Description
Kenneth **Poon** *MClinPsy, Ph.D.* 	Kenneth is Professor at the Psychology and Child & Human Development Academic Group at the National Institute of Education, Nanyang Technological University. He also serves as Associate Dean, Education Research, as well as Co-Director of the Centre for Research in Child Development. Trained as a clinical psychologist and as an early interventionist, he is an active researcher aiming to engage in research on the development of and what can be done to improve the lives of persons with neurodevelopmental disabilities. Kenneth currently serves on the Boards of Rainbow Centre, the National Council of Social Service, Catholic Family Life, and the International Association for the Scientific Study of Intellectual and Developmental Disability. He has previously served the community as a member of the technical review committee for the Academy of Medicine Singapore-Ministry of Health Clinical Practice Guidelines for Young Children with Autism Spectrum Disorders and the steering committee of the Enabling Masterplan 2012–2016.

Tan Sze Wee
BA (Social Work &
Psychology, NUS),
Postgrad Certificate
(Monash University),
Executive Certificate
(Lee Kuan Yew School
of Public Policy)

Sze Wee is the Executive Director of Rainbow Centre. Sze Wee has over 24 years of experience in the social service sector and started her career as a social worker in community mental health care and disability. Having worked in direct practice, managed programmes and now leading an organisation, Sze Wee believes that social workers can effect immense change at different levels – for a client, a community, an organization and even a nation. Whether supporting clients or colleagues, She believes that change happens when people can draw on their own strengths and realize their potential to live fulfilling lives. Sze Wee is interested in innovative models of service and management. She currently serves as President of the Singapore Association of Social Workers and has been serving on the YMCA FACES Committee since 2008.

Manoj **Pathnapuram**
M.Sc (Speech &
Hearing)

Manoj has more than 25 years of clinical, training and management experience in the fields of Disability, Early Intervention and Special Education. He is the Director of Accessibility Services in Rainbow Centre where he oversees the Allied Health and Employability Services. Manoj also has a Masters in Speech Language Pathology & Audiology and extensive post-graduate clinical specialization certifications. In addition to clinical areas, Manoj is passionate about teaching and developing people.

Faridah Ali Chang
M.A (Research)
Registered
Psychologist (S'pore)

Faridah is the Principal Psychologist with Rainbow Centre's Family Empowerment Programme (FEP) supporting caregivers who face challenges with their children & youths with disability. Her experience at Rainbow Centre and in the area of disability spans more than 28 years. She is also the Principal Trainer & Consultant with Rainbow Centre Training & Consultancy (RCTC). Faridah actively seeks the opportunity to mentor psychologists and other allied health professionals. She believes that professionals should strengthen their clinical competency and continue to grow into a more compassionate practitioner in their work with persons with disabilities and their families. Faridah focused her graduate research on the *Quality of Life of Adults with Multiple Disabilities and their Parents*.

Kenneth Lyen
*MA (Oxon), BM BCh
(Oxon), FRCP
(Glasgow),
FRCPCH (UK), DCH
(London), FAMS
(Singapore), PBM
(Singapore), Consultant Paediatrician*

Dr Kenneth Lyen is a graduate of Oxford University Medical School. He did his specialty training at the Hospital for Sick Children at Great Ormond Street Lonon, and he carried out research at the Children's Hospital of Philadelphia. His special interests are in endocrinology and neuropsychology. He started the Developmental Assessment Clinic at the Singapore General Hospital in 1984 and managed the clinic for disabled children at the National University Hospital (1983–1989). He was on the editorial board of the Singapore Medical Journal (1998–2003). He has published over 40 papers in endocrinology, neurology, and childhood disabilities, and coauthored 15 books on education, mental health of children, parenting, creativity and musical theatre. In 1986, Dr Lyen was invited by the late Dr Ee Peng Liang to establish the Margaret Drive Special School, which was opened the following year. He was instrumental in starting the first programme in Singapore for autism spectrum disorders. He helped establish the Rainbow Centre in 1992, which now manages three special schools, and he was chairman of the Rainbow Centre from 1992 to 1998. In 2022, Dr Lyen was awarded the National Day Public Service Star (BBM) for his work helping the developmentally challenged and autistic individuals. He was the former chairman of the Medical Commission of the Singapore Red Cross, an advisor to the board of the Rainbow Centre, and President of the Rotary Club of Singapore North in 1999. For leisure he is a music composer and has written and staged over 30 musicals in Singapore, most of them to raise funds for the Rainbow Centre.

List of Authors

Name of Author	Description
Dawn **Chik**	Dawn is a Senior Music Therapist and has a Bachelor of Art in Music Therapy (Keyboard). Dawn has worked with Rainbow Centre since 2015, when she first returned home from her studies. She first heard about using music as a form of therapy when she was fifteen, and she knew then that music therapy was what she wanted to further her studies in. Dawn enjoys listening to music and you can hear her humming when she is around. In her other role as mum, Dawn is often making up silly lyrics and singing to her two young children about what's going on around them.
Belinda **Chua**	Belinda is Head of the Employability Services unit in Rainbow Centre. She holds a Bachelor Degree in Banking and Financial Management with Second Upper Class Honours from the University of London. She started her journey in social services with Rainbow Centre in 2018, as an Administration Manager at the Admiral Hill School. Prior to that, she spent around 12 years in the private and public sectors specialising in product management, strategic planning and policy development. She is passionate about making work possible for Rainbow Centre students and hopes to bring about meaningful work engagements for them in the post 18 space.

(*Continued*)

Name of Author	Description
Calvin **Eng**	Calvin is a Senior Project Executive with Rainbow Centre's Development & Innovation. He is a board certified music therapist by profession, and a curious generalist by nature. Health and social care are one of his interests, and the Arts his passion. He is on a journey to advocate how music can play a role in improving healthcare, quality of life, well-being and society. At other times, Calvin enjoys taking care of his bonsai!
Goh Ting Ying	Ting Ying (TY) is a Senior Manager of the Workability Programme under Employability Services. She holds a Bachelor in Sports Science University of Western Australia and has completed a Higher Certificate in Autism (HCIA) at Autism Resource Centre. With 7 years of job coaching experience, TY trains and supports her students with relevant work readiness skills on the ground.
Lynette Hanah **Gomez**	Lynette is the Deputy Principal of Rainbow Centre Margaret Drive School. She is a special needs educator who has served for 19 years and continues to be passionate about teaching and growing the wonderful children and youth in special education. Lynette is keen to innovate and drive special education to evolve with the changing needs of our children and the world around us, in order to enable and equip them to be strong participants in our society and live a meaningful life.
Hong Kai'en	Kai'en is a Senior Occupational Therapist and has a Bachelor of Science (Hons) in Occupational Therapy from Trinity College Dublin. Kai'en's interest lies in working with persons with special needs within the community. She believes that early intervention is essential in laying the foundation for children

Name of Author	Description
	with developmental needs and values a holistic approach in which the child's family and other community partners are involved in the intervention process.
Kay **Huang** Shujuan	Kay was a Senior Manager of the Workability Programme under Employability Services. She holds a Bachelor of Arts degree with honors in English Language from NUS, where she learnt about autism, and has since been focussed on serving clients with autism and other disabilities.
Kang Poh Sim	Sim has a Masters in Science in Speech Pathology and is one of the longest serving and experienced speech therapists at Rainbow Centre. She is a Principal Speech Therapist who is generous in sharing her knowledge and experiences with the therapists that she supervises or mentors.Sim is currently part of RC's Family Empowerment Programme where she coaches caregivers of children and youths with disabilities. She finds her work with these caregivers very fulfilling and enriching.
Koh Kheng Wah	Kheng Wah is the Head of Technology at Rainbow Centre. Coming form a background of Electrical Engineering and a Master of Business Administration. Kheng Wah has over 20 years of international experience leading teams in innovation, development, and marketing of technology products and services. He is passionate about developing innovative solutions that deliver sustainable social impacts.

(*Continued*)

Name of Author	Description
Christy **Lee-O'loughlin**	Christy is currently DIrector of Good Life Services. She led the pilot project 'School to Community' that developed the Good Life Transition Toolkit used for person centered transition planning across Rainbow Centre's schools. She hopes people with disabilities can live their vision of good life and we can co-create a truly inclusive society with them. Christy holds a Bachelors in Special Education and a Msc in Counseling Psychology.
Cynthia **Lee**	Cynthia is Assistant Director of Good Life Services and Allied Professional Services. Trained as a social worker, she was part of the team which developed the Good Life Transition Toolkit, now used for life planning with young adults in the Connected Communities Services, which aims to provide person-centred planning for young adults with disabilities to plan for good quality of life.
Janice **Leong**	Janice is the Deputy Director, Early Intervention Services. She has a Masters in Science, Speech-Language Pathology. She began her journey as a speech therapist in Rainbow Centre 11 years ago. In her current role, Janice is involved in the management and leadership of the staff in the Early Intervention Services, and is especially inspired when high quality collaborative teams are built to journey alongside families of the little ones.
Bernice **Lim** Miaoxin	Bernice is a Job Coach from Micro Business Academy under the Employability Services Unit. She holds a Diploma in Business and Social Enterprise from Ngee Ann Polytechnic.

Name of Author	Description
Jean **Loo**	Jean practises advocacy and community mobilisation with a focus on disability inclusion in Singapore. At Rainbow Centre, she leads the Advocacy and Community Engagement team and oversees OOSH, its student care services. Jean co-founded Superhero Me, an inclusive arts movement and currently advises its strategic projects and partnerships. For her commitment to inclusion through the arts, she was conferred the Singapore Youth Award 2018 and Nanyang Outstanding Young Alumni Award 2019. She also serves on the Panel of Advisers to the Youth Court.
Grace **Low**	Grace is a Board-Certified Music Therapist at Rainbow Centre where she works with children with special needs. She received her Bachelor of Music in Music Therapy with a minor in Psychology from Berklee College of Music in Boston, United States. She had the opportunity to work with various populations in different settings across her years of experience, including students and adults with special needs, community music therapy, adults with dementia, adults undergoing neurorehabilitation, and palliative care. She is also currently serving as the Secretary in the Association for Music Therapy Singapore.
Karina **Lou**	Karina Lou is an established music educator. She holds a Bachelor of Arts (Hons) Music from Goldsmiths, University of London and Masters of Music Education at the National Institute of Education, Singapore. She is well versed with the ABRSM syllabus and comfortable teaching all grades for examination attainment or for enjoyment. Besides teaching, her research interests span Music Education

(*Continued*)

Name of Author	Description
	and Music Therapy for Individuals with Autism. She collaborated briefly with Rainbow Centre during her graduate research to learn how music is used by the Music Therapists to engage their students with autism.
Trina **Liew**	Trina is a Senior Speech Language Therapist with a Master of Pathology Studies and Master of Science in Music, Mind & Brain. She has over ten years of experience working in the special education setting. She is constantly thinking out of the box to improve the communication and mealtime abilities of children and youths with special needs. She strongly feels that partnering families is key to empowering them to carry out the strategies successfully within the home and community. Mentoring young SLTs is also an area that she is passionate about.
Nursidah **Malik**	Nursidah is a Senior Manager of the Artability Programme under the Employability Services Unit. She holds a Bachelor degree in Communications from Monash University, a Diploma in Special Education (DISE) from NIE and Master degree in Education (Special Education) from NTU. Nursidah started her journey in Rainbow Centre in 2005 as a volunteer and fell in love with the students. She became a special education teacher in the same year and never looked back since.
Eileen **Oh** Kai Ling	Eileen has 15 years of experience working with children with autism and is currently a Lead Teacher in the Junior Programme at Admiral Hill School. She holds a Bachelor of Science (Statistics) with a Minor in Economics from NUS. She is passionate about fostering partnerships with families and community agencies, and building a team of compassionate and competent teachers to bring the best out of her students.

Name of Author	Description
Eileen **Soh**	Eileen is a Senior Speech-Language Therapist, Assistant Lead Allied Professional, and has a Master of Science (Speech and Language Pathology). She has been with Rainbow Centre Yishun Park School since 2013. Eileen began as a learning facilitator and developed an interest in the field of special education before pursuing a career in speech therapy. She is part of a multi-disciplinary team that provides speech, language and feeding interventions for students aged 15-18 years old. Eileen also contributes to the transition management of the students to integrate them into the community post-graduation. She is passionate about providing AAC services to give her students a voice to participate as part of their good life.
Tan Seok Hui	Seok Hui completed a Master of Science (Speech Language Pathology) and joined Rainbow Centre – Yishun Park School in 2021. Having been interested in the development of children's language in her previous role as a researcher, she finds Augmentative and Alternative Communication (AAC) assessment and intervention in her current role as a speech therapist both interesting and fulfilling. She enjoys the process of building rapport with students when at school, and lindy hop and tap dance outside of school hours.
Tan Yeok Nguan	YN is a warm soul that has married education, design and social service. He provides human-centred and inclusive practices for persons of all abilities and has led inclusive design projects with partners such as National Youth Council, Changi Airport Group and National Arts Council etc. He was formerly from Design Singapore Council and National Council of Social Service where he advo cated the importance of human-centric and inclu sive

(Continued)

Name of Author	Description
	design, overseeing innovative projects that sought to uplift the experiences for persons with disabilities and caregivers. If he is not around, you will likely find him trekking in remote natural places, away from Wi-Fi.
Jimson **Tham**	Jimson is Assistant Director (Therapy Services). As an occupational therapist, Jimson is passionate about enhancing the capabilities of children with special needs to connect with people and the world around them. He finds it meaningful when children can use their voices to interact with their loved ones, and finds joy and purpose in playing with different materials and people. As a leader, he believes connection and collaboration between stakeholders are key to successes in supporting our children and their families.
June **Tham-Toh** Syn Yuen	June has been a part of the evolution of the social service landscape for four decades since 1982 when she joined the Association for Persons with Special Needs. She retired from Rainbow Centre as the Executive Director after serving 25 fulfilling and meaningful years transforming it into one of the largest social service agencies. June was one of the authors and editors for three editions of the Rainbow Dreams. She received the inaugural Tote Board scholarship to attend the Strategic Perspectives in Nonprofit Management at Harvard University in 2008, the NCSS Social Service Fellowship award from 2016 and the Skillsfuture Fellowship award in 2020. Today, June contributes as a Social Service Fellow. In 2018, she co-chaired to organize the inaugural Early Intervention Conference in Singapore.

Name of Author	Description
Toh Ee Ming	Toh Ee Ming is a freelance writer and journalist. Her work has been published in the Associated Press, Al Jazeera, South China Morning Post, Southeast Asia Globe, among others. She is passionate about social issues and serving the community. In 2019, Ee Ming became befriender to Keith, a graduate of Rainbow Centre.
Jessica **Wee**	Jessica is currently Principal at Rainbow Centre Yishun Park School, where she has served for 13 years. As a leader, she believes in supporting them to pursue their passion and goals. A significant part of Jessica's experience has been school leadership, people and change management, project management, developing strategic partnerships, talent recruitment and capability building. She also advises one of RC's strategic initiatives on mobility training and independence. Her personal philosophy is having the serenity to accept the things she cannot change, courage to change the things she can, and the wisdom to know the difference.
Sharifah Masturah **Yokoyama**	Sharifah is a special education practitioner with over 30 years of experience in Rainbow Centre. She is also Principal Trainer with Rainbow Centre Training & Consultancy. Sharifah is driven by the belief that every person, regardless of their different needs, has the right to participate fully in the community and to have the same choices, opportunities and experiences as everyone else. Very much a teacher at heart and a life-long learner, Sharifah has led, mentored and developed beginning and experienced special education teachers to develop their teaching competencies. Sharifah has a Master in Education (Special Education) and is also a certified Mindfulness trainer.

Contents

Section 1

Introduction and History

This section presents an overview of the development of the landscape towards a more inclusive society for children and young adults with disabilities. It also introduces this history of how schools for children with autism and developmental disabilities were formed.

1 Towards a Caring and Inclusive Landscape

June Tham-Toh Syn Yuen

What are the significant milestones in the development of the disability landscape and the emerging trends creating a vision of a more caring and inclusive Singapore?

THE EARLY YEARS

Comprising mainly of volunteer professionals and parents of children with special needs, services for persons with disabilities were initiated and managed by Voluntary Welfare Organizations (VWOs), now known as Social Service Agencies (SSAs). Fundraising and human resources were the responsibilities of the individual charities providing services to meet the needs of specific disabilities. Before 1992, the preceding agency, the Singapore Council of Social Service (SCSS) of the National Council of Social Service (NCSS), was the national coordinating body of the social service sector. It met the needs of the disabled and disadvantaged by raising funds under Community Chest, the fundraising arm of SCSS, for all its registered charities and organised events to create awareness and support for the sector. A significant initiative by SCSS was the setting up of Margaret Drive Special School in 1987 to provide early intervention and special education programmes for children with intellectual and multiple disabilities, and in 1989, for children with autism. Today, the school is run under the umbrella of Rainbow Centre Singapore and spans three campuses.

Formed in 1992, NCSS, a statutory board under the Ministry of Social and Family Development, is the national umbrella social service body for over 450 SSA members with a mission to provide leadership and direction in enhancing their capacities, advocating social service needs, and strengthening strategic partnerships for an effective social service ecosystem.

ADVISORY COUNCIL FOR THE DISABLED

Chaired by the then Education Minister Dr Tony Tan, the report and recommendations by the Advisory Council for the Disabled (ACD) were published in 1988. This proved to be the turning point for many initiatives which spearheaded coordinated partnerships and involvement of various Government ministries and voluntary agencies for a holistic approach to providing and improving the quality of services for the disability sector.

Recommendations in the ACD report that were implemented included allocating land and defining space norms for VWOs to create new purpose-built special education (SPED) schools to cater to the specific needs of the children using a co-funding model from the Ministry of Education (MOE) and self-fundraising by the VWO. This enabled Rainbow Centre Singapore to build and open the first purpose-built special education school with special facilities and features in Singapore to cater to the special needs of her students in 1998. Co-funding for operating budgets of SPED schools by MOE and the Community Chest was a great relief for VWOs, enabling them to direct their focus to the quality and delivery of services. The introduction of the Certificate in Special Education programme, which was later upgraded to Diploma in Special Education (DISE), by the National Institute of Education played a significant role in the professional development of untrained teachers working in the SPED schools. This direction has undoubtedly contributed to the quality planning and delivery of lessons and positive learning outcomes for their students. Today, apart from the DISE course for the disability sector, other training programmes are offered by Rainbow Centre Singapore, Autism Resource Centre (Singapore), Social Service Institute (SSI) of NCSS, Ngee Ann Polytechnic, Nanyang Polytechnic, Temasek Polytechnic and the National University of Singapore (NUS), providing a range of courses for teachers, social workers and allied health professionals.

Another significant milestone arising from the ACD Report was the setting up of a child development programme in 1991 by the Ministry of

Health to provide diagnostic assessments and referral of children diagnosed with a developmental disability to early intervention and special education programmes provided by SSAs. Today, this programme, provided at the KK Women's and Children's Hospital and the National University Hospital, serve as the national referral centres for children diagnosed with developmental issues.

UNITED NATION CONVENTION OF THE RIGHTS OF PERSONS WITH DISABILITIES (UNCRPD)

Singapore signed the United Nation Convention on the Rights of Persons with Disabilities (UNCRPD) in 2012, and cemented its commitment in 2016 by undertaking collaborative efforts to build a caring and more inclusive society.

Enabling masterplans

Recognising the need for greater inclusivity in our society, a series of masterplans were published. The first came out in 2007 and produced a national road map outlining the vision to fully integrate persons with disabilities into the community. It adopted a life course approach charting the development of programmes and services for the disability sector. In 2016, the Ministry of Social and Family Development (MSF) went further and confirmed it under the UNCRPD. Four key thrusts were recommended by the Steering Committee:

1. Improving the quality of life of persons with disabilities.
2. Supporting caregivers
3. Building the community
4. Building an inclusive society

Key Initiatives Implemented:

1. Special Education Schools
More purpose-built SPED schools led by Ministry of Education leaders were established, and extension of the upper age limit from 18 to 21 years.

2. Early Intervention Programmes for Infants and Children
Increased support for Early Intervention Programmes for Infants and Children (EIPIC) aged up to six years, and expanded subsidies for needy children receiving EIPIC.

3. Mainstream School Developmental Support Programme
Starting a Development Support Programme (DSP) to provide early intervention services for children with mild developmental delays in their natural setting within mainstream childcare settings and kindergartens. Additional resources and facilities to support children with mild special needs to promote integration and inclusiveness and enhance their learning in the mainstream schools.

4. Employment Services
Setting up of Employment SG Enable (SGE) in 2013 dedicated to providing information and referral services, administering grants and other forms of support to persons with disabilities and caregivers, and offering job coaches to enhance the employability and employment options for persons with disabilities. Special Employment Credits are given to employers as an incentive to hire persons with disabilities. Workfare Income Supplement scheme to supplement wages of low-income persons with disabilities to enable them to achieve financial independence.

5. Designing Jobs and Workplace
The existing Open Door Programme (ODP) set up to re-design jobs; offer workplace modification, conduct training and job placement plus provide support services was enhanced in 2013.

6. Mobility Enhancement
Ramps and public transport system to enhance accessibility in the community.

7. New Technology
Setting up of a new technology facility in Enabling Village to enable the accessibility of assistive technology for education, employment and independent living. In addition, the Government expanded coverage and subsidies for those who require assistive technology.

8. Social Services

A Social Service Institute (SSI) was set up to provide a range of training courses under NCSS with the mission to upgrade the quality of social service professionals in their professional knowledge and competency in the social service sector.

9. Early Childhood

The Early Childhood Development Agency (ECDA) was established in 2013 by the Ministry of Social and Family Development (MSF) to serve as the regulatory and developmental authority for the early childhood sector. The agency works to ensure that every child has access to affordable and quality early childhood education and services, and provides subsidies and grants to support the sector. The National Institute in Early Childhood (NIEC) was set up in 2019 to work with ECDA as a key partner as well as with MOE to offer courses in early childhood and early intervention for children with special needs. The Social Service Skills Future Tripartite Taskforce (STT) was set up under ECDA to establish a road map and identify paths and training for progressive career and professional development of early childhood and early intervention leaders and educators. This important direction will not only enhance their professional capabilities and competence but also upgrade the professional status of early childhood and early intervention professionals for impactful outcomes, leading to a quality and sustainable sector.

Compulsory Education Act

The Compulsory Education Act effected in 2019 to include all children aged seven to twelve years with special needs in government-funded SPED schools finally became a reality four years after the recommendation was included in the Enabling Masterplan 2012–2016. This is an important milestone in Singapore's vision towards national inclusiveness and indeed a reaffirmation that every child matters regardless of his or her learning challenges, and leaving no child behind.

With this legislation, all children with mild special needs attend mainstream schools while those with moderate and severe special needs attend SPED schools. To ensure that a child with a developmental issue has early access to special education, steps to ramp up capacity in these schools were made. The Act provides exemption to children with severe special needs and medical conditions from attending in a school setting. Instead, they are given access to a home-based programme that meets their educational and developmental needs. As for parents who wish not to enrol their children in a SPED school, they may seek exemption from the rule and MOE will consider them on a case-by-case basis.

INCLUSIVE EDUCATION

Inclusion, as a value, supports the right of all children to function in their communities, regardless of their diverse abilities. Driven by the belief that an inclusive education values children as individuals and enables them to feel belonged, allowing them to participate and achieve, the Lien Foundation and AWWA Ltd collaborated and conceived Kindle Garden, Singapore first purpose-built inclusive preschool in 2016 in the Enabling Village.

The success of Kindle Garden as an inclusive preschool and the growing demand for inclusive preschools prompted the setting up of a workgroup by MSF to look at how children with special needs can be better integrated into preschools. In response to the demand from parents, more preschools began opening their doors to accept preschoolers with mild developmental issues. They have stepped up teacher training, opened more inclusive preschools and carried out manpower recruitment to meet the growing demand.

Students with mild special needs and who are able to adapt to the mainstream school curriculum are integrated in mainstream education schools and tertiary institutions. Mainstream schools are provided with additional professional resources by MOE to support their learning. Allied educators trained in autism spectrum disorder or dyslexia, as well as educational psychologists are deployed in all primary schools to support the learning and behaviour of these students when needed. Many of them require special arrangements to facilitate participation in classrooms and activities. Students with difficulty in social skills may face challenges having friends, and this is where attention and support need to be provided by all members of the school community to encourage acceptance of their special needs.

Ms Sun Xueling, Minister of State for Social and Family Development, and Education, said, "The InSP pilot is part of a concerted effort by ECDA and our partners to enhance inclusion and support for children with developmental needs. Through this initiative, we aim to cultivate an inclusive environment from the early years that embraces each child's unique abilities, and enables all children to learn together, develop friendships, thrive and feel a sense of belonging. When we start young, we have the best chance to foster shared values. I hope parents, preschools and early intervention providers can give their fullest support in making our preschools more inclusive" (Early Childhood Development Agency, 2021)

The success of an inclusive school or educational setting depends on the provision of a supportive environment, positive relationships among everyone and equal opportunities to participate in activities alongside other children where possible. An inclusive environment not only provides opportunities to have an impact on the importance of empathy and acceptance in typical developing children from a young age but also enables those with special needs to develop a positive sense of self-worth. Values of compassion and graciousness should begin at home as well as in an environment that promotes inclusiveness in the early years.

EMERGING TRENDS AND NEEDS

With the growing trends in the disability landscape, there is a need to prepare for changes and emerging needs to enhance services to enable persons with disabilities gain independence so that they can live and work in an inclusive environment within our community.

Four key trends affecting the disability landscape:

(a) Persons with Disabilities Live Longer
With medical advances and effective medical and early interventions, many persons with disabilities live longer and outlive their parents. As persons with disabilities live longer, it is paramount to enable them to achieve their true potential and gain independence and skills through effective vocational training and job coaching for better sustainable employment opportunities in an inclusive work environment and within our community. It is heartening to see the emergence of social enterprises to train and employ them. One of the many successful initiatives is the Professor Brawn Café set up by the Autism Resource Centre (Singapore). For those with moderate and severe disabilities, more day activity centres, employment

training centres and residential facilities are needed to serve this group of persons with disabilities.

(b) Growing Number of Persons Diagnosed with Autism

Services for children with autism in Singapore was first introduced at Margaret Drive Special School in 1989 as a collaboration with NUS. The programme caters specifically to children with autism with moderate and high needs for support. It expanded in 1995 under Rainbow Centre Singapore to cope with the long waiting list. In 2002, to address another gap in the landscape, a deliberate collaboration between Rainbow Centre Singapore and Autism Resource Centre (Singapore) presented a joint proposal named "Project Platinum" to the Minister for Education for a centre to integrate students with autism spectrum disorder into the mainstream education community. As a result, Pathlight School was conceived and opened in 2004 as the first autism specific school for high-functioning children with autism. The school is run under the umbrella of the Autism Resource Centre.

The Child Development Programme at KKH saw 5,292 cases with autism in 2017 as compared to 2,584 in 2011, an increase of 51%. There is a need for more services to support this group. MOE has approved the building of three more autism specific schools by Autism Resource Centre (ARC), Rainbow Centre Singapore (RC) and AWWA Ltd. These will add on to the existing seven SPED schools, namely Pathlight School (ARC), Rainbow Centre Margaret Drive School, Rainbow Centre Yishun Park School, Rainbow Centre Admiral Hill School St. Andrews Autism School, AWWA School and Eden School. It should be noted that children with mild and moderate intellectual disability with autism are also enrolled in other SPED schools run by the Association for Persons with Special Needs (APSN) and MINDS. While more schools are being built for children with autism, there is an urgent need to recruit manpower and train them.

(c) An Aging Population

Singapore has one of the most rapidly ageing population in the world. With the shrinking of family sizes, ageing parents who are caregivers face difficulties in caring for their grown-up children with disabilities. This is a common concern shared by parents, "What will happen to my child when

I am not able to take care of him/her or when I am no longer around?" There is a dire need for more facilities and services to be expanded for youth and adults with special needs.

(d) Support for Caregivers

Parents are the main caregivers of their children. Their understanding and acceptance of their children's needs and abilities, and their positive involvement in their children's development is crucial, especially in the early years as well as throughout their lives. Therefore, programmes to train and empower caregivers with services to provide short-term respite for them and support for older caregivers need to be expanded and be accessible to all parents in a language that suits them.

CONCLUSIONS

Singapore celebrated her 50th year of independence in 2015. As a multi-racial city state with such a short history, we are making progressive and significant milestones towards building an inclusive society where everyone including persons with disabilities is treated with equal rights and dignity. The 1988 ACD Report, signing of the UNCRPD in 2012 and rectification in 2013, the inclusion of children with special needs aged seven years to 12 years in the Compulsory Education Act in 2019, the three Enabling Masterplans from 2007 to 2021, as well as the collaborative efforts and commitments of the Government, NCSS, SSAs, training institutions, prominent donors and community partners and volunteers are testimonies of possibilities towards building a caring and inclusive nation.

As Singapore continues her commitment to build a truly inclusive and sustainable landscape for persons with disabilities and their families, and to work with greater impact towards the vision, we hope to see profound changes and outcomes in the following:

- Societal attitudes towards persons with disabilities evolve,
- Families with children with disabilities are better supported to integrate into and participate in social activities in our community,
- More inclusive workplaces where persons with disabilities are treated and accepted with respect,

- Collaboration of stakeholders for a holistic strategic road map and implementation of initiatives to meet the emerging needs of more facilities and services for youth and adults with moderate and severe disabilities, and
- Extension of the Compulsory Education Act to start from preschool age.

REFERENCES

Early Childhood Development Agency (28 October 2021). Launch of Inclusive Support Programme (InSP) Pilot. To strengthen inclusion and support for children with developmental needs in preschools (Press Release). https://www.ecda.gov.sg/PressReleases/Pages/Launch-of-Inclusive-Support-Programme-(InSP)-Pilot.aspx

Ho, L. Y. (2018). *Building an Inclusive Early Childhood Intervention Ecosystem in Singapore 1988–2017*, Singapore Paediatric Society.

Ho, L. Y. (2021). Current Status of the Early Childhood Developmental Intervention Ecosystem in Singapore. *Singapore Medical Journal 2021, 62*(1 Suppl), S43–S52.

The Enabling Masterplan 2012–2016 (2012). Ministry of Social and Family Development Singapore. https://www.msf.gov.sg/policies/Disabilities-and-Special-Needs/Documents/EM2%20progress%20report.pdf

Enabling Masterplan 2017–2021 (2017). Ministry of Social and Family Development, Singapore. https://www.msf.gov.sg/policies/Disabilities-and-Special-Needs/Documents/Enabling%20Masterplan%203%20%28revised%2013%20Jan%202017%29.pdf

Soong, C. M., Tan, J. C. S., Mahesh, M., Teo, H. F, Ong, C. H. L., & Teoh, W. Q. (2019). *EIPIC Consultancy Recommended Practices for Early Intervention in Singapore*. KK Women's & Children's Hospital, Singapore.

Population White Paper: A Sustainable Population for a Dynamic Singapore (2013). Strategy Group, Prime Minister's Office, Singapore. https://www.strategygroup.gov.sg/media-centre/population-white-paper-a-sustainable-population-for-a-dynamic-singapore

Tham-Toh, J. (2012). Integration-A Shift in Perspective. In J. Tham-Toh, K. Lyen, K. Poon, E. H. Lee & M. Pathnapuram (Eds.). *Rainbow Dreams* (3rd ed.) (pp. 385–395). Singapore Armour Publishing.

Tham-Toh, J., & Poon K. (2012). The Development of Special Education in Singapore. In J. Tham-Toh, K. Lyen, K. Poon, E. H. Lee & M. Pathnapuram (Eds.). *Rainbow Dreams* (3rd ed.) (pp. 22–32). Singapore Armour Publishing.

2 History of Schools for Children with Autism in Singapore

Kenneth Lyen

SPECIAL EDUCATION

Before 1985, children on the autistic spectrum did not receive a diagnosis and were grouped together with developmentally delayed individuals. The first school for these children was started in 1962 by the Singapore Association for Retarded Children, which was renamed Movement for the Intellectually Disabled of Singapore (MINDS) in 1985. A few schools which catered for children above the age of 7 years were started.

When Dr Kenneth Lyen returned to Singapore in 1983 from his overseas postgraduate studies, he joined the Department of Paediatrics at the National University of Singapore (NUS). He was asked by Professor Freda Paul, who looked after developmentally delayed children, to take over her clinic as she was about to retire. When Dr Lyen took over this clinic looking after over 1,000 intellectually and physically challenged children, he realised there was a gap in the services provided. There were no educational or rehabilitation therapies for children under the age of 7 years, who numbered over a couple of hundred. When Dr Lyen was invited to be on the school management board of the MINDS schools, they had just started a programme for children under 7 years old, which was named the Early Intervention Programme. However, there was very limited classroom space, which prevented the programme from expanding.

In 1985, Dr Lyen approached the Community Chest of Singapore, a charity body under the Singapore Council of Social Service. He proposed to the then-president Dr Ee Peng Liang that a separate school, run independently, be started for intellectually as well as physically challenged children under the age of 7 years. This was immediately accepted. Dr Lyen then approached an Oxford University colleague, Dr Tay Eng Soon, who was the Minister of State for Education, to look for a place to start the early intervention programme. Dr Tay found a disused primary school along Margaret Drive, which became the first school for younger special needs children in Singapore, known as Rainbow Centre at Margaret Drive. It started taking in students in 1986.

CHILDREN WITH AUTISM

While running the clinic for special needs children at NUS, Dr Lyen noticed that there were a number of children who had speech delay, socialising difficulties, and obsessionally repetitive behaviours, all pointing toward autism spectrum disorder. He consulted a senior child psychiatrist who, to his surprise, remarked that there were no autistic children in Singapore.

He soon realised that the definition of autism used by some Singapore psychiatrists was based on Leo Kanner's 1943 definition, which required autistic children to have zero speech, no socialising abilities, and extremely obsessional repetitive behaviours. When Dr Lyen reviewed the children attending the Developmental Clinic, he noted that his patients had a milder form of autism, with some speech, some social impairments, and repetitive behaviours, more like the behavioural spectrum described in 1944 by Hans Asperger.

He was able to convince both the Ministry of Education as well as the Ministry of Community Development to start a new special programme devoted to helping children on the autistic spectrum. This was approved in 1987, and once again Dr Lyen approached Dr Ee Peng Liang of the Community Chest to provide funding, which he approved. There were spare classrooms in the Rainbow Centre at Margaret Drive, and so, the programme was started there. This was the first programme for children with autism in Singapore.

APPLIED BEHAVIOUR ANALYSIS

Structured Teaching for Exceptional Pupils (STEP) Programme

In a stroke of perfect timing, a renowned clinical psychologist Dr Vera Bernard who had a special interest in childhood autism had moved to

Singapore. She approached Dr Lyen in 1988, offering her help, which he accepted with alacrity. Dr Bernard then explained that she would use Applied Behaviour Analysis which was started by Ivar Lovaas in 1965 for children with autism. Dr Vera Bernard had worked under Professor Bernard Rimland at the University of California San Diego, and he had also supported Lovaas' Applied Behaviour Analysis. Dr Bernard renamed it the Structured Teaching for Exceptional Pupils (STEP) programme, and it has remained the mainstay of management of autistic children, evolving over the years. The highlight of this programme is that therapy is individualised, a philosophy which the Rainbow Centre had embraced when it started the Early Intervention Programme. Another aspect of the STEP programme is that it has a structured format for developing a child's individual potential skills, including visual, auditory, physical, and other abilities. It also recruited parents or other caregivers to learn and become involved in the training using positive behavioural reinforcements, and not aversion. Over time, the students who attended the STEP programme learnt to speak more and socialise better. Their obsessional behaviours also diminished, compared to the children on the waiting list. Parents and caregivers were enlisted to help, and have remained an important component of the programme.

THE RAINBOW CENTRE

The STEP programme was started in 1989 with 12 students. Since then, the number has progressively increased to the current enrolment of over 700. It became important to have an executive director to manage both the STEP programme as well as the rest of the school. Mrs June Tham was headhunted and invited to join the Margaret Drive school. Initially, she did not want to leave her position in another special needs school, but agreed in 1989 to become the executive director of the school.

Mrs Tham believed in a holistic approach to special needs education, and so, in addition to the Applied Behaviour Analysis approach of physiotherapy and occupational therapy, she started music therapy and hydrotherapy. She also involved parents and caregivers in the training, and networked with other organisations helping special needs children.

The Margaret Drive school expanded rapidly and was soon unable to cope with the increasing number of students. A second school was needed, and this was started in 1992; the new school is currently located at

Yishun Park. Both schools took in younger children on the autism spectrum, under the age of 12 years. To manage two schools, an umbrella body — the Rainbow Centre — was officially established in 1992. Most of the members of the new governing board were the same as the original founding body. In 2018, a new school — the Woodlands Campus — was started, making it the third school under the Rainbow Centre.

OTHER SCHOOLS FOR CHILDREN WITH AUTISM

In 2004, some members of the Rainbow Centre were approached by the Ministry of Education to help start a school for autism spectrum children above the age of 7 years. Several Rainbow Centre board members volunteered to help start Pathlight School, which was led by Denise Phua. This school served students who were capable of pursuing the standard Singapore school examinations, such as the Primary School Leaving Examinations and the General Certificate of Education examinations. An additional education track was started for those found to be suitable for vocational skill certifications. Pathlight School launched the Satellite School Model in 2005 in which its secondary schools students were physically located with their teachers in several partner mainstream secondary schools such as Chong Boon Secondary School and Bishan Park Secondary School, for fuller social and academic integration.

There are now many more schools in Singapore serving children with autism, including Grace Orchard, Eden School, and St. Andrew's Autism Centre. The older schools of MINDS and Association for Persons with Special Needs also take in students with autism. There is now an Autism Resource Centre, as well as several centres that organise co-curricular activities. As for older persons on the autism spectrum, there are now job training programmes, helping them with finding employment in the food and beverage industry, gardening, working in an office, computing, etc.

CHILDREN WITH SPECIAL NEEDS IN MAINSTREAM SCHOOLS

Singapore has recognised that there are children within mainstream school settings whose special needs require additional support beyond what is usually available in schools. Services supporting such students, particularly those with mild disabilities, have been steadily developing. However, the 21st century has seen great leaps in services for children with special needs, in line with the government's focus on making Singapore a more inclusive society.

In the sections that follow, we will describe two developments in mainstream schools since the 1970s, as well as other organisations supporting special needs students who are attending them.

PSYCHOLOGICAL SUPPORT

In 1970, the Ministry of Education established the Schools Social Work and School Psychological Services, and this was later renamed the Psychological Services Branch. Staffed by educational and associate psychologists, the aim was to provide support to students with special needs in mainstream primary schools. This branch also provides support to the Allied Educators' Learning and Behavioural Support.

Another initiative to provide early intervention to students who required support in their acquisition of literacy skills was started under The Learning Support Programme, introduced in 1992. This was subsequently expanded in 1999 to provide the same screening and support for students who were weak in mathematics.

Currently, all trainee teachers must receive a 12- to 36-hour introductory course on special needs education to help accommodate and support students with learning difficulties. In addition, 10% of primary and 20% of secondary school teachers receive over 100 hours of training to further assist students with special needs in mainstream settings.

FINANCIAL SUPPORT

As the school population grew, the existing facilities were unable to support the students' needs. When the time came for a new purpose-built building, the team embarked on fundraising initiatives. As a member of the Rotary Club of Singapore North, Dr Lyen took up the mantle for fundraising. Support was also given by other charity bodies such as Lions Club, Lee Foundation, and Tsao Foundation.

FUTURE CHALLENGES

Ideas for future development include:

1. Lifespan Approach

The first is to adopt a lifespan philosophy that surveys the entire life of a person on the autism spectrum and introduce new programmes. This requires more training, and jobs support. The next task is to find ways of looking after those on the more severe end of the spectrum, especially when their parents and loved ones pass on. Who will look after them?

2. Different, Not Disabled

The second challenge is raised by the higher functioning autistic individuals. They do not want to be labelled "disabled", but to be regarded as "differently abled". In other words, they do not want autism to be regarded as an abnormality or a pathological disease. They want to be seen as merely different. One repercussion of this is that mainstream schools need to be capable of becoming inclusive.

3. Inclusive Education

The education system should be more inclusive. Children have different abilities and interests, but we should not partition them into isolated schools. They can still join in other activities such as sports, art, music, dance, etc. We need to develop the mindset that we are all part of a family. This is already starting to take place in some nursery schools and kindergartens. Many of them are accommodating children on the autism spectrum. Hopefully, this will be extended to older age groups.

4. Prevention is Better than Cure

It is a paradox that if autism is not recognised as a disease or disorder, then why should one even attempt to prevent it occurring. One reason is that people at the severe end of the spectrum have many difficulties coping with day-to-day living, and some may have associated disorders such as epilepsy, attention deficit hyperactivity disorder, anxiety and depression. This is a controversial issue and needs further discussion.

5. New Technologies

Creating new technologies to help people on the autistic spectrum should be given more funding. Enhancing communication, facilitating the integration of special needs children into society, and allowing them to travel, shop, and enjoy leisure activities can be developed further.

Resources

Autism Resource Centre https://www.autism.org.sg/
Eden School https://www.edenschool.edu.sg/
Grace Orchard School https://www.graceorchardschool.com/
MINDS Schools https://www.minds.org.sg/for-children/schools/
Pathlight School https://www.pathlight.org.sg/
Rainbow Centreh ttps://www.rainbowcentre.org.sg/
Tham-Toh, J., Lyen, K., Poon, K., Lee, E. H., & Pathnapuram, M. (Eds.) (2012). *Rainbow Dreams* (3rd ed.). Singapore Armour Publishing.
St. Andrew's Autism Centre https://www.saac.org.sg/

Section 2

Support Across the Lifespan

This section describes programmes and services for clients with autism and other developmental disabilities during their early years, school years and early adulthood, as well as Rainbow Centre's experience of continuum of care towards good lives of our clients.

3 Early Intervention

Janice Leong

*"A treatment method or an educational method that will work for one child may not work for another child. The one common denominator for all of the young children is that early **intervention** does work, and it seems to improve the prognosis."*

Temple Grandin

INTRODUCTION

Case No. 1: Eric, who just turned one year old, is the newest addition to the family. He has a *jie jie* (elder sister) who is in Primary One this year, and *gor gor* (elder brother) who is 4 years old, and goes to a childcare centre during the day. Every morning, Eric's mummy, Suzanne, drops him off at his grandmother's place before heading to work. She works as an English teacher at a kindergarten. Victor, who is Eric's daddy, drops off the other two children before heading home for some rest. He starts his work as a food delivery driver slightly before lunch time, and often works till past dinner time. Suzanne joins Grandma in the caring of Eric once she knocks off from work. Eric was born with cerebral palsy and has been seeing a physiotherapist (PT) at the hospital since birth.

Teacher Naomi was introduced to the family during the first early intervention session at their home. Victor and Suzanne shared that they were taught some exercises by the PT to carry out with Eric, but confessed that it was hard to find time during the day to carry them out. Teacher Naomi spent some time understanding the routine at home and together with

Suzanne and Eric's grandmother, started looking at learning opportunities throughout the day. In that way, intervention can be embedded into daily activities and there would be no need to find extra time for exercises. As Teacher Naomi tried these out during her home-based session, and with further discussion with the family and other team members, six goals were set up with some of them relating to motor skills, while others encouraged social communication and development of feeding within the home environment.

Case No.2: Kayden has attended Rainbow Centre since he was 3 years old. Now six, he was going to transition from centre-based services to preschool-based services in the DS-Plus (Development Support Plus) programme. Teacher Shu had the opportunity to observe Kayden in his Rainbow Centre class a few times and also had a handover discussion with Kayden's Key Worker and Individual Education Plan (IEP) Team on the goals he has achieved and progress he has made in the past few years. Teacher Shu also connected with Kayden's family to find out their hopes and dreams for Kayden, especially as he progresses towards Primary One the following year. Kayden's preschool teachers shared that Kayden is a bright and lovable boy. However, they struggle with his behaviour in class at times; he screams at the top of his voice when he does not get his way during play time with his peers. This causes his classmates to avoid playing or even interacting with him as they are afraid of him.

Kayden has a diagnosis of autism and is unsure about how to approach his friends or resolve conflicts. He is able to read and spell, but when asked questions during story time or "Show and Tell", Kayden gives single-word answers and finds it hard to string them into a complete sentence. As Teacher Shu started observing him at the preschool during different points of the school routine, she was able to introduce strategies that helped Kayden organise his thoughts into sentences. Teacher Shu also had the opportunity to co-plan lessons with his preschool teacher, and co-teach during "Learning Centre" time. In that way, Kayden had the opportunity to practise some problem-solving skills while interacting with his friends, with support from his early intervention (EI) teacher and preschool teacher. The collaboration is paying off as Kayden grows more and more confident in communicating his thoughts within the classroom setting.

Both Eric and Kayden are two of the many students and their families whom we serve at Rainbow Centre Early Intervention (RC EI) Services.

Key tenets of Rainbow Centre Early Intervention Services

The Rainbow Centre Early Intervention team journeys with families and their children 6 years and below by providing support for them to grow, learn and achieve their developmental milestones. The three tenets of our Early Intervention Services ensure that intervention is holistic and relevant. They are:

1. Family members are important partners
2. Focus on daily routines and natural environments
3. Transdisciplinary team approach

The gear diagram (Fig 1) below illustrates that the three tenets are interlinked and work together to produce the best results. Each of the tenets is explained in the following section.

Figure 1.   Key Tenets of RC EI Services

Tenet 1: Families are important partners

For a young child, parents, siblings, and significant caregivers are the world. They are the constant in a child's life and spend the most time with them. For this reason, the family is the child's biggest resource, and it is imperative to involve the family as an essential partner in the intervention process. Support given is not just in the care of the child but extends to the family from the first contact. This support aims to empower a family's sense of confidence and competence about their child's current and future learning development.

The recognition that family is important in the intervention process is referred to as Family-Centred Practice (FCP). It is one of the philosophical foundations of RC EI Services and has the goal of promoting active participation of families in decision-making related to their child's intervention. FCP results in joint service planning, which is crucial in supporting families to achieve the goals they identify for their child and the family as a whole.

FCP is based on three basic considerations: (a) acknowledging that families have unique circumstances, hence needing individualised and flexible, responsive practices; (b) including participatory opportunities and experiences to strengthen new and existing parenting abilities; (c) practices that build relationships between families and professionals who work together to achieve mutually agreed outcomes and goals. This promotes family competency and development of the child (DEC, 2014).

By embracing FCP, the programme believes in acknowledging the individuality and strengths in each family to foster a positive relationship between the professionals and the family. This is crucial for achieving the best possible outcomes for a child and the family.

In FCP, the family is involved throughout the early intervention journey from the initial assessment to goal setting and goal evaluation. Figure 2 shows how families are engaged as fully participating members of the team in the entire assessment and intervention process at RC.

Tenet 2: Focus on daily routines and natural environments

Daily routines refer to the child's daily activities that occur with some regularity and that are not professionally set up (e.g., meal times, play times, bath time, travelling). Natural environments refer to settings where these

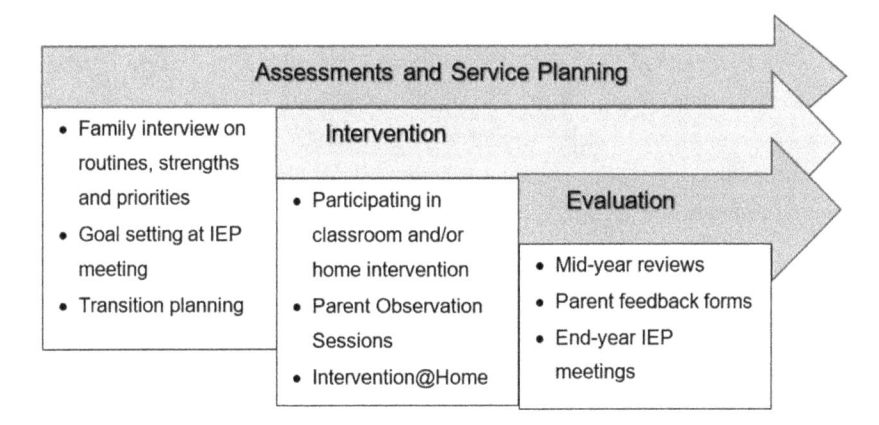

Figure 2. Family Involvement in RC EI Services

daily routines typically take place and may include home, school, and community settings.

RC EI Services strives to deliver intervention in the child's natural environments to leverage the learning opportunities found in daily routines. As daily routines are meaningful, predictable, and occur numerous times throughout the day, they offer various learning opportunities for the child to generalise the skills gained in the centre. Integrating intervention into daily routines and natural environments also help to enhance their daily functioning at home and the community (Jennings *et al.*, 2012) thus enhancing the family's dynamics as a whole.

Here is an example of the principle in action with our student, Eric. Eric's family has expressed priority in helping him to request using words (e.g., "I want biscuit"). In the family interview, the team found that meal times provided naturally occurring opportunities for Eric to ask for desired items that he would be motivated to request for. Therefore, the professional team and family decided to use meal times to create opportunities for Eric to practise requesting, by providing his desired food and then strategically prompting and responding to his communication.

Kayden, our student with autism, is another example. Kayden loves playing with LEGO bricks. His preschool teacher noticed that Kayden wanted to build with LEGO bricks with his friends but approached them by taking away their bricks. To him, this caught his friends' attention but they became angry, causing them to move away from him. During "Learning Centre" time, his teachers took the opportunity to facilitate a turn-taking LEGO activity, allowing Kayden to practise some scenarios and communication skills that he was taught during his pull-out individual session, on how to approach his friends to play together. These skills were then extended to other turn-taking activities during other lessons, allowing Kayden to practise them over and over again.

Tenet 3: Transdisciplinary team approach

Given the nature and complexity of intervention services for young children with disabilities or those who are at risk of developmental delay, the intervention team comprises various professionals (e.g., teacher, speech language therapist, occupational therapist, physiotherapist, psychologist). A transdisciplinary (Trans-D) approach is adopted by RC EI Services to facilitate collaboration within the team and to guide service delivery. As the dynamics among the team members involved in the care of a child with unique needs can be a defining success factor in the early intervention process, it is therefore essential to have a common understanding of the expectations and scope of participation of team members.

The transdisciplinary team approach is defined by professionals from different disciplines working together seamlessly, overcoming the disciplinary boundaries and maximising communication and cooperation (Woodruff & McGonigel, 1988). The Trans-D approach considers all perspectives of the child's development, thus viewing them as an integrated and interactive whole, rather than a collection of separate parts.

There are five indicators in the Trans-D approach that RC EI adopts, and each is incorporated into the RC EI journey:

Parents/caregivers are team members: Their priorities are taken into consideration during goal-setting and they are also involved in the progress monitoring of their child.

Collaborative effort in planning and decision making: Team members do not work in silos, but meet regularly and work together in making decisions and delivering intervention. The professional team meets weekly or fortnightly to share observations and strategies, and to plan lessons and intervention sessions.

Shared Vision on Individual Education Plan (IEP) Document: The IEP document is a common document that reflects the team's agreement on the vision and goals for the student and family. The IEP is formulated in collaboration by all team members, including the student and/or the family.

Role release: While the team comprises different professionals, the strategies are not delivered in isolation, but are shared and delivered across team members.

Key Worker (KW) and Key Therapist (KT): A KW, usually the teacher, is identified to be the main liaison for the family. The KT is identified depending on the student's most salient area of needs at that point in time. The KW and KT are the two main team members involved in the engagement of the family and the intervention of the child.

Figure 3 illustrates that all these indicators are equally important in practising the transdisciplinary team approach in RC EI Services.

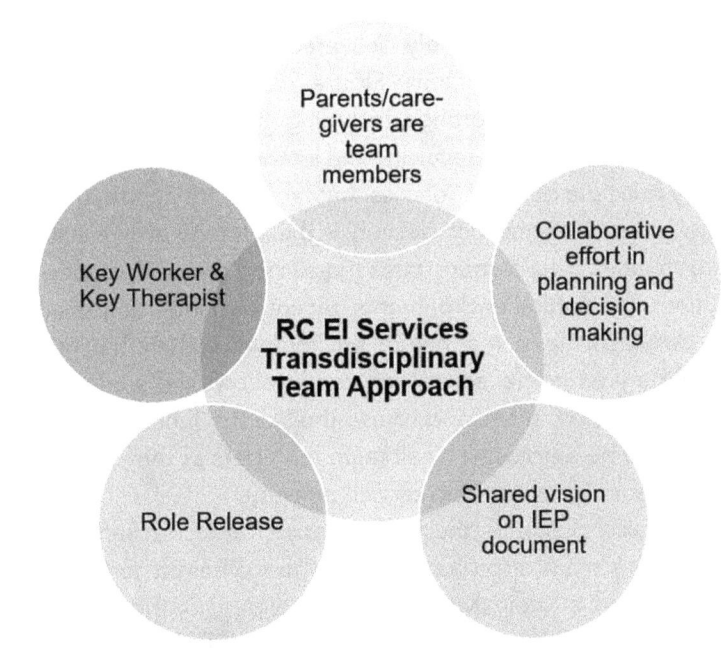

Figure 3. RC EI Services Transdisciplinary Team Approach

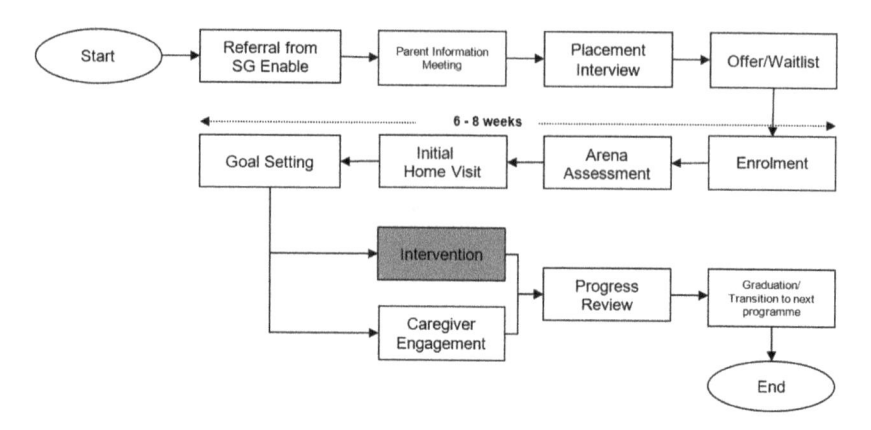

Figure 4. Intervention in the RC EI journey

Approaches in Rainbow Centre Early Intervention

Intervention refers to the part of the early intervention journey where services are delivered to achieve the goals set forth in the IEP. Hence, intervention should begin once goals have been set and agreed upon (Fig 4).

Intervention is collaboratively delivered by everyone on the team: teachers, therapists, and the family. Figure 5 also shows that intervention can take place in multiple settings, including in the home with the family being the interventionists or receiving the intervention. This demonstrates the first key principle of RC EI Services that families are important partners.

At the centre of the service delivery is the strategy of embedding the goals into routines. This demonstrates the second principle of focusing on daily routines and natural environments. By entrenching the goals into the student's daily activities across natural environments where he/she spends the most time (i.e., home, school, centre), it allows the student to have more practice opportunities and to use the skills in functional ways. This strategy should be employed by all team members as they work with the student to ensure consistency in service delivery.

Figure 5 also illustrates the third principle of RC EI Services — the transdisciplinary team approach. Despite the different team members providing support in their own domains of expertise, the whole system centres around achieving the student's common IEP goals and transition planning. Therapy is no longer delivered in isolation as in a multidiscipli-

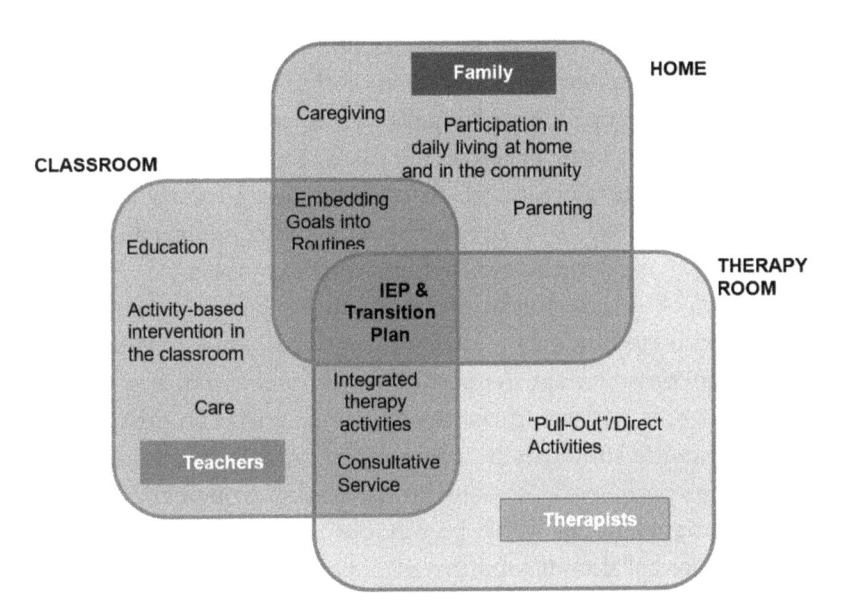

Figure 5.   Intervention Service Delivery in our centre-based services

nary approach (except for special cases), but integrated into activity-based intervention in the classroom with the therapists and the teachers working closely together. As role release gradually takes place, the therapists' role gradually transforms into a consultative one.

While the team works collaboratively, each domain expert has their own main settings in which they operate.

An even greater emphasis on collaboration in the community

In 2017 and 2019, RC EI services expanded from a centre-based service to include a home-based and preschool-based service respectively. This is in recognition of the importance of bringing the intervention into the community context of our students.

In our home-based services, our Key Workers and Key Therapists do not bring a "therapy bag" along with them for the sessions. Our objective when in the home is to look for materials and resources within the environment, and together with the family or caregiver, to then create intervention opportunities within an activity in that environment. This increases the success of the intervention being repeated and carried out outside of the weekly sessions. A good understanding of the family's routines outside the home also allows us to include in our plans strategies that can be embedded within the community. For example, during a weekly trip to the supermarket, the family can practise language and communication goals while labelling or making choices for fruits and vegetables.

Up to 70% of our students attend a preschool childcare centre or kindergarten and these students may need some additional support within their preschool environment. As part of our programming, and with the support of parents and preschool teachers, our team can provide consultation to provide strategies or teaching resources that will benefit the students in their preschool classroom. With the existing number of students with developmental needs within preschools, there is an urgent need to establish deeper collaborative partnerships between EI professionals and early childhood (EC) educators.

Moving forward: Making Every Preschool Inclusive (MEPI)

Making Every Preschool Inclusive (MEPI) is an ongoing collaborative project between Rainbow Centre and two preschools in Singapore (St. James' Church Kindergarten and PAP Community Foundation), funded by the Lien Foundation. The project seeks to uncover a model of collaboration that guides inclusive practices in Singapore with a strong focus on the collaborative teaming approach.

While strengthening our support and services for our students in their preschools and childcare centres via the government-funded DS-Plus service, together with our partners, Rainbow Centre is interested in exploring how an established approach towards inclusion through the collaborative teaming model could look like in the local context. Through the project, a practice guide will be developed, and it will guide the partnership between EI providers and EC educators. At the same time, the MEPI Training Programme is developed and piloted through the project, where Rainbow Centre hopes to contribute in capability building of EI and EC professionals as Singapore moves towards the inclusion of students in the community.

With the ongoing project evaluation by the Centre of Evidence and Implementation and the completion of the project in 2023, we are looking forward to sharing findings and our learning from this experience with the sector and other like-minded professionals.

In April 2021, the Early Childhood Development Agency Inclusive Preschool Workgroup provided in their report a tiered framework on how support and inclusion of children with different levels of developmental needs can be enhanced in an inclusive preschool sector. With these ongoing shifts in the early childhood and early intervention sector, MEPI will pave the way for a model in which these partnerships can take place. At the same time, Rainbow Centre will continue to enhance our specialist support to the children with higher needs through our centre-based and home-based services.

There is so much more for Rainbow Centre Early Intervention Services to learn and to contribute in the years to come; indeed, what an exciting time for our little ones and their families!

RESOURCES

Early Childhood Development Agency
(a) Early Intervention Services: https://www.ecda.gov.sg/Parents/Pages/EarlyIntervention.aspx
(b) Parent's Guide for Early Intervention: https://www.ecda.gov.sg/Documents/Parents/Parent's%20Guide%20for%20Early%20Intervention.pdf
SG Enable
Early Intervention Programme for Infants & Children and Development Support Plus: https://www.enablingguide.sg/im-looking-for-disability-support/therapy-intervention/early-intervention-programme-for-infants-children

REFERENCES

Alexander, S., & Forster, J. (2012). *The Key Worker Resources for Early Childhood Intervention Professionals*. ECII.

Bricker, D., & Cripe, J. (1992). *An activity-based approach to early intervention*. Paul H. Brookes Publishing.

Bruder, M. (2010). Early Childhood Intervention: A Promise to Children and Families for Their Future. *Council for Exceptional Children, 76*(3), 339–355.

Case-Smith, J., & Holland, T. (2009). Making Decisions About Service Delivery in Early Childhood Programs. *Language, Speech, and Hearing Services in Schools, 40,* 416–423.

DEC. (2014). *DEC recommended practices in early intervention.* The Division For Early Childhood of the Council for Exceptional Children.

Foley, G. M. (1990). Portrait of the arena evaluation. In E. Gibbs, & D. Teti (Eds.), *Interdisciplinary assessment of infants: A guide for early intervention professionals* (pp. 271–286). Baltimore: Paul H. Brookes.

Jennings, D., Frances, M., & Woods, J. (2012). Using Routines-Based Interventions in Early Childhood Special Education. *Dimensions of Early Childhood, 40*(2), 13–23.

King, G., Tucker, M., Desserud, S., & Shillington, M. (2009). The Application of a Transdisciplinary Model for Early Intervention Services. *Infants & Young Children,* Vol. 22, No. 3, pp. 211–223.

McGonigel, M. J.-M. (1994). The transdisciplinary team: A model for family-centered early intervention. In L. J. Johnson, R. J. Gallagher, & M. J. Lamontagne (Eds.), *Meeting early intervention challenges: Issues from birth to three* (pp. 95–131). Baltimore: Paul H. Brookes.

Scott, S., & McWilliam, R. (2000). *Scale for Assessment of Family Enjoyment Within Routines (SAFER).* University of North Carolina, Chapel Hill: Frank Porter Graham Child Development Center.

Woodruff, G., & McGonigel, M. J. (1988). *Early Intervention Team Approaches: The Transdisciplinary Model.* ERIC Publications.

The School Years

Lynette Gomez, Sharifah Masturah Yokoyama and Jessica Wee

"It takes a whole village to raise a child."
This is very true at Rainbow Centre.
We work with various systems and subsystems to fulfil the needs
of the student and their families
in order to enhance their quality of life.
We set the vision for the student with their families and then
create the plan towards this vision.
If the plan doesn't work, we change the plan, but never the
vision.
And we do this together as a team, the whole village.

Karnatie Junid, Senior Social Worker
Rainbow Centre Margaret Drive School (RCMDS)

What does "a whole village to raise a child" mean? During the school years at Rainbow Centre (RC), teams of professionals come together to develop our students, in the hope that they become adults who are empowered and thriving in their communities. This shared vision is the core belief of everyone who makes up those teams — the educators, allied professionals, social workers, community partners — working hand-in-hand with the student and his family.

When it comes to developing a young person, it is not possible to do it alone without collaborating with the family, the people who are most important to the student. Whatever the student learns in school, it is important that he can generalise the skills at home. Therefore, families play an important role in the whole process of developing our students during their school years.

What about learning? What are we learning from one another? The professional teams at school need to learn more about the student from the families, as there will be in-depth information that only the family would know, and such information could support the team when planning and working on the student's Individual Education Plan. Within the professional teams, members can learn more about the strategies to support the student's learning or manage behaviour by learning from other team members who have strong skills and knowledge in their specific discipline. Families can also learn more about the teaching strategies that can be used at home to strengthen the learning and development of the student. This could benefit families beyond the school years too. Such teaming is therefore a critical enabler for our students' holistic development, as they stand to benefit from the strong and effective partnership. It allows for meaningful plans to be created and monitored to achieve the shared vision.

From age seven to 18, students spend 11 years in our schools. How may we maximise this opportunity to push their potential?

HOLISTIC EDUCATION AND DEVELOPMENT

The Rainbow Centre Special Education Curriculum has six core domains: Language and Communication, Numeracy, Daily Living, Social and Emotional, Physical Development, and Vocational Education. These six domains highlight the key areas of development that our students would need in order to live a Good Life and participate safely in the community. This forms the core of community based learning and participation that RC's holistic education and development approach is based upon.

The RC Educational Outcomes are aligned to the Ministry of Education Special Education framework, and adapted to RC's philosophy, culture and student profiles. Our curriculum has been designed to not only be holistic, but also person-centred, developmentally appropriate, collaborative, coherent, and of high expectations of our students.

The RC Education Outcomes are shown in the diagram below:

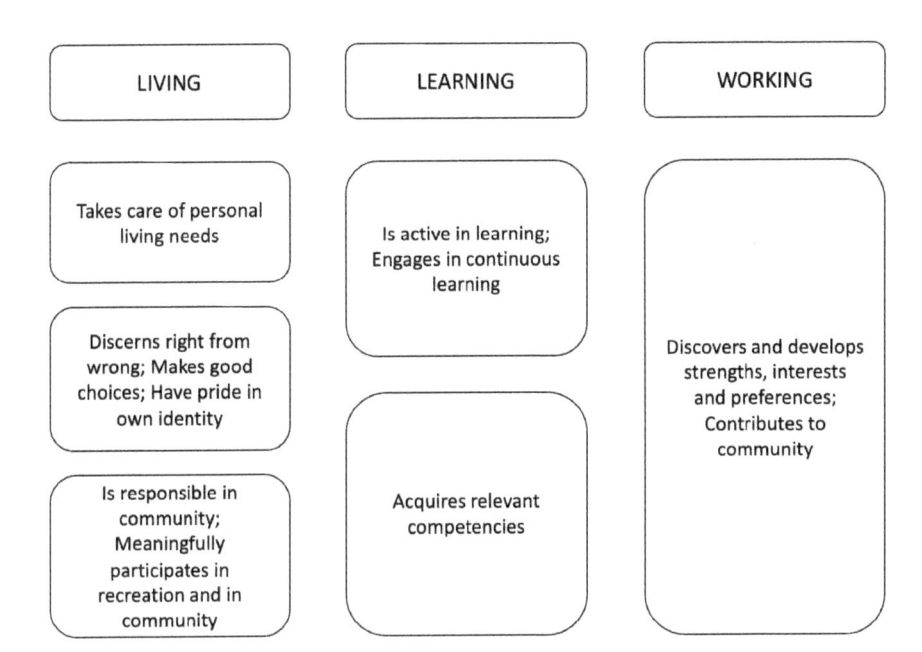

Under the *Living* outcome, our students are supported to live independently and interdependently with and within their community. Therefore, they develop a sense of responsibility for themselves, that is, being an active participant in society as well as willingly participating in meaningful activities for themselves, within the community. Participation in the community also means having good social skills in order to develop friendships and positive relationships.

Under the *Learning* outcome, the main objective is in having our students be active in their learning, generalising the skills they acquire and build on their existing skills, for example, communication and independent travelling skills. These skills can be strengthened, so that our students are always able to stay connected in their community.

The aim of the *Working* outcome is for our students to discover and develop their strengths, interests, and preferences while also contributing to their community. Another intended outcome is that our students will meet with higher success in their post-school options and contributing well to their homes and families, to the centres that they may be enrolled in and for those who can work in supported or open employment, then to contribute well in their job roles.

These *Living*, *Learning* and *Working* outcomes are developed through the RC school's programming approach.

THE RC PROGRAMME

These 12 years are split into three programmes, namely the Junior, the Middle and the Senior programme. Each programme has its own focus as well as five main outcomes, which support the holistic development of the RC student in the areas of self, communication, social skills, and personal safety.

Junior Programme (7–10 years old)

The junior programme focuses on building foundational knowledge and skills in self-care and self-management in daily living. These foundations are enhanced and contextualised across the other two programmes as the student grows and develops.

At a young age, it is critical for students to develop strong learning skills, like starting a task, following instructions, staying on task, and completing tasks. Another important area of development at this age is developing self-regulation skills, that is, skills that enable the student to manage his emotions as well as the various environmental factors that may affect him. These skills will also support the student's ability to gain access to learning and maintain engagement in his learning as well.

The primary outcomes are related to communication, self-regulating and work habits, which are key skills to access learning. The development of social skills enables the student to learn to accept others — perhaps in shared space with others — interact with others in a group setting and develop teamwork skills. Together, these outcomes provide the student with a strong foundation for future learning, as well as in social interaction with peers and trusted or familiar others. We hope that this would also create a desire to contribute to and participate in teams and social activities beyond school. Meeting basic daily living needs, keeping safe and being able to seek help are the foundational skills for self-care and self-management, leading to independence.

At this fundamental age, students also require support from both the school as well as their families and would greatly benefit from a keen partnership between the two. This is because the skills that our students learn in school must be generalised and maintained across a period of time.

Middle Programme (11–14 years old)

"My journey as a special education teacher has been driven by the belief that every student/child regardless of their different needs, is able to participate fully in discovering themselves and exploring in the community. Middle Programme outcomes such as communicating effectively gives them the opportunities, choices and experiences just like any other individual. When we know the strengths and interests of our students, we are halfway through helping them in having a more meaningful life!"

Zaidah Binte Mazelan, Assistant Lead Teacher
Rainbow Centre Yishun Park School (RCYPS)

The middle programme facilitates the transition into adolescence, when our students are beginning to explore and understand who they are by discovering their strengths, interests and preferences. The focus of this programme is on discovering self, and exploring the wider community. This stage is a critical bridging stage before the students enter the Senior Programme and develop skills to support post-school living.

Understanding more about themselves, knowing what they like or do not, and knowing how to help themselves when required are critical for successful post-school outcomes. In the middle programme, our students learn ways to find out more about themselves as well as their needs and wants, so that they can achieve their goals in the most productive way.

To do so, they have to be open to new experiences, attain some level of flexibility and accept change as part of the real world. With a firm understanding of themselves, our students are in a better and safer position to explore the wider community and start thinking about their place and responsibilities in society. This encourages the building of their own value systems and aids in their decision-making processes, which are important skills when they are starting to build friendships.

Being able to develop and maintain friendships is another key skill in adolescence. Interactions in this context will enhance their social communication skills. RC uses a strengths-based approach that focuses on what a student can do and wants to do. This approach enables students to have a sense of personal identity and agency as they transit into adulthood.

Senior Programme (15–18 years old)

In the Senior Programme, our students are guided to form a sense of personal agency and interdependence with the community as they transition into adulthood. With their value systems, knowledge, self-regulation, and communication skills developed and strengthened from the Junior and Middle programmes, students are now encouraged to contribute to and/or participate in the community in different ways.

The senior programme focuses mainly on transition to adulthood, where being able to make good choices, expressing one's thoughts and opinions, and possessing resilience and adaptability are critical outcomes. Living and engaging interdependently within the community calls for a mix of independence and dependence. Students must know how to nurture positive relationships and take on shared responsibilities. They must also be able to access information, resources, and services as an adult while knowing how to seek support in these areas. The senior programme outcomes are aligned to and support the domains of the RC Good Life transition plan that facilitates their transition from school to adulthood.

Important areas of focus for all students

As part of the three programmes during the school years, skills in the three important areas of Communication, Mobility, and Social Emotional skills are developed in all our RC students.

Communication

"Imagine going a day with no one responding to you. Now, imagine a year, or even years! Communication is essential for us to feel empowered and included. Our clients need to feel understood and also be able to understand what is happening around them. We do this when we provide the support needed for them to share to share their thoughts with us, and when we present what we say in a way that they can understand too."

**Michelle Cheong, Senior Speech & Language Therapist
Rainbow Centre Margaret Drive School (RCMDS)**

It is important to focus on communication for our students. All of us are social animals and have a desire and a need to connect to the environment and people around us. It is of course no different for our RC students. The impact of having strong communication skills is being heard, being connected with others and advocating for self. In order for our students to acquire these skills, numerous opportunities must be created, with communication partners playing a critical role in this area. Families must also believe in the power of communication and support our students by not only learning to use their communication systems, but also in using them as frequently as possible in ALL authentic settings.

MOBILITY TRAINING

"Mobility training helps our students to safely navigate their key environments, enabling them to interact with the world, including the home school and community.

Being MOBILE is an important prerequisite skill that enables and enhances individual student access to teaching and learning within, and across, academic and functional domains.

Implementing Orientation and Mobility Training for the students at RC can surely also 'broaden the student's awareness of the environment, resulting in increased motivation, independence and safety'."

**Emmanuel Prabhu, Senior Teacher
Rainbow Centre Yishun Park School (RCYPS)**

Being able to travel and move around independently means that our students will have a better chance to access community services and participate in community activities. Hence at RC, our schools develop travelling skills milestones that we support our students to achieve, from the foundational level at Junior programme to more advanced skills levels in the Middle and finally Senior programmes.

As the outcome is on independence and participation in the community, our schools offer Community-Based Instructional activities where our students hone their mobility skills while out and about in the community. This independence in mobility can be specially curated for our students to meet their individual needs, through close partnership with families and community partners. The independence our student achieves is based on the effort and aspirations of everyone, especially the student, enabling the student to achieve his highest level of independence.

SOCIAL-EMOTIONAL SKILLS

> "Social and emotional well-being is a balanced and healthy way of interacting with people in one's environment, and the ability to respond to one's own emotions. This has great impact on one's quality of life."

> **Susan George, Lead Psychologist**
> **Rainbow Centre Margaret Drive School (RCMDS)**

Another key area of focus is on developing strong social-emotional skills which impacts self-esteem, self-determination, and self-management. Social-emotional well-being is at the core of our students' development. With strong social-emotional skills, our students are well-balanced and able to learn new things, can acquire some flexibility to adapt to changes, and are able to manage their own emotions well, which therefore support them when participating in the community.

A critical area of focus in social-emotional development is self-determination

It has always been perceived that people with special needs have difficulty developing skills associated with self-determination and problem solving, given their characteristic difficulty with self-awareness, awareness of others, engagement, and social-emotional understanding. The conversations with families and stakeholders, and most importantly, observing and listening to our students and young adults share their transitioning manoeuvres in school, and from school to home and the community, highlighted the need to develop self-determination skills and attitudes. Indeed, self-determination skills and attitudes are enablers across the lifespan.

Opportunities to make choices are infused throughout a student's day. Experiences with making choices 'teach' students that they can exert some control over their environment. It is indeed delightful to watch the smiles from our students as they express their choices within or between instructional activities, with whom they engage in the various tasks and activities, as well as with different people in their learning spaces. A number of core strategies, such as using concrete teaching materials and visual support, structuring the environment for clarity and predictability, and using repeated experiences, are incorporated and woven into daily routines and school programmes.

Early on in the Junior Programme, students are introduced to learning opportunities that promote the attitude of self-determination through the concepts of 'working from one task to another' and 'task completion' in their work system. During situations which require the students to put on shoes or learn to brush their teeth independently, visual support and checklists are introduced for them to monitor progress towards their goals. Reinforcers and rewards are introduced to celebrate progress and a positive attitude to learning.

As students move on to the Middle Programme, other components of self-determination are introduced, including decision-making, problem-solving skills, as well as building and maintaining friendships.

Choreographing situations for students to be actively involved in decision-making provides an opportunity for their 'voice' to be heard. In the spirit of continuously innovating teaching and learning, targeted opportunities were embedded into routine school activities, while several new exciting programmes were implemented.

The Mobility Intentional Learning via Education & Support or The MILES Programme @YPS is one example of a programme that encompasses the various self-determination skills. From being introduced to move around the learning spaces within the school ground in the Junior Programme, students in the Middle and Senior Programme are engineered to explore the community around them. Besides acquiring independent mobility skills, they learn to make choices, solve problems, make decisions, as well as build values related to being resilient and adaptable.

Aligning with the RC vision of enabling the young people we serve to go beyond their disabilities by being empowered, included in the community, and being able to live a thriving life, the enrichment programme known as Watch-Out-World (WOW) was implemented in the three RC campuses. The aim of WOW is to help students become young adults who are continuously learning, adaptive to new contexts, and able to engage in and contribute to the community as per their interest and talent. This programme provides students with training in higher order skills such as critical thinking and problem solving, communication and collaboration, as well as creativity and innovation.

WOW has three aims:

1. **Enrich**: Train our students to become better thinkers and problem solvers, stronger communicators and collaborators, and be more creative and innovative;
2. **Explore**: Nurture the enjoyment of learning and enhance person-centred growth through engaging our students to explore their interests and areas of potential talent;
3. **Excel**: Provide development for excellent performance and achievement for students who demonstrate high level talent in a specific domain.

The practice of self-determination skills in the repertoire of students' learning in RC has brought about many positive ripple effects. The exposure to the rigour and discipline in sports, engagement with people in the community, and empowerment through working in teams have brought the students to new terrain in areas of self-management and self-advocacy. Our teachers used to be the ones advocating for our students with regard to inclusion and diversity. Interestingly, our students are now being enabled and empowered to advocate for themselves, and learning skills on how to be assertive, how to effectively communicate their perspective, and how to negotiate, including how to compromise. This was done by embedding opportunities for self-advocacy within the school day, including working out their preferred schedules, arranging their apparatus and resources needed to prepare for training (sports), and participating in transition planning.

While several characteristics of people with disabilities may impact the development of the skills related to self-determination, the team at Rainbow Centre stays optimistic and creative that with educational support and accommodation, these skills can be acquired and sustained. Breaking down skill steps, using concrete examples, and embracing generalisation for further practice in different settings with different people will ensure that teaching and learning is authentic, future-oriented and holistic.

PARENTSHIP

Parents are the child's first teachers. But sometimes, educators forget this and leave the parents out of the education planning process. Rather than talking about partnership, Dr Kyle Palmer, Distinguished Principal of Missouri Association of Elementary School Principals in 2013 mooted the idea of having a mindset of parentship, where parents are viewed as key partners with a voice to be heard in how schools are run. At Rainbow Centre, we strive to uphold this belief through our approaches and strategies in our three schools in the hopes of achieving the following outcomes:

- Families understand their child's abilities and special needs, and are implementing developmentally and contextually appropriate best parenting practices.
- Families are socially connected and participating in the community.
- Families are resilient to general life stressors as well as parenting-related stressors.
- Families know where to turn to for help and are able to advocate for their needs.
- Families and children have positive interactions.

Families go through different seasons of their lives as their child grows up. The family dynamics also change with the developmental growth of the child, requiring schools to constantly adjust the support given to the families. RC adopts a tiered approach to family engagement as outlined in the figure below.

The *Universal* level is targeted at all families with a focus on education, support, information giving, and building social networks. It comprises mainly school based engagements through various modes such as home visits, class observations, case conferences, class dojo, and term letters.

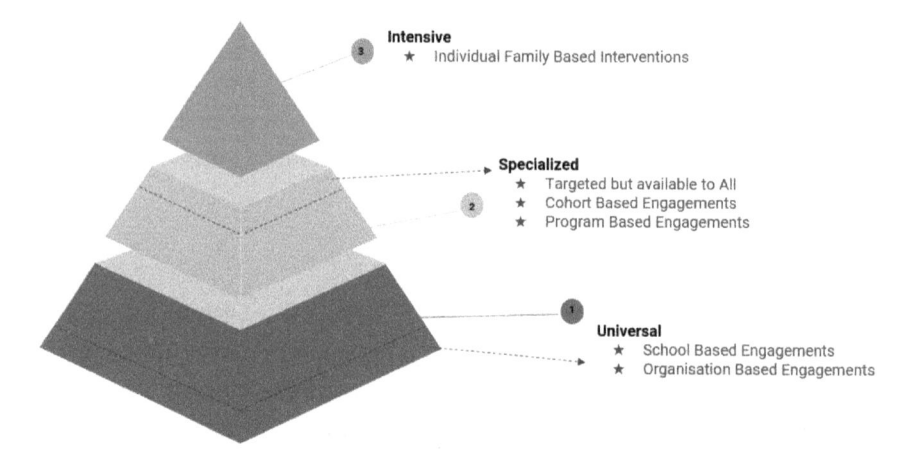

TIERED APPROACH & ACTIONS

The *Specialised* level is targeted at cohort based or programme based engagements. There is also targeted support for specific communities such as fathers, single parents or siblings. The modes of engagement are monthly drop-in sessions for caregivers and parents who spend time in school, cohort parent connect, semester outings, programme orientation for new parents, and envisioning exercise with the Senior Programme families.

The Intensive level is where a customised intervention plan is developed for each individual family and their child. When necessary, additional support through programmes such as the Family Empowerment Programme would see the school professionals working closely with the families at risk for a dedicated period of time.

One of the lessons which educators learn rather quickly is the importance of communication — especially timely, open and clear communication with parents. Transparency and timely communication always works. Communicate frequently and in the way that works best for each family via phone, email, text message or handwritten notes.

It is essential to assume every family wants the best for their children, and parents do look to the school as the expert. As such, the school has a responsibility to guide them on what they need to do for their children to achieve success.

At Rainbow Centre, we share frequently with parents the successes of their children in school to encourage them to generalise these skills at home.

When COVID-19 hit us, we needed to implement home-based learning and various safety management measures in the school such as mask-wearing and temperature-taking. These were not helping with promoting family relationships; in fact, parents felt alienated and alone when managing their children at home.

The schools had to adapt quickly to the new normal of teaching and changing the approach of engaging parents. To support learning on the home front, the schools provided parents with home-based resources, conducted virtual lessons and equipped parents with follow-up on the lessons at home.

Parents who are proactive in collaborating with teachers was a huge morale booster for the latter. More importantly, it gave a whole new meaning to collaboration. The pandemic had accelerated the progress of parents' participation and collaboration, which provided a structure for schools to continue post-COVID 19.

CONCLUSION

It is truly amazing how the buzz, action, conversations and narratives are evolving in the learning and teaching spaces in our Rainbow Centre campuses. We salute each and every member at Rainbow Centre for their boldness in the ongoing reflective inquiries and explorations, as well as possessing the courage to innovate and develop pathfinding tools as we redesign various learning environments and teaching moments that are needed to meet the current and future challenges of the real community. Of course, the 'adventurers' in this continuous exciting expedition towards making teaching and learning engaging, inclusive and real are our students and their very supportive families.

REFERENCES

Palmer, K. (2022). Parentships in PLC at Work®: Forming and Sustaining School-Home Relationships with Families (An action plan for meaningful school improvement). USA: Solution Tree Press

Rainbow Centre. (2018). *Your guide to the curriculum.* Rainbow Centre.

5 Transitions to Adulthood: Charting Good Life

Christy Lee-O'Loughlin and Cynthia Lee

INTRODUCTION

Exiting one life stage and going to another is often celebrated by graduation ceremonies along with the excitement of welcoming the new. However, such transition points for people with autism and other developmental disabilities and their families can often be marked by anxiety and apprehension. In particular, transitions to adulthood can provoke much stress.

Adulthood demands more independence and autonomy than the preceding life stage calls for. It also signifies family life cycle changes such as the siblings of youths with autism also possibly entering adulthood, and parents becoming older. To add to the stress, the post-18 services for young adults with autism or other developmental disabilities can be limited. This is especially more so for those with severe to moderate needs who attend special education schools in Rainbow Centre. For them, the precipice of Post-18 — the commonly used term — is even deeper, wider and more challenging to navigate.

At Rainbow Centre, we see the challenges faced by our students who are not well prepared for life after graduation, and those of parents with children who have significant disabilities, where their options are few and limited. In 2016, we asked how we could better share knowledge and vision among students, parents, and professionals of students' post-school goals and the transition resources necessary to support their needs and interests; how we could ensure meaningful roles for the students and parents in the transition decision-making process; and how we could increase the options for students with significant disabilities to ensure no one would be left behind.

What resulted from our inquiry was a clearer scope of what quality of life means for our students with significant difficulties, and a process for how best to plan and prepare them towards that goal.

This chapter outlines the Good Life Transition Planning process which has been used in Rainbow Centre since 2017. Students with moderate to severe autism as well as multiple disabilities participate in this process when they turn 14 years old. This is aligned with the year students enter into a curriculum focused on forming a personal agency and interdependence with the community. This planning process is facilitated by transition facilitators using an Understand-Involve-Connect framework spelled out in the Good Life transition toolkit.

This chapter will also insights and ongoing challenges we face as we continue to implement this process. You will find how best practices of transition planning, including person-centred planning; active involvement of the youth, their families and the community; the use of a transition facilitator; and collaboration among stakeholders are implemented.

OUR UNDERGIRDING BELIEFS

Four undergirding beliefs guided the development of our person-centred planning approach. Firstly, we believe that everyone wants a Good Life. The "Good Life" for a person with a disability is not very different from yours or mine. While we have different life aspirations and motivations, we all desire a good quality of life. Secondly, everyone has a voice. Often not heard because of their difficulty to communicate verbally, we forget that our students have a voice and want to be heard. Professionals and the people around our students have a role to help express those voices and ensure that our students are able to communicate their wants and desires. Thirdly, our students' aspirations need to be listened to before any assessment of ability. Often, the focus is on the ability of our students to do something instead of their desire or wish to do something. It is important that we learn and listen to what our students want and their aspirations before considering whether they can do it.

Lastly, there is power in the community. Drawing reference from the Assets Based Community Development approach, the community is a reservoir of emotional support, resources and networks waiting to be uncovered and tapped on. There is potential in partnering the untapped resources in the community in building a community of care around our students.

THE GOOD LIFE TRANSITION FRAMEWORK: UNDERSTAND-INVOLVE-CONNECT

Understand
Establish understanding
of who the youth is; his or
her strengths, preferences,
abilities and aspirations

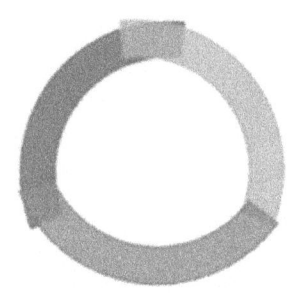

Involve
Envisioning and
co-creating a good
life with the youth
& family

Connect
Activating connections
within the community
to achieve youth's &
family's visions.

Understand-Involve-Connect is a model of managing transitions of persons with disabilities (PWDs) and their families alongside them, and organising support around them by connecting them to their community. Key to this approach is that things should be done with people, not to them. A fundamental tenet of the approach is that there are assets available in people and the community to be tapped on for solving problems together. Learning with and about PWDs, their families, and the community they live in, and working with them to find creative solutions is the basis of this model, rather than prescribing a service to them.

Essentially, this is a resource-based approach to support PWDs and families with reference to the Asset Based Community Development approach. It views resources as varied, rich, expandable and renewable as opposed to services-based practices where resources are commonly viewed as fixed and limited. More importantly, this approach moves away from the risk of creating services that often remove PWDs from the community and sometimes from their families. Providing services where they are needed honours their right to live, love, work, add value to, play, and pursue their life aspirations just as others do in their community.

DOMAINS OF A GOOD LIFE

At Rainbow Centre, a Goodlife Toolkit is used by transition facilitators to guide the process of transition planning. It is inspired by the Charting the Life Course Guide developed by the Missouri's University Center for Excellence in Developmental Disabilities Education, Research and Services and contextualised for Singaporean families and aligned to the Ministry of Education Special Education Living, Learning and Working (LLW) framework. There are six domains of a Good Life.

Being Engaged: In particular, because working outcomes are often perceived narrowly as employment and this aspect is a challenge for many Rainbow Centre graduates, working is framed as being 'engaged' under the Good Life in an attempt to facilitate discussions. Being engaged includes participating in interest groups (such as sports, arts, crafts, music), meeting up with family and friends, volunteering, and learning new skills. It recognises that life is more than simply going to school or working. An engaged lifestyle will bring meaning to our lives and keep us mentally active.

Being Safe: Feeling and being safe allows us to enjoy our lives without the fear that we could be harmed physically, psychologically, or financially. Being safe is most often about keeping ourselves out of dangerous situations or having the skills to avoid a dangerous situation. This is especially important as students with autism are often found missing and unable to intentionally protect themselves in the community because of their difficulties in understanding social cues and communication. Hence, we need to ensure that we develop a safety plan and support the practice of being safe.

Being Independent: Recognising that everyone has limits helps reframe what being independent means. There will be certain things that we cannot do, or do not want to do. By starting to make everyday decisions such as what to wear, what to eat, or choosing friends and the activities to participate in, we begin to know our limits. This helps us to make important decisions like how to use our money and where to stay. Increasing independence gives us the confidence to live the life we want.

Being Healthy: Being healthy allows us to live full and active lives and be part of the community. To be healthy, we may require health care for conditions related to the disability as well as health care that meets our needs as a whole person. We can acquire information and tools to make healthy lifestyle choices. A healthy lifestyle will see us exercising regularly, eating healthy foods in healthy proportions, and using medicines wisely, among other habits.

Being Included and Heard: When we are heard and our opinions valued in our community, we move away from being seen as someone requiring assistance in all aspects, and becoming an individual who is seen and valued by the people around us. We become better able to advocate for ourselves and others. We can participate in discussions about what we require and what affects us. We can contribute to design for services and spaces to address accessibility issues, co-creating inclusive communities for everyone.

Being Connected: When we are connected to families and friends and engaged in meaningful relationships, we live a more fulfilling life. Friendships and relationships are essential in our lives. We receive care and concern from our families and friends and reciprocate by doing the same. Being connected means that we are able to receive support from and provide support to the right people.

Every person's good life is different. However, through the 6 domains, we make sure that we include the considerations for all parts of one's life. This is important for someone like Alice, for example, who has Autism with limited post-18 service options such Day Activity Centre (DAC), sheltered workshop much less open employment. For Alice, a good life that was planned when she was 15 now looks like this:

— Folds clothes with adapted folding board, gets paid for pasting labels on egg-carton and selling microgreens (Engagement)
— Hikes with YMCA Hiking Club and Good Life Befrienders, hikes with her family and participates in Running Hour (Health and Being Connected)

UNDERSTAND: A PERSON CENTRED APPROACH

A person-centred approach is often a recommended practice for improving the transition planning process.[3,5,6] It is a co-creation process which involves organising support and resources around one person to define and create a good life for that individual. We start by getting to know this person as a whole person. This 'whole person' orientation as opposed to disability management or service focused approach seeks to truly understand the experience of people with disabilities from their own perspective.

In the first phase of the Good Life Transition planning, the focus is on developing an understanding of their likes, dislikes, interests and preferences. Co-creation of a Good Life plan can only happen when we have a good understanding of our students and their interests, with person-centred information collated by a transition facilitator. It forms the backdrop and focus of the transition planning going forward — serving to keep the person in the centre of decision making and resourcing of support needed.

One of the key challenges of understanding our students' likes, dislikes, interests and preferences is their limited exposure to a wide range of interests and activities. Hence, they are not able to tell us what they like or not like. We have learned that curriculum focus and supporting families to expose their youth to a variety of age appropriate activities are necessary for long-term planning of how youths will develop a sense of self, their abilities and discover their interests and talent along the way. With a limited repertoire, many areas of their good life can be compromised , such as ways they can be engaged, things they can do to stay healthy, and how they can be connected, among others.

INVOLVE: A PROCESS OF EMPOWERMENT

"Nothing about me without me" is a common slogan and a core principle in person-centred planning. What this means in practice for us in Good Life Transition planning, is the direct involvement of our youths as well as their parents and family members in their transition planning. Youths and their families share about who they are and their dreams for a good life, and the way they like to be supported towards their dreams.

In the context of the culture of Rainbow Centre , we see ourselves as service providers. As service providers, we naturally do things *for* our clients instead of doing things *with* them. Instead of inviting them to participate in the conversations and hearing from them what they truly want, we often decide for them based on our assessment of their needs and ability. As we begin to invite them into the conversation of planning their Good Lives, we provide them with a platform to be truly heard. It is about self-advocacy and self-determination.

However, hearing the voices of our youths and their families can sometimes be challenging due to anxiety, as well as difficulty in social interaction and communication. These need to be mediated through pre-planning and employment of strategies to build rapport and to structure the planning sessions. Though challenging, listening to the youths and their families has been full of surprises. We have heard youths share interests and dreams which their parents did not know about. Some parents were surprised by what their children revealed as they did not think that their children had dreams or interests. Alex, now 24, whose interest was to make friends and earn money, now works full time at a laundry service provider and still visits his old teachers at Rainbow Centre. As professionals, we have learnt to hold back our professional judgement on what is best for them. We learned to ask not whether someone 'can' do something but to focus on what they want to do. And our role is to support them towards doing it.

Parents and immediate family members' voices are also important and are included in the planning process. Sometimes it's a small voice of not daring to hope for too much. Other times, it's a powerful voice, speaking on behalf of the missing voice of our youth. Both voices, and the many in between, having their say in their own life empowers them and is key to ownership of their process and sustaining the efforts in the transition. Other than the involvement of the youth and immediate family members, the *family envisioning* and planning process also saw the involvement of the youth and others such as aunts, godparents, domestic helpers, neighbours, friends and people who care deeply for the youths. Hearing them share their hopes and dreams for the youth and their family is comforting and heartening for they are the ones who will journey with the youths and their immediate family members.

Other than involvement in their child's transition planning process, parents of graduating students also come together to discuss their fears and hopes. Even though not all are equally resourced and ready for the future in the same way, they share similar experiences and this allows them to support each other in their journey.

Stakeholder engagement in the transition of the youth is a critical factor for successful transition.[2] This entails resourcing commitment and logistics of getting everyone into the same room. Securing alignment with organisation leaders and implementers is the first step.

CONNECT: ACTIVATING THE POWER OF COMMUNITY

The answers to what needs to happen in order to meet the dreams and hopes of how people with disabilities would like to live are clear: Resources in the community need to be activated. The Connect phase of the process is grounded on the belief that the community is a reservoir of emotional support, resources and networks we can activate for our PWDs to be connected to and included in the real world.

Reviewing and planning what a typical week may look like while in school and after graduation is one way of ensuring smooth transition.[5] In this phase of the transition planning, the aim is to create a self-directed plan where our youths are meaningfully engaged. This is challenging when resources are limited. It requires development of partnerships and collaborative relationships which are beyond the usual service provisions. In response to what matters most for the person and how they want to be supported as gathered from the earlier planning stages, we started a Good Life Befrienders programme and Young Adult Activities! (YAA!) Many had shared their desire to have friends with whom to do things they enjoy and also to participate in activities of their interests.

The Good Life befrienders connect over similar interests, and they are passionate about working with the youths and finding ways to fulfil their good life plans. Our Good Life Befrienders also seek to develop meaningful friendships with our students. In a friendship where there is reciprocity, our students become contributing members where they provide support, care and concern to their befrienders. YAA!, a social activity club, provides opportunities for our youths to participate in diverse activities and to be connected with their peers. Our youths are able to decide and choose which activities they would like to participate in or be exposed to. They get to pick up new interests and skills when participating in the activities and bond with their peers. Rainbow Centre has also started Connected Communities Services where life coaches continue to build connections and expand networks after they graduate.

A significant factor affecting quality of life is social inclusion and participation.[4] Thus, ensuring our youths and their families are part of their local as well as the wider community is critical. Many of our youths have only two connections — family and school. The process has sought to connect our youths beyond these connections. However, sustaining the connections and continuing to expand the connections is a challenge. There is ongoing efforts to enrol more GoodLife befrienders, to match them to our youths and facilitate enduring friendships. Activities for young adults need to be more varied, not only to ensure that they are meaningfully engaged, but also to offer the young adults ample opportunities to pursue lifelong learnin Rainbow Centre. Our youths will thrive only when their gifts are recognised, supported and used in communities. We need partners in the community who are able to go beyond including them to valuing them as resources and assets in our society.

CONCLUSION: LOOKING AHEAD TOGETHER

The good life transition planning process is not one that starts at only age 15 to prepare our youths with autism and other developmental disabilities for adulthood. The vision of a good life, our Rainbow Dream, starts the moment they enter Rainbow Centre. Every decision has an impact on the good life trajectory. The good life articulated in the six domains creates the language and shared goal for the person we serve, their families and all of us in Rainbow Centre. Beyond special education, caregivers can still continue to use the good life domains to guide them throughout their lives. With the guide, the caregivers can engage any post-18 stakeholders who can then support and design the programmes and lifelong learning to make their good life a reality.

This person-centred transition planning process is also not simply a planning process in itself. Beliefs and values of personhood, empowerment, and inclusion, underpin the process. Successful and sustainable implementation of the process requires a change in culture and mindset that is only possible through systemic changes at the organisational, community and national levels. As with such changes involving paradigm shifts and systems integration, there are tensions to work through, dynamics to learn from and manage, as well as possibilities to welcome. The work of charting a good life and looking ahead with them at what's possible and also managing some of the challenges described in this chapter mirrors the uncharted emerging hope that our youths and their families are confronted with during their post-18 transition. We are in this with them!

We invite you to join us on the change and action required on different levels: individual, organisation, community and national for person-centred planning and support to truly benefit our youths with autism and other developmental disabilities, and to truly honour the social model of disability that Singapore had endorsed with our signing of the UN Convention on the Rights of Persons with Disabilities in 2012.

REFERENCES

1. Certo, N. J., Luecking, R. G., Murphy, S., Brown, L., Courey, S., & Belanger, D. (2008). Seamless transition and long-term support for individuals with severe intellectual disabilities. *Research and Practice for Persons with Severe Disabilities (RPSD)*, *33*(3), 85–95.
2. Goh, A. & Malik, N. (2021). Stakeholders' involvement in the transition to adulthood for youth with disabilities. *Special Needs in Singapore*, *10*, 193–217.
3. Kaehne, A., & Beyer, S. (2014). Person-centred reviews as a mechanism for planning the post-school transition of young people with intellectual disability. *Journal of Intellectual Disability Research*, *58*(7), 603–613. http://doi.org/10.1111/jir.12058
4. National Council of Social Service. (2017). Understanding the quality of life of adults with disabilities. https://www.ncss.gov.sg/press-room/publications/detail-page/UnderstandingPersonswithDisabilities
5. Robertson, J., Emerson, E., Hatton, C., Elliott, J., McIntosh, B., Swift, P., Krijnen-Kemp, E., Towers, C., Romeo, R., Knapp, M., Sanderson, H., Routledge, M.,

Oakes, P., & Joyce, T. (2005) The Impact of Person Centred Planning. Lancaster: Institute for Health Research, Lancaster University.

6. Sanderson, H., Jeanette T. & Jackie K. (2006). The emergence of person-centred planning as evidence-based practice. *Journal of Integrated Care*, *14*(2), 18–25.

Section 3

Medical Aspects

This section details the diagnosis, causes, manifestations and characteristics of autism and other developmental disabilities. It also addresses frequently asked questions from parents and caregivers, examines the facts and myths of autism and the effects music has on autism.

Diagnosis

Kenneth Lyen

INTRODUCTION

Diagnosing autism spectrum disorder is a challenge because there are no definitive biochemical or genetic tests, nor any brain imaging scans that can confirm the diagnosis. We rely entirely on history taking and clinical behavioural observations. This too can be very difficult because the manifestations of autism may not be apparent in the first few years of life. Furthermore, the condition can range from mild and moderate to severe.

The spectrum of autism ranges from the verbally fluent and slightly socially withdrawn individual at the mild end, to the nonverbal and socially isolated loner at the severe end. Some people on the mild end may not wish to be labelled autistic and prefer to be viewed as "different". Children at the severe end, on the other hand, need a lot of help, including early intervention, speech and occupational therapy, as well as long-term supportive care. Early diagnosis can lead to early intervention therapy, which can have long-term benefits. Finally, to qualify for early intervention special education and to apply for financial help, a diagnostic label is generally required by many institutions.

DEFINITION[1–3]

Autism is a common but complex neurodevelopmental disorder characterised by early-onset difficulties in social communication and unusually restrictive repetitive behaviours and interests. It manifests as a wide spectrum, ranging from a mild hesitancy in communicating with others, to someone who barely talks to anyone else. It encompasses the person who physically displays obsessionally recurring movements, to the savant with exceptionally gifted mathematics or artistic talents.

The early signs of autism are often subtle, but become clearer during the second and third year of life. Autism is not a transitory problem; one does not grow out of autism, but some of the signs become less prominent as one gets older. Autism is a lifelong condition.

Early signs

Early signs of autism include barely babbling, not using gestures such as pointing, and not responding to others by waving or nodding. Although poor eye contact is often listed as a feature of autistic children, this is an unreliable sign in Asians because they mostly have poor eye contact as part of Asian culture. They may display repetitive behaviours like flapping their hands or spinning the wheels of a toy car. They may pay more attention to objects than people, and although they can hear perfectly well, they may not respond when their name is called.

DIAGNOSIS[4]

Before we can make a diagnosis of autism, an important question needs to be answered: "Is autism one condition, or is it several overlapping conditions?" Is it a single diagnosis or is it a composite of several diagnoses? The clinical presentation of autism is variable with a diversity of expressions, and therefore the diagnosis can be challenged or refuted. Without a definitive diagnosis, could we have misdiagnosed autism in some cases?

If we can link relevant and replicable investigations to the clinical manifestations, we can formulate a hypothesis of cause and effect. Unfortunately, at the moment, we have neither unequivocal clinical findings nor clearcut investigatory findings.

The problem is compounded by the fact that there is a myriad of diagnostic tools for autism, and there is no consensus on which one of these tests is the most accurate.

Medical examination

The doctor does a thorough clinical examination, and checks carefully for hearing, eyesight, as well as neurological and other medical signs. Conditions associated with autism, such as attention deficit hyperactivity disorder (ADHD), epilepsy, fragile X syndrome, tuberous sclerosis, Rett syndrome, insomnia, are also looked for. Tests that might be considered include blood test for low thyroid hormone, electroencephalography, and other investigations.

Classifying systems

- Diagnostic and Statistical Manual 5th revision (DSM-5)
- International Classification of Diseases 10th revision (ICD-10)

The DSM-5 and the ICD-10 are classifying systems, not diagnostic tests. They list the major components to consider, and guide one towards considering whether or not to refer someone for a more definitive diagnosis.

Diagnostic and Statistical Manual 5th Edition (DSM-5)

The American Psychiatric Association introduced the Diagnostic and Statistical Manual to guide the classification of many psychiatric disorders, and it is now in its 5th edition. The DSM-5 lists two major areas that need to be present in order to consider someone with autism.

1. Social communication and interaction deficits

The autistic individual prefers to be alone and there is little social reciprocity. They do not seem to want to share interests with others, and there can be verbal as well as nonverbal communication difficulties. There appear to be problems developing and maintaining friends. As they get older, they may have difficulty with small talk and reading facial expressions, which can make them seem insensitive. They may take what is said quite literally, for example when asked to "take a seat", they may pick up a seat and take it elsewhere.

2. Restricted or repetitive behaviours, interests and activities

Children may line up toys in a ritualistic way, flap hands, pace up and down, and imitate words or phrases repeatedly. They may be fixed on certain routines, preferring the same sequence of activities like dressing themselves and having breakfast before brushing their teeth. There can be restricted patterns of interests like having specific in-depth knowledge of astronomy or dinosaurs. Some individuals are distracted by background noise so they cannot focus on what is said by others.

Diagnostic tests[5]

To make a definitive diagnosis of autism, these are the commonly used tests:

- Autism Diagnostic Interview
- Autism Diagnostic Observation Schedule
- Checklist for Autism in Toddlers
- Childhood Autism Rating Scale
- Gilliam Autism Rating Scale

It is uncertain which method is the most accurate because there has not been a large-scale trial comparing one method with another.

All diagnostic tests agree that autism is a spectrum disorder and varies significantly from person to person. The above descriptions may not be found in everyone. Some may require more, and others less support in their daily lives. A small percentage (probably 10% or less) show special abilities in visual memory, art, music, maths and science.

Prevalence[6–8]

The prevalence of autism differs from one country to another, ranging from 1:59 in the US to 1:150 in Singapore.

According to a 2021 report[9], there has been a 787% increase in the incidence of autism in England during the past two decades. However, the authors do not think this is a real increase in the number of cases, but rather, an increase in the number of cases diagnosed due to more aware-ness of the condition.

Table 1. Prevalence of autism in different countries (World Health Organization 2020)

Country	Prevalence
United States	1 in 59
Canada	1 in 66
Ireland	1 in 78
South Korea	1 in 91
Hong Kong	1 in 99
Saudi Arabia	1 in 99
India	1 in 113
China	1 in 125
England	1 in 128
Japan	1 in 128
Thailand	1 in 128
Taiwan	1 in 129
Russia	1 in 130
Germany	1 in 138
France	1 in 144
Australia	1 in 150
Singapore	1 in 150

Associated conditions[10]

Another confounding factor is that some autistic persons may have other associated conditions. Some 30% will have intellectual disability, over 30% have ADHD and between 10%–20% will have epilepsy. Other associated diagnoses include obsessive-compulsive disorder (OCD), and gastrointestinal disorders. Clinically, it is important to decide whether or not these comorbidities should be viewed as part of the autistic diagnostic spectrum, or should they be classified as additional separate diagnoses? Paediatricians tend to take the latter route and separate autism from the other comorbidities, and this appears to be the current consensus.

Are boys more likely to be autistic?

Another finding that also needs to be explained is the apparent predominance of males diagnosed with autism. There are several publications suggesting that boys are five times or more likely to be diagnosed with autism than girls. However, recent studies suggest that the diagnosis of autism in girls is frequently missed because they display less repetitive behaviours, their restricted range of interests tend to be considered as normal for girls, and the assessors have fewer issues with smaller vocabulary and delayed learning. Most current researchers assert that in the community, the male:female ratio is about equal.

CONCLUSIONS

Teamwork is the foundation of coping with autism. The good news is that there are now quite a number of organisations, schools, psychological and medical services that can help. The problem is trying to find the best option for your child and family. The Internet can overwhelm you with too much information, and the most attractive site may not offer the best advice or therapy. Discuss it with as many people as possible, including teachers, psychologists, doctors, and other parents.

Autism is a challenge at many levels. Educationally, it requires us to reduce class size and to individualise the curriculum and pace of instruction, and to employ positive rather than negative methods of teaching. It affects families and caregivers, requiring them to adapt their child's physical environment and activities, and to plan for the long term. Some individuals on the more severe end of the autism spectrum may need lifelong support and care. This may require intervention from the state to plan for the long term. Philosophically, autism forces us to rethink whether we should label people on the spectrum as disabled, disadvantaged, exceptional, or differently able. Ideally, in the long run, we want an inclusive society that does not discriminate against anyone.

Resources

Autism Link Malaysia https://www.autism.my/

Autism Resource Centre (Singapore) https://www.autism.org.sg/
Autism Spectrum Australia https://www.autismspectrum.org.au/
National Autistic Society (UK) https://www.autism.org.uk/
Rainbow Centre (Singapore) https://www.rainbowcentre.org.sg/
St. Andrew's Autism Centre (Singapore) https://www.saac.org.sg/
Wings Melaka (Malaysia) http://www.wingsmelaka.org.my/

REFERENCES

1. Frith, U. (2008). *Autism: A very short introduction*. Oxford University Press.
2. Fletcher-Watson, S., & Happé, F. (2019). *Autism: A new introduction to psychological theory and current debate*. Routledge.
3. Casanova E. L., & Casanova, M. F. (2019). *Defining Autism*. Jessica Kingsley Publishers.
4. Gallo, D. P. (2010). *Diagnosing Autism Spectrum Disorders*. Wiley-Blackwell.
5. ABA Centers of America. *How is autism diagnosed?* https://www.abacenters.com/how-is-autism-diagnosed-screening-testing-and-diagnosis/
6. Statista. Prevalence of autism 2020. https://www.statista.com/statistics/676354/autism-rate-among-children-select-countries-worldwide/
7. Russell, G., Stapley, S., Newlove-Delgado, T., Salmon, A., White, R., Warren, F., Pearson, A., & Ford, T. (2021). Time trends in autism diagnosis over 20 years: a UK population-based cohort study. *The Journal of Child Psychology and Psychiatry*, 63(6), 674–682. https://acamh.onlinelibrary.wiley.com/doi/10.1111/jcpp.13505
8. Wikipedia. Epidemiology of autism. https://en.wikipedia.org/wiki/Epidemiology_of_autism
9. Vennells, L. (2021). Number Diagnosed With Autism Jumps 787 Percent In Two Decades. *Neuroscience News*. https://neurosciencenews.com/austim-rate-increase-19368/
10. Furfaro, H. (2018). Conditions that accompany autism, explained. *Spectrum News*. https://www.spectrumnews.org/news/conditions-accompany-autism-explained/
11. Tsang, L. P. M., How, C. H., Yeleswarapu, S. P., & Wong, C. M. (2019). Autism spectrum disorder: early identification and management in primary care (Singapore). *Singapore Medical Journal*, 60(7). 324–328. http://www.smj.org.sg/article/autism-spectrum-disorder-early-identification-and-management-primary-care
12. Cherney, K., & and Seladi-Schulman, J. (2021). Everything you need to know about autism spectrum disorder. Healthline. https://www.healthline.com/health/autism

7 Causes of Autism

Kenneth Lyen

INTRODUCTION

Autism is a common but complex neurodevelopmental disorder characterised by early-onset difficulties in social communication and unusually restrictive repetitive behaviours and interests. It manifests as a wide spectrum, ranging from a mild hesitancy in communicating with others, to someone who barely talks to anyone else. It encompasses the person who physically displays obsessionally recurring movements, to the savant with exceptionally gifted mathematics or artistic talents.

Trying to discover the causes of autism is like finding one's way through a dense forest with only the guide of a global positioning system, which sets the general direction you want to travel, but does not help you overcome the obstacles that can block your progress.

Because autism is a complex condition, there are potentially many causes.[1] We can stratify the causes into several layers. The basic layer consists of the underlying genetic and environmental causes which interact with each other. The genes express themselves in many ways, including biochemically and neurodevelopmentally. The next layer to explore is the brain: How the structure, neurocircuitry, and function of the brain modulate behaviour. Environmental influences are still pervasive, and can alter a child's behaviour before or after birth. The factors potentially affecting foetal or child development are numerous, and may include food, infections, toxins, etc.

Diagnosis of autism[2]

An important question that needs to be answered: "Is autism one condition, or is it several overlapping conditions?" Is it a single diagnosis or is it a composite of several diagnoses. The clinical presentation of autism is variable with a diversity of expressions, and therefore, the diagnosis can be challenged or refuted. Without a definitive diagnosis, how do we prove which cause is the right one? Could we have misdiagnosed autism in some cases?

Ideally, autism is a single diagnosis which can be securely verified. Conventionally, the diagnosis of a medical condition is based on a reliable set of symptoms and signs, supported by clear results of investigation. This is the problem with autism. As there is a spectrum of clinical symptoms, signs and investigatory results, the diagnosis is often somewhat inconclusive. Thus, at the moment, we do not have a definitive clinical diagnosis for most individuals suspected of being on the autism spectrum.

If we can link relevant and replicable investigations to the clinical manifestations, we can formulate a hypothesis of cause and effect. Unfortunately, at the moment we have neither unarguable clinical findings nor clearcut investigatory findings.

Autism has a myriad of possible causes. This makes it difficult to pin down which aetiology is the dominant one. To date, there are no indisputable scientific experiments, no incontrovertible imaging or genetic findings that can pinpoint the main causes. For example, genetic probes which are the most promising research findings, have led to the discovery of hundreds of possible genes linked to autism. It is confusing. But, complexity itself does not negate that one is on the right track. It just makes it harder to prove the aetiology or aetiologies.

Associated conditions[3]

Another confounding factor is that some autistic persons may have other associated conditions. Some 30% will have intellectual delay, and between 10%–20% will have epilepsy. Other associated conditions include attention deficit hyperactivity disorder, large heads, obsessional compulsive behaviour, and gastrointestinal symptoms, etc. Each of these symptoms can be due to a separate diagnosis in its own right. Clinically, it is important to decide whether or not these comorbidities should be viewed as part of the autistic diagnostic spectrum, or they should be disassociated into different categories. This will be explored later.

Epidemiology[4]

The prevalence of autism is between 0.6%–2% of the population. Over the past few decades, the prevalence has been increasing.

This increased prevalence could be due to heightened public awareness, or the relaxation of the diagnostic criteria by the American Psychiatric Association in their Diagnostic and Statistical Manual 5th edition (DSM-V). These two explanations have been questioned. If indeed there is a real increase in its prevalence, we need to explain why.

Another finding that also needs to be explained is the predominance of males diagnosed with autism. It is estimated that autism is between three to five times more common in males compared to females. Is this an artefact due to the underdiagnosis of autism in females? Or is it a real observation? If indeed there is a male predominance, can we explain it by

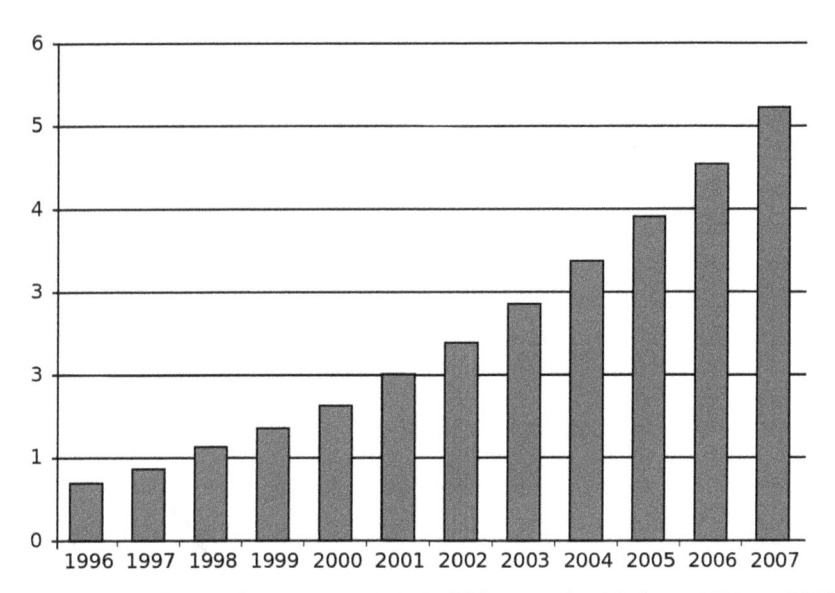

Figure 1. Prevalence of autism per 1,000 children in the US from 1996 to 2007 (Wikipedia)

attributing it to the influence of male hormones in antenatal brain development, or are there any other theories?

GENETIC CAUSES

Why are genes linked to autism?[5-7]

It originates from the famous studies of identical and non-identical twins. When one twin has autism, then an identical twin has a 60% to 90% chance of developing it. In contrast, a non-identical or fraternal twin of the same sex shares the autistic diagnosis around 30% of the time, compared to boy-girl twin pairs that only share the diagnosis about 20% of the time. The concordance rate for differently-aged siblings is about 10%, while the general population risk ranges from 0.5% to 1.8% depending on the country being surveyed.

The fact that the identical twin concordance rate is not 100% suggests that there must be other factors involved, most probably environmental.

Hunt for variants or mutations

Humans match one another quite closely, with 99.9% of the order of their base pair DNAs identical with one another. The non-identical 0.1% are known as variants and are either non-functional, or they may contribute to disease risk, and may even protect one from diseases. Gene variants can arise from mutations. Nowadays, the terms variants and mutations are used interchangeably but some would keep the definitions separate.

Are variants or mutations inheritable? Yes and no. Some variants can cause inheritable diseases, like those associated with autism. Fortunately, they are relatively rare. Below are some of the inheritable causes of autism.

Inheritable causes of autism

How might genes give clues to help us understand the cause of autism? One way is to study inherited conditions that are associated with autism, like the ones below:

(a) Fragile X Syndrome[8]

Inheritable forms of autism are relatively rare. For example, there is an abnormality of the X-chromosome, known as the Fragile X Syndrome. This is a sex-linked (X-linked) dominant condition and 50% of the affected children will develop autism. Fragile X Syndrome is associated with the FMR1 gene, and it causes multiple repeats of the base pairs. This results in hyperactivity of the glutamate receptor in the brain.

Researchers developed a mutant mouse that lacked the FMR1 gene and reproduced the hyperactive glutamate receptor. When they reduced the glutamate receptor activity, it resulted in increased dendritic neuronal density and hippocampal protein synthesis. Another group increased Gamma-AminoButyric Acid (GABA) by giving an agonist, baclofen; it increased synaptic protein synthesis and increased neuronal density in the spinal cord.

(b) Tuberous Sclerosis[9]

Tuberous sclerosis is an autosomal dominant disorder affecting one of two chromosomes. One has a variant called TSC1 which is located on chromosome 9q34.3 and the other is known as TSC2 found on chromosome 16p13.3. It causes a problem in the mammalian target of rapamycin signalling pathway in the hippocampus. A group of researchers looked at mice with deficits in one or two TSC1 genes in the cerebellum and noticed that the mice showed decreased neuronal activity, abnormal social interactions, and repetitive behaviours. Treating these mice with rapamycin improved neuronal activity and behavioural deficits.

Another group of scientists developed mutant mice missing one copy of TSC2 resulting in cognitive deficits. They were able to treat adult mice with rapamycin which improved synaptic plasticity and behavioural deficits.

(c) Rett Syndrome[10]

Another condition also involving the X-chromosome is Rett Syndrome. The gene affected is known as MECP2, and only girls are affected. A unique feature of this syndrome is the obsessional hand-washing motions. They have an awkward gait, developmental delay, and the condition worsens progressively. The mutations of the MECP2 gene results in abnormal neurons.

A mutant mouse lacking the MECP2 gene was developed, and these mice displayed some symptoms resembling Rett Syndrome. When they reactivated the MECP2 gene back to normal in adult mice, these mice regained some normal functioning including normalising neuronal signalling in the hippocampus, which is found in autism.

(d) Phelan-McDermid Syndrome[11]
Deletion of part of chromosome 22 in the region of 22q13.3, also known as the Shank3 gene, causes a disease known as Phelan-McDermid Syndrome. This is inherited as an autosomal dominant, and is associated with autism.

(e) Chromosome 16
Chromosome 16 is interesting because not only is it associated with tuberous sclerosis (see above), but other parts of this chromosome, such as the regions 16p11.2 and 16p12.1 are associated with autism, delayed development and recurrent seizures.

The syndromes listed in Table 1 are frequently associated with autism, and they are inherited in an autosomal or sex-linked dominant manner. But they are relatively rare. By understanding the pathophysiology of these genetic disorders linked to autism, we can gain deeper understanding into the causes and potential treatment of autism.

The majority of persons with autism do not have any family history. They arise discontinuously, and therefore, they are most likely due to new impromptu mutations, also known as de novo variants.

Table 1.   Autism-related syndromes

Syndrome	Associated Gene(s)	Proportion of Patients with the Syndrome that have Autism	Proportion of Autistic Persons who have the Syndrome
(a) Fragile X	FMR1	25% males, 5% females	1%–2%
(b) Rett Syndrome	MECP2	100%, all females	<0.5%
(c) Tuberous Sclerosis	TSC1, TSC2	20%	1%
(d) 22q deletion	SHANK3	High	1%
(e) 16p11 deletion	Unknown	High	1%

De novo variants[12]

De novo variants of the genes are usually thought to arise spontaneously and quite passively. Most do not cause any problems. But sometimes, they can result in serious conditions, including autism. Spontaneous mutations may occur in either the sperm or the ovum before or after fertilisation. They are not inherited from earlier generations as they arise unexpectedly, but they will affect the offspring.

Genome-wide linkage studies

To link genetic causes to autism, one of the methods is to do a genome-wide linkage study. This is achieved by trying to identify chromosome regions or loci that are inherited by affected individuals more frequently than expected by chance. The scope was widened to search for all DNA variations in all families, whether several members are involved, or if only one member has autism.

Whole Exome Sequencing (WES)[13]

Thanks to the human genome project, an international scientific research project, all the base pairs or genes that make up human DNA were identified and mapped . The project started in 1990 and was completed in 2003.

Whole Exome Sequencing (WES) has revolutionised the study of genes in autism. Using this new technology, scientists can look at all 21,000 genes comprising 180,000 exome nucleotides, which constitute about 0.6% of the 30 million base pairs of the entire human genome.

Although several hundreds of gene variations are found in autistic subjects, when they looked at the function of these genes, they were able to group them into their different functions. One group of variants were involved in the neurons, influencing the neuronal cell adhesion molecules, thereby affecting the function of nerves, while another group affected a ubiquitin pathway, which helps in the synthesis of new proteins, and the destruction of defective proteins.

With current whole exome sequencing, we can explore all the exome genes at the same time. This not only widens the search, but simultaneously cuts down the time taken for research.

Other genetic challenges

There are still several challenging problems awaiting clarification:

Firstly, there are hundreds of genes associated with autism, some of them affecting nerve cell development and function, and others affecting gene expression, a phenomenon known as epigenetics. Looking at the wide spectrum of autism, it seems quite likely that these different genes interact with one another and converge in producing the clinical picture of autism.

Secondly, the genes are expressed at different times of development. Some of them are active in early embryonic life, others later, and some after birth.

Thirdly, genes can affect different organs differently, and each organ can in turn interact with one another, perhaps altering their functions.

Overall, between 10%–20% of people with autism have a de novo genetic mutation.

NEUROLOGICAL CAUSES

Brain pathophysiology[14]

Exploring the genetics is only the first step in our attempts to understand the causes of autism. The next step is to understand the neuroanatomy and the neurophysiology of the autistic brain and how it differs from the non-autistic brain. Fortunately, recently there have been major advances in mapping the form and function of the brain and the nerve connections.

The brain has billions of nerve cells or neurons. However, in autism, these neurons are not communicating with one another appropriately. Researchers are trying to pinpoint which parts of the brain are affected, and the mechanisms of the problems that are found in autism.

Functional magnetic resonance imaging (fMRI)[15,16]

One major advance in understanding the function of the brain is the development of fMRI. This detects increased oxygen that is supplied to active brain nerve cells.

There have been many studies using fMRI to see how the brains of autistic individuals differ from neurotypical brains. For example, autistic persons are said to be less sociable compared to non-autistic people, and this has been correlated with decreased activity in certain brain areas linked to social interactions.

Diffusion tensor imaging magnetic resonance imaging (MRI)[17]

Diffusion tensor imaging is a form of MRI that detects the flow of water along the white matter of the brain. In so doing, it shows the white matter connections in the brain.

Children with autism have increased connections of the shorter nerve fibres closer to one another, and decreased connections with distant parts of the brain.

Magnetic resonance spectroscopy[18]

Another new development in magnetic resonance imaging is modifying conventional MRI to see a specific set of brain chemicals. For example, one can now measure Gamma AminoButyric Acid (GABA), an inhibitory transmitter, as well as glutamate, which is an excitatory transmitter. Autistic children have a higher glutamate concentration, and lower GABA concentrations in their occipital cortex, suggesting that there is imbalance with increased excitation and decreased inhibition.

It is postulated that the ability to excite and inhibit brain function can be used to filter sensory information. Failure to dampen excitatory stimuli can, for example, enhance loud sounds or visual stimulation, which many autistic individuals do not tolerate well.

Knowing the neurotransmitters involved, adults with autism have undergone a trial where they were treated with riluzole, which blocks the pre-synaptic release of glutamate and facilitates GABA activity. Preliminary data are encouraging.

Electroencephalography (EEG)[19,20]

Epilepsy occurs in 1%–2% of the general population but in 10%–20% of those with autism. An abnormal EEG occurs in about 2%–4% of the general population but in over 40% of those with autism. These statistics suggest that the autistic brain may harbour some underlying disorder.

The use of simple resting state EEG has inconsistent results. But, when combined with eye-tracking manoeuvres, the results correlate significantly with autistic subjects.

CONCLUSIONS

Finding the causes of such a complex condition as autism is highly challenging. Advances in genetics have uncovered hundreds of genes linked to autism. The precise mechanisms by which genes lead to autism are still being explored. The other major areas of research are in the area of brain imaging, using fMRI, diffusion tensor MRI, and magnetic resonance spectroscopy. They have also unravelled geographic areas and the function of these brain regions in relation to autism. These investigations have also been used to determine the efficacy of the treatment of autism.

FUTURE CHALLENGES

Hopes for the future include:

(a) Prevention
Prevention is better than cure. If we can discover the causes of childhood developmental conditions, we may be able to prevent more of these states. Already, the incidence of Down Syndrome and cerebral palsy has fallen. I hope that autism will follow suit. Whole genome sequencing during pregnancy or at birth may lead to earlier identification of autism before or shortly after birth, and which can potentially lead to some form of intervention or therapy to correct biochemical deficiencies. Advances in gene therapy or genome editing can one day correct mutations for many genes.

(b) Inclusive Education
Different, not disabled. I do not believe in segregating children with differences into separate schools or institutions. Children have different abilities and interests, but we should not partition them into isolated schools. They

can still join in other activities such as sports, art, music, dance, etc. We need to develop the mindset that we are all part of a family.

An enhanced understanding of the neurophysiology of autism can help us better understand human neurodiversity, and how each individual has their own unique brain connectivity and function.

(c) New Technologies
Creating new technologies to help the disabled should be given more funding. Enhancing communication, facilitating the integration of special needs children into society, and allowing them to travel, shop, etc with ease can be developed further.

(d) Stem Cells
Stem cells may one day be developed to produce different types of cells, either to replace neurons affected by autism, or to do research into the drugs or toxins that can influence these stem cell neurons.

(e) Dark Matter
We are currently looking at protein-related exome genes which comprises only 1% of all our genes. We have barely started looking at the "dark matter" non-protein related intron in genes. Like dark matter in the universe, we have a long way to go, but we may be surprised by where this research might lead to.

(f) Infant Brain Imaging Study
Ongoing studies using conventional MRI scans coupled with EEG and eye tracking tests, were applied to children between 6 months and 2 years old. These children are followed up with repeated MRI scans and psychological tests to detect early autism. The objective is to see if there are any early structural changes in the brain of children that can predict autism, which hopefully can lead to earlier intervention.

Recommended videos

Burrows, C. (2020, October). *Improving Future Diagnosis of Autism Using Brain Imaging.* https://www.youtube.com/watch?v=Gfp2emVQUYo

Chung, W. (2017, March). *Is Autism Genetic?* https://www.youtube.com/watch?v=1lqupCqbes4

Kolevzon, A. (2020, October). *The Benefits of Genetic Testing in Autism.* https://www.youtube.com/watch?v=b9nCihlhhk0

Sprouts. (2021, July). *Autism Spectrum: Atypical Minds in a Stereotypical World.* https://www.youtube.com/watch?v=j3PrAqJ-H9k

REFERENCES

1. Wikipedia. Causes of autism. https://en.wikipedia.org/wiki/Causes_of_autism
2. Wikipedia. Diagnosis of autism. https://en.wikipedia.org/wiki/Autism
3. Furfaro, H. (2018). Conditions that accompany autism, explained. *Spectrum News.* https://www.spectrumnews.org/news/conditions-accompany-autism-explained/
4. Wikipedia. Epidemiology of autism. https://en.wikipedia.org/wiki/Epidemiology_of_autism
5. Hadley, D., & Hakonarson, H. (2022). Genetics of autism spectrum disorders. *Medscape.* https://emedicine.medscape.com/article/2024885-overview#-showall
6. Zeliadt, N. (2021). Autism genetics, explained. *Spectrum News.* https://www.spectrumnews.org/news/autism-genetics-explained/
7. Sarris, M. (2014). Twins study finds large genetic influence in autism. *Interactive Autism Network.* https://iancommunity.org/autism-twins-study
8. National Fragile X Foundation. Fragile X and Autism. https://fragilex.org/understanding-fragile-x/fragile-x-syndrome/autism/
9. TSC Alliance. (2013). TSC and Autism Spectrum Disorders. https://www.tscalliance.org/about-tsc/signs-and-symptoms-of-tsc/brain-and-neurological-function/tsc-and-autism-spectrum-disorders/
10. Deweerdt, S. (2019). Rett Syndrome's link to autism, explained. *Spectrum News.* https://www.spectrumnews.org/news/rett-syndromes-link-to-autism-explained/
11. Oberman, L. M., Boccuto, L., Cascio, L., Sarasua, S., & Kaufmann, W. E. (2015) Autism spectrum disorder in Phelan-McDermid Syndrome: initial characterization and genotype-phenotype correlations. *Orphanet Journal of Rare Diseases, 10*(105). https://ojrd.biomedcentral.com/articles/10.1186/s13023-015-0323-9
12. Alonso-Gonzalez, A., Rodriguez-Fontenla. C., & Carracedo, A. (2018) *De novo* Mutations (DNMs) in Autism Spectrum Disorder (ASD): Pathway and network

analysis. *Frontiers in Genetics.* https://www.frontiersin.org/articles/10.3389/fgene.2018.00406/full

13. Yu, T. W. *et al.* (2013). Using whole exome sequencing to identify inherited causes of autism. *Neuron, 77*(2). 259–273. https://www.ncbi.nlm.nih.gov/pmc/articles/PMC3694430/

14. Brasic, J. R. (2021). Autism spectrum disorder. *Medscape.* https://emedicine.medscape.com/article/912781-overview#a3

15. Gabrielsen, T. P., Anderson, J. S., Stephenson, K. G., Beck, J., King, J. B., Kellems, R., Top, D. N., Jr., Russell, N. C. C., Anderberg, E., Lundwall, R. A., Hansen, B., & South, M. (2018). Functional MRI connectivity of children with autism and low verbal and cognitive performance. *Molecular Autism, 9*(67). https://molecularautism.biomedcentral.com/articles/10.1186/s13229-018-0248-y

16. Lau, W. K. W., Leung, M., & Lau, B. W. M. (2019). Resting-state abnormalities in autism spectrum disorders: A meta-analysis. *Scientific Reports, 9*(3892). https://www.nature.com/articles/s41598-019-40427-7

17. Solsoa, S., Xu, R., Proudfoot, J., Hagler, D. J., Jr., Campbell, K., Venkatraman, V., Barnes, C. C., Ahrens-Barbeau, C., Pierce, K., Dale, A., Eyler, L., & Courchesne, E. (2016). Diffusion tensor imaging provides evidence of possible axonal overconnectivity in frontal lobes in autism spectrum disorder toddlers. *Biological Psychiatry, 79*(8). 676–684. https://www.sciencedirect.com/science/article/pii/S0006322315005697

18. Ford, T. C. & Crewther, D. P. (2016). A comprehensive review of the ^{1}H-MRS metabolite spectrum in autism spectrum disorder. *Frontiers in Molecular Neuroscience, 9.* https://www.frontiersin.org/articles/10.3389/fnmol.2016.00014/full

19. Bosl, W. J., Tager-Flusberg, H., & Nelson, C. A. (2018). EEG analytics for early detection of autism spectrum disorder: A data-driven approach. *Scientific Reports, 8*(6828). https://www.nature.com/articles/s41598-018-24318-x

20. Shapiro, K. & Goh, S. Why and when are EEGs Recommended for Children with autism? *Cortica.* https://www.corticacare.com/care-notes/why-and-when-are-eegs-recommended-for-children-with-autism

8 Medication

Kenneth Lyen

INTRODUCTION

Currently, no medicines have been proven to significantly improve the core symptoms of autism, namely the communication and socialising difficulties, and the restrictive repetitive movements.

Medicines can help with certain specific behaviours such as reducing self-injury, anxiety, aggression, depression, and abdominal symptoms.

Medicines may also be used to treat some of the conditions associated with autism, including attention deficit hyperactivity disorder (ADHD), obsessional compulsive behaviour, and epilepsy.

Main targets for therapy

The main targets for therapy are to improve communication and social skills, promote academic functioning, decrease negative behaviour, and ultimately to improve the quality of life of the autistic individual.

The proven ways of achieving most of these goals are not through medication, but rather through special education with trained teachers and therapists in a small class, preferably started early in the child's life. The interventions include occupational therapy, physiotherapy, social skills training, speech and language therapy, and the use of music, art and sports to enhance all the therapies.

TREATMENT OF SPECIFIC BEHAVIOURS

Autistic individuals can sometimes display difficult behaviours that cannot be readily ameliorated by talking persuasively and in a comforting manner.

Manifestations of anxiety, depression, aggression and self-injury may occasionally need medical treatment. Because some of these symptoms may occur at the same time, many of the medicines used overlap. For example, antidepressants may also help reduce anxiety.

Anxiety[1,2]

Although anxiety is not part of the diagnostic criteria of autism, it is a symptom frequently experienced by autistic persons. Anxiety includes the feeling of unease, having worries or fears; when severe, these symptoms can interfere with the autistic individual's lifestyle. We advise trying to reduce anxiety through exercises, engaging in art, music, and social interactions, as well as mindfulness training. If these are not effective, then one might have to try destressing through counselling, and sensory integration training. If none of these suggestions are effective, then it may be all right to consult a doctor, and some may consider prescribing risperidone or clonidine.

Depression[3]

Some autistic individuals experience depression. Early warning signs include feeling sad, inattention, becoming more on edge and anxious, losing appetite, and becoming more sleepy. Repetitive-compulsive behaviours may increase, and they may be more cranky and agitated, have more emotional or aggressive outbursts. They may hurt themselves through biting their fingers, or become obsessed with death and suicide. Sometimes, depression may be triggered by people refusing to give the autistic persons what they want, or they may be bullied at school or online . We try counselling and behavioural therapy if appropriate. Failing which, medicines may be helpful. Antidepressants include fluoxetine, clonazepam, which some doctors might consider prescribing.

Aggressive behaviour, temper tantrums, self-injuries[4-7]

Another set of behavioural issues ranges from irritability, aggression to temper tantrums and self-injurious actions. The initial management is to calm the person down, isolating them in a safe quiet room where there are no sharp or potentially dangerous instruments or furniture. If this type of therapy is ineffective or if the person is at risk of harming either other people or themselves, then medical treatment may have to be considered. These include risperidone or aripiprazole. These medicines need close monitoring.

Cognitive enhancers[13]

The use of medicines that help nerves transmit signals — cholinergic-enhancing medicines — may help some autistic individuals improve their memory, attention, ability to interact with others, as well as help them to speak, think clearly, and perform regular daily activities. An example of such a medicine is donepezil, but its efficacy is controversial. Side effects include nausea, vomiting, diarrhoea, loss of appetite and frequent urination.

Social responsiveness[14,15]

Autism is characterised by poor social communication. Not surprisingly, there have been some attempts to enhance socialising, one of which is a peptide hormone, oxytocin. This hormone is normally produced in the base of the brain, a region known as the hypothalamus, and promotes positive pro-social warm feelings. It plays a role in social bonding. Some studies have shown that giving oxytocin improves socialising in autistic people. The medicine is administered intra-nasally.

Sleep disturbances[16]

Autistic people may have difficulty falling asleep, and wake up several times in the middle of the night. Melatonin is a hormone released by the pineal gland located deep within the brain. It is normally released at night-time and is involved in the control of the sleep-wake cycle. It is quite widely used by the general public for treating insomnia and jet lag. Studies have shown that melatonin can sometimes help autistic people who have sleep disturbances.

CONDITIONS ASSOCIATED WITH AUTISM

Attention Deficit Hyperactivity Disorder (ADHD)[8-10]

About 30% of children on the autism spectrum have ADHD. This means they are easily distracted, and have difficulty focusing on a given task. Some of them cannot keep still and wander around aimlessly, others have intermittent impulsivity in which they suddenly do things unexpectedly.

Examples of lack of impulse control seen in autistic children include disruptive behaviours when they interrupt you when you are in the middle of doing something; when others are playing together, they may intrude. Some may blurt out an answer even before you have finished asking the question, and others may have difficulty controlling their emotions and suddenly become angry.

There are several medicines available for managing ADHD, and some doctors will choose either methylphenidate or atomoxetine.

Epilepsy and Abnormal Electroencephalogram (EEG)[11]

Epilepsy occurs in around 10–20% of children from two to 17 years old. This compares to 1%–2% of the general population who have epilepsy. Valproic acid is an anti-epileptic drug which is effective in autistic children who also have abnormal EEGs. Side effects include drowsiness and hair loss.

Obsessive Compulsive Disorder (OCD)[12]

Some children on the autism spectrum display repetitive movements such as hand flapping, clapping, running up and down, rocking to-and-fro, etc. It is hypothesised that the purpose of these behaviours is to enable the autistic person to cope with an unpredictable and slightly threatening environment. The repetitive movements are occasionally misdiagnosed as epilepsy or obsessive compulsive disorder (OCD). There is a distinction between diagnosis of OCD and autism; while both will exhibit repetitive behaviours, people with OCD are fully conscious of their repetitive behaviours, while autistic individuals do them without self-awareness. The treatment for OCD may not work for autism.

MEDICINES AND DIETS THAT DO NOT WORK

There are no large double-blind placebo-controlled trials for the treatments and medicines listed below. However, many parents believe that they work. Provided they do not do any harm, and are not prohibitively expensive or time-consuming, and if they do not displace therapies that are proven to work, then it is probably all right for parents and patients to continue with the therapies below, but please consult a medical doctor first.

- Anti-Fungal and Anti-Yeast Medication
  - Anti-Yeast Medication
  - Flagyl (metronidazole)
  - Diflucan (fluconazole)
  - Nystatin
- Cannabis and Marijuana
- Chelation Therapy
- Complementary Alternative Medicine
- Transcraniosacral Magnetic Stimulation
- Essential Oils
- Faecal Microbial Transplantation
- Herbs and Homeopathic Treatments
- Hyperbaric Oxygen Therapy
- Iridology
- Magnets
- Neurofeedback Therapy
- Secretin
- Special Diets
  - Gluten-free (wheat)
  - Casein-Free (dairy)
  - Gluten-Free plus Casein-Free Diet
  - Sugar free
  - Removal of food dyes
- Vitamin and Supplement Therapy
  - Vitamin A
  - Vitamin B6
  - Vitamin B12
  - Vitamin C
  - Vitamin D

- Magnesium
- Dimethylglycerine
- Calcium
- Omega 3 Fatty Acids

REFERENCES

1. Sarris, M. (2018). What anxiety treatments work for people with autism? *Interactive Autism Network*. https://iancommunity.org/what-anxiety-treatments-work-people-autism

2. Nadeau, J., Sulkowski, M. L., Ung, D., Wood, J. J., Lewin, A. B., Murphy, T. K., May, J. E., & Storch, E. A. (2011). Treatment of comorbid anxiety and autism spectrum disorders. *Neuropsychiatry, 1*(6). 567–578. https://www.ncbi.nlm.nih.gov/pmc/articles/PMC3809000/

3. Chandrasekhar, T., & Sikich, L. (2015). Challenges in the diagnosis and treatment of depression in autism spectrum disorders across the lifespan. *Dialogues in Clinical Neuroscience,. 17*(2). 219–227. https://www.ncbi.nlm.nih.gov/pmc/articles/PMC4518704/

4. Fitzpatrick, S., Srivorakiat, L., Wink, L., Pedapati, E., & Erickson, C. (2016). Aggression in autism spectrum disorder: presentation and treatment options. *Neuropsychiatric Disease and Treatment, 12.* 1525–1538. https://www.dovepress.com/aggression-in-autism-spectrum-disorder-presentation-and-treatment-opti-peer-reviewed-fulltext-article-NDT

5. Canitano, R., & Scandurra, V. (2008). Risperidone in the treatment of behavioral disorders associated with autism in children and adolescents. *Neuropsychiatric Disease and Treatment, 4.* 723–730. https://www.ncbi.nlm.nih.gov/pmc/articles/PMC2536539/

6. Blankenship, K., Erickson, C. A., Stigler, K. A., Posey, D. J., & McDougle, C. J. (2010). Aripiprazole for irritability associated with autistic disorder in children and adolescents aged 6–17 years. *Pediatric Health, 4*(4). 375–381. https://www.ncbi.nlm.nih.gov/pmc/articles/PMC3043611/

7. LeClerc, S., & Easley, D. (2015). Pharmacological Therapies for Autism Spectrum Disorder: A Review. *Pharmacy & Therapeutics, 40*(6). 389–397. https://www.ncbi.nlm.nih.gov/pmc/articles/PMC4450669/

8. Sturman, N., Deckx, L., & van Driel, M. L. (2017). Methylphenidate for children and adolescents with autism spectrum disorder. *Cochrane Database of Systematic Reviews, 11.* https://www.ncbi.nlm.nih.gov/pmc/articles/PMC6486133/

9. Ghanizadeh, A. (2013). Atomoxetine for treating ADHD symptoms in autism: a systematic review. *Journal of Attention Disorders, 17*(8). 635–640. https://pubmed.ncbi.nlm.nih.gov/22544388/

10. Rudy, L. J. (2020). How OCD Compares With Autism. *VeryWell Health.* https://www.verywellhealth.com/autism-vs-obsessive-compulsive-disorder-260344

11. Viscidi, E. W., Triche, E. W., Pescosolido, M. F., McLean, R. L., Joseph, R. M., Spence, S. J., & Morrow, E. M. (2013). Clinical Characteristics of Children with Autism Spectrum Disorder and Co-Occurring Epilepsy. *PLoS ONE, 8*(7). e67797. https://www.ncbi.nlm.nih.gov/pmc/articles/PMC3701630/

12. Smith, P. (2018). Understanding the Relationship Between Autism, OCD, and Repetitive Behaviors. *Autism Spectrum News.* https://autismspectrumnews.org/understanding-the-relationship-between-autism-ocd-and-repetitive-behaviors/

13. Srivastava, R. K., Agarwal, M. & Pundhir, A. (2011). Role of Donepezil in Autism: Its Conduciveness in Psychopharmacotherapy. *Case Reports in Psychiatry, 2011.* 563204. https://www.ncbi.nlm.nih.gov/pmc/articles/PMC3420777/

14. Bernaerts, S., Boets, B., Steyaert, J., Wenderoth, C., & Alaerts, K. (2020). Oxytocin treatment attenuates amygdala activity in autism: A treatment-mechanism study with long-term follow-up. *Translational Psychiatry, 10.* Article 383. https://www.nature.com/articles/s41398-020-01069-w

15. Wright, J. (2017). Oxytocin spray boosts social skills in children with autism. *Spectrum.* https://www.spectrumnews.org/news/oxytocin-spray-boosts-social-skills-children-autism/

16. Gagnon, K., & Godbout, R. (2018). Melatonin and Comorbidities in Children with Autism Spectrum Disorder. *Current Developmental Disorders Reports, 5*(3). 197–206. https://www.ncbi.nlm.nih.gov/pmc/articles/PMC6096870/

9 COVID-19 Pandemic

Kenneth Lyen

INTRODUCTION

COVID-19 has engulfed the whole world, causing deaths, serious medical and psychological problems, and upsetting the economy of many countries. The virus keeps on mutating, making it almost impossible to exterminate.

While the earlier variants of COVID-19 did not affect children as much as it did older people, the newer mutations, like the Omicron variants, are attacking more children, especially the unvaccinated. The Omicron variant is less dangerous than the Delta variant, but it is far more contagious, and because higher numbers of people are infected, it is unleashing major problems in healthcare services for both children and adults.

The effects of COVID-19 on children can either be primary, that is, the virus directly enters and attacks the brain and body, or secondary, where the body invokes an immune response to the virus. The result of measures taken by the authorities to restrain the spread of the virus can also affect children.

The pandemic has affected the mental health of everybody, but autistic individuals are some of the worst hit.

COVID-19 INFECTION

Symptoms and signs in children[1]

Children are usually spared the symptoms of COVID-19. However, some may develop symptoms a few days (usually about six days) after exposure to someone with the condition. The commonest presenting symptoms are cough and fever. Other symptoms are listed below:

- Cough that can become productive of phlegm
- Fever
- Chest pain, shortness of breath
- Loss of smell or taste
- Changes in the skin, such as discoloured areas on the feet and hands, or skin rash
- Sore throat
- Nausea, vomiting, abdominal pain or diarrhoea
- Shivering and chills
- Muscle aches and pain
- Extreme fatigue
- Severe headaches
- Blocked nose

Fortunately, the life-threatening complications of COVID-19 are rarer in fully vaccinated children.

Lockdowns and other restrictions[2]

To slow down the spread of COVID-19, authorities have imposed lockdowns, social distancing, restrictions on large gatherings, and the wearing of masks.

Some schools were closed and classes were conducted online; many non-academic pursuits like sports, arts, music and community service, were restricted for a year or two.

EFFECTS ON CHILDREN

Changes in routines[3-5]

Autistic children are particularly affected by the school closures and having to stay at home all day. They might not understand why their normal daily routines have changed, and some may become anxious, stressed and frustrated. This may lead to even more behavioural and communication problems.

Children with autism are often resistant to changes in their routines. They may have become used to going to school each day and look forward to interacting with their peers and teachers. This interaction might motivate them to learn better in school.

At the same time, parents and caregivers may have difficulty struggling to balance their professional and family responsibilities while caring for their children who are stranded at home.

Benefits of staying at home

Not all autistic children are badly affected by staying at home. There is increased contact time between child and parents. If the caregivers are loving, sensitive and gentle, this can improve communication and bonding between loved ones. They may play more games together, learn new hobbies, etc (see below).

Online learning at home

Online learning at home shot up during the pandemic. Physical exercises decreased, and research has shown that obesity bloated in more than 10% of Singapore children. In contrast, poverty and food insecurity increased in poorer countries.

Non-academic activities like sports, art, music, dance, and theatre also slumped due to school closures or being cooped up at home. This has led to some serious mental problems including anxiety, depression and misbehaviour.

TACKLING MENTAL PROBLEMS

It is important to try to identify emotional problems as early as possible, so that intervention can be initiated. The early signs of these disturbances are listed below:

Anxiety

Early signs of anxiety include:

- Feeling nervous or tense
- Feeling restless or on edge
- Feeling excessively tired
- Sleep disturbances
- Asking the same questions repeatedly
- Irritable, aggressive, temper tantrums, meltdowns
- Social withdrawal
- Less physically active, more sedentary
- Playing less
- Excessive online screen time
- Tightness of muscles or muscle cramps
- Abdominal pain or discomfort
- Shouting more
- Sweating more profusely

Depression

Early signs of depression include:

- Reduced appetite
- Sleep problems
- Poor mental concentration and not paying attention
- Reduced self-esteem and self-confidence
- Ideas of guilt and unworthiness
- Social withdrawal
- Harbouring thoughts of self-harm or suicide

If identified early, one can intervene by talking to the child, and if necessary, referring them for counselling.

MANAGING AUTISTIC CHILDREN [6-8]

Children with autism are found to be more likely to become infected with the COVID-19 virus with higher death rates. Vaccination has been shown to be safe in autistic children.

Caregivers can do the following to help autistic children cope better at home:

- Try to explain why there are changes in their routine, using visual explanations where possible.
- Structure time for schoolwork and play. Draw up a routine and allow the child to make choices.
- Take a break between study and games.
- Use different coping strategies, such as listening to preferred music, counting numbers, drawing pictures, and taking deep breaths.
- Encourage regular physical exercise, do sports, go for walks.
- Play games, work on puzzles, read books, learn a new hobby.
- Visit less crowded places like gardens, zoos, museums, and shopping centres.
- Make time for social connections whenever possible.
- Draw out times for meals, snacks and drinks.
- Regulate access to screen time.
- If the child is sensitive to noise, try to find a quieter environment, or provide headphones for them to block out noise.

CONCLUSIONS[9–11]

COVID-19 has changed everyone's lives, and it does not appear to be going away any time soon. Autistic children can be affected quite seriously, both physically and mentally. The pandemic has been associated with an increase in anxiety, depression, and disruptive behaviour. One needs to be sensitive to any changes in the children's moods or activities. Connect more with the child by talking and playing, discuss the problems with their teachers, and seek additional support like consulting a counsellor early, before the condition turns into a tragedy.

REFERENCES

1. Mayo Clinic Staff. (2022). COVID-19 in babies and children. *Mayo Clinic*. https://www.mayoclinic.org/diseases-conditions/coronavirus/in-depth/coronavirus-in-babies-and-children/art-20484405
2. Dalabih, A., Bennett, E., & Javier, J. R. (2022). The COVID-19 pandemic and pediatric mental health: advocating for improved access and recognition. *Pediatric Research*, *91*. 1018–1020. https://www.nature.com/articles/s41390-022-01952-w

3. Benton, T., Njoroge, W. F. M., & Ng, W. Y. K. (2022). Sounding the Alarm for Children's Mental Health During the COVID-19 Pandemic. *JAMA Pediatrics, 176*(4). e216295. https://jamanetwork.com/journals/jamapediatrics/fullarticle/2788911

4. Ford, T., Mathews, F., & Benham-Clarke, S. (2021). The impact of COVID-19 on the mental health of children and young people in the UK: what the research says. *The Conversation*. https://theconversation.com/the-impact-of-covid-19-on-the-mental-health-of-children-and-young-people-in-the-uk-what-the-research-says-172653

5. Abramson, A. (2022). Children's mental health is in crisis. *American Psychological Association, 53*(1). 69. https://www.apa.org/monitor/2022/01/special-childrens-mental-health

6. Lugo-Marín, J., Gisbert-Gustemps, L., Setien-Ramos, I., Español-Martín, G., Ibañez-Jimenez, P., Forner-Puntonet, M., Arteaga-Henríquez, G., Soriano-Día, A., Duque-Yemaila, J. D., & Ramos-Quiroga, J. A. (2021). COVID-19 effects in people with Autism Spectrum Disorder and their caregivers: Evaluation of social distancing and lockdown impact on mental health and general status. *Research in Autism Spectrum Disorders, 83*. 101757. https://www.ncbi.nlm.nih.gov/pmc/articles/PMC7904459/

7. Salomon, S. H. (2021). 5 Things People With Autism and Their Caregivers Should Know About COVID-19 Vaccines. *Everyday Health*. https://www.everydayhealth.com/autism/things-people-with-autism-and-caregivers-should-know-about-covid-19-vaccines/

8. Eske, J. (2021). How to manage autism during the COVID-19 pandemic. *Medical News Today*. https://www.medicalnewstoday.com/articles/autism-and-covid-19

9. Rosenthal, E., Franklin-Gillette, S., Jung, H. J., Nelson, A., Evans, S. W., Power, T. J., Yerys, B. E., Dever, B. V., Reckner, E., & DuPaul, G. J. (2021). Impact of COVID-19 on Youth with ADHD: Predictors and Moderators of Response to Pandemic Restrictions on Daily Life. *Journal of Attention Disorders, 26*(9). 1223–1234. https://pubmed.ncbi.nlm.nih.gov/34920689/

10. Nigg, J. (2021). Mental Health, ADHD, and COVID-19. *Psychology Today*. https://www.psychologytoday.com/us/blog/helping-kids-through-adhd/202104/mental-health-adhd-and-covid-19

11. Toms, S. (2021, June 25). Covid-19: Singapore schools tackle mental health amid pandemic stress. *BBC News*. https://www.bbc.com/news/world-asia-56720368

10 Effects of Music on Individuals with Autism

Karina Lou

INTRODUCTION

History of music therapy

Music has been in existence since ancient times; it has been prevalent in the empires of China, Egypt, Greece, and Rome.[1] Music was not only used for entertaining purposes but also as healing therapy. Pythagoras (c 570–495 BC) observed that the body and soul could be affected by music, and Plato (428–348 BC) famously wrote that "music is the medicine of the soul".[2] In the Bible, it was said that King Saul's depression was alleviated by David's harp-playing. The native Americans also believed in the therapeutic effects of music, and the United States Indian Bureau contains 1,500 songs used for healing by native Americans.

After the world wars, music was used to heal post-war trauma among patients who had been wounded.[3] Although music has been used for the treatment of emotional problems, its use did not become better defined until a group of music therapists in the USA came together and formed the National Association for Music Therapy (NAMT) in 1950. One of the specific goals was to use music to treat children with autism in regular music classrooms.[4]

Experimental studies to assess the efficacy of music therapy on children with autism was initiated in the 1960s by several experimental studies, including the 1969 study by Stevens and Clark, published in the *Journal of Music Therapy*. They studied autistic boys 5–7 years of age and they found that music therapy was beneficial using the Ruttenberg's Autism

Scale for assessment.[5] Since this and other publications, music therapy has gained widespread use.

How does music affect the brain?

It has been observed that music can improve a child's mood and anxiety, singing can help speech development, dancing can help muscle development, learning an instrument can improve motor coordination, and group music activities can develop self-confidence and social skills. As music has such widespread actions, it is only natural to ask why and how it works, especially in individuals with autism.[6] In recent decades medical technology has enabled us to explore the inner workings of the brain neuroanatomically, electrophysiologically, as well as biochemically. These advances have occurred concurrently with a more precise definition of autism. Without a better diagnosis of autism, scientific research into the autistic brain remains imprecise. Another reason why it is important to delineate the boundaries of autism is that it is often accompanied by comorbid conditions such as attention deficit hyperactivity disorder, depression, obsessive-compulsive disorder, bipolar disorder, epilepsy, sleeping disorders, and other conditions. Improvement in these comorbid conditions following music exposure may complicate the interpretation of experimental findings.

Neuroanatomy

It has been observed that the brains of children with autism are different from non-autistic neurotypical children. Using functional magnetic resonance imaging which detects connectivity between brain regions, it has been observed that there is reduced connectivity between those areas involved in in facial recognition, understanding what other people are thinking, and in knowing one's self.[7] These are precisely the major manifestations of autistic symptoms. Another study showed that the areas of the brain associated with language and speech were decreased whereas those parts of the brain handling music was increased.[8] These findings correlate with the speech problems of individuals with autism and the relative conservation of music abilities. A neuroimaging study comparing children with autism listening to music versus those that were not exposed to music showed significant improvements in brain connectivity. The improved brain connections persisted over time.[9] Thus this study supports the beneficial effects of music therapy in children with autism.

Biochemistry

Understanding the biochemistry of autism and the effects of music therapy has the potential to compare music therapy with other forms of therapy including art therapy, physical exercise and medicines.[10,11] It has been shown that the autistic brain has an imbalance between excitatory and inhibitory impulses which in turn is due to defects in neurotransmitters which signal nervous impulses. Levels of the neurotransmitter serotonin are excessive in autistic individuals and this leads to lowering of reelin and oxytocin. The latter is also referred to as the "feel-good" chemical, and hence low levels of oxytocin can lead to depression and social withdrawal. Music has been shown to improve oxytocin levels. There are also studies to see if pharmaceutical agents may have benefits in modifying the behaviour of ndividuals with autism.

CONCLUSIONS

Scientific research is helping understand the effects of music on autistic individuals. Over the decades we realise that music has multifactorial roles in individuals with autism. It calms their nerves, it allows them to express themselves better, it can help improve attention span. Students with autism receiving music therapy often show reduced negative behaviours, and music helps them become more sociable to their fellow students.[12] Children who have challenging communication skills are also noted to improve. Studies have shown that this therapy restores the cognitive functioning of the brain because music uses both hemispheres. This neurophysiological and biochemical approach gives scientific credibility to the therapies being employed.

The multi-sensory stimulation created by music makes the students with autism coordinate several activities simultaneously, like visualising and at the same time feeling emotionally while hearing the music. As music therapy builds on their strengths, children with autism with unique talents in music can be identified. Some have perfect pitch, and they can even distinguish the slightest change in pitch.[12] This too can help them build confidence in themselves and some can develop their talents to make a career in music. Some children with autism have shown that music can boost their memory, enhance their self-esteem and socialising skills with their peers. Music has such wonderfully diverse benefits to individuals with autism. Music enhances the learners' joint attention as they sing together or play together with their instruments.[13]

In summary, the benefits of music therapy supported by research studies are listed here:

- Improved attention span
- Reduced anxiety
- Learning more effectively
- Reduction in stimming
- Improved socializing, and more positive behaviours
- Music is incorporated into a form of nonverbal self-expression and expressing emotions
- Improved verbal skills
- Improved interpersonal skills through shared play, listening and taking turns
- Able to Integrate auditory, visual and tactile senses that autistic individuals struggle with
- Improved gross and fine motor skills through dance and learning a musical instrument
- Becoming more flexible coping with new tasks

Music is an inborn sensory faculty inside us. Individuals with autism enjoy music, and it is an ideal tool to supplement their education. Music educators can collaborate with other therapists to enhance their services with children with autism. The different treatment modalities complement each other, so that equipping educators with different skills sets enable them to serve the students better. They will improve their communication, social and behavioural skills. Thus, through music therapy, the challenges faced by an individual with autism can be addressed.

REFERENCES

1. Marcheva, P. (2018). Musical art as a means for developing emotional skills in children with special educational needs. Knowledge International Journal, *28*(3), 1057–1061. https://doi.org/10.35120/kij28031057p

2. Dobrztnska, E. *et al*. (2006). Music therapy – history, definitions and application. *Archives of Psychiatry and Psychotherapy, 8*(1), 47-52.

3. Sandoval, E. (2016). Music in peacebuilding: A critical literature review. *Journal of Peace Education, 13*(3), 200–217. https://doi.org/10.1080/17400201.2016.1234634

4. Reschke-Hernandez, A. E. (2011). History of music therapy treatment interventions for children with autism. *Journal of Music Therapy, 48*(2), 169–207.

5. Stevens, E. & Clark, F. (1969). Music therapy in the treatment of autistic children. *Journal of Music Therapy, 6*, 98–104.

6. Sharda, M. *et al*. (2018) Music improves social communication and auditory–motor connectivity in children with autism. *Translational Psychiatry, 8*, 1–13. doi: 10.1038/s41398-018-0287-3

7. Wei, C. *et al*. (2015). Autism: reduced connectivity between cortical areas involved in face expression, theory of mind and the sense of self. *Brain*, 138, 1382–1393. https://www.ncbi.nlm.nih.gov/pmc/articles/PMC4407191/

8. Lai, G. *et al*. (2012). Neural system for speech and song in autism. *Brain*, 135, 961–975. https://academic.oup.com/brain/article/135/3/961/263918

9. Jones, R. M. (2018). Music tunes the brain in autism. *Science Translational Medicine*, 10, 466. https://www.science.org/doi/10.1126/scitranslmed.aav6056

10. Fatemi, S. H. (editor, 2015). *The Molecular Basis of Autism*. Springer-Verlag. ISBN: 978-1-4939-2189-8

11. AutismBrainNet (2020). The serotonin system in the autism brain. https://www.autismbrainnet.org/2020/04/10/the-serotonin-system-in-the-autism-brain/

12. Bharathi, G., Jayaramayya, K., Balasubramanian, V., & Vellingiri, B. (2019). The potential role of rhythmic entrainment and music therapy intervention for individuals with autism spectrum disorders. *Journal of Exercise Rehabilitation*, 15(2), 180–186. https://doi.org/10.12965/jer.1836578.289

13. Geretsegger, M. *et al*. Music therapy for people with autism spectrum disorder. *Cochrane Database Syst Rev* 2014. https://www.ncbi.nlm.nih.gov/pmc/articles/PMC6956617/

11 Questions by Parents

Kenneth Lyen

INTRODUCTION

Just as there is a spectrum of autistic individuals, there is also a spectrum of families into which they belong. Some families are thrown out of balance when they are challenged with a child who needs extra support and management. Others cope with the myriad of difficulties with self-assurance. Here we will focus on the more severe end of the autistic spectrum that poses stresses upon their families. What are the challenges facing them?

COPING WITH AN AUTISTIC FAMILY MEMBER

1. How can we come to terms with the diagnosis?
Approach: It can come as a shock to learn that your child has autism. None of us are prepared for this, and we will go through a wide range of emotions ranging from fear to anxiety and despair. We love our child so much, and we want to give them the very best in life, but now we fear the worst, our hearts suffering agonising pain. Initially, you may deny the diagnosis, and later, you might become angry and even depressed, before finally beginning to accept the diagnosis. Some of your friends may try to convince you that autism is not a disease, but simply a different condition that will sort itself out in the end. But this will probably not help your grief.

It is important to try to obtain more information, either through websites, books, or talking to recognised teachers, psychologists or medical specialists about the diagnosis. Given the characteristics of autism, it is important that you and your family seek professional advice early, as this can help you learn how to engage and connect with your child, and to become more flexible and understanding of your child's behaviours, feelings, and development.

2. How should we deal our other family members' reactions to the diagnosis?

Approach: You may have begun to accept the diagnosis of your child, but then you have to inform other members of your family. Each one will probably respond differently. Perhaps you might want to talk to each member separately, including your spouse, siblings, grandparents, and other caregivers. The reason is that autism is a lifelong condition that requires teamwork and long-term management. This can only come about when everybody accepts and understands the condition and learns how to work together to cope.

Having a child with autism can be very lonely for you. It is not uncommon for parents to keep the child's diagnosis hidden from their friends and colleagues and even immediate family. It is probably better not to conceal your child's condition from others, because eventually, you will need to enlist the help of your friends, neighbours and other members of the community.

3. How should we accept our child?

Approach: Accept your child as they are. Accept their idiosyncrasies, their unusual mannerisms, and their quirks. There are times they will be exasperating, like crying for long periods, and nothing you do will stop the crying. Don't give up. Engage with them, love them. Children will grow up and change with time. You too will learn to adapt.

4. How do we change the physical environment of our home?

Approach: Autistic children are sensitive to the environment. As such, the home environment should be safe. Avoid getting furniture with sharp corners. Keep dangerous implements away. Cover electric sockets with electric plug protectors. Construct window grilles to keep the child safe within the confines of the home.

Reduce noise because many autistic individuals have sensitive hearing and cannot withstand loud noise. This also applies to television, radio, home cinemas, and bright lights. Many autistic people do not tolerate lights that are too glaring.

Have a variety of safe toys. Some autistic children like to line up objects, like cars, so perhaps one should not buy too many similar vehicles.

5. Should we set a timetable?
Approach: Yes, autistic children learn and develop better with a predictable programme. You should set up a detailed structured schedule that can be followed every day. This includes waking up at around the same time, brushing teeth, washing face, toileting, changing clothes, having breakfast, playtime, exercise time, etc., all the way to bedtime.

6. How should we communicate with our child?
Approach: Some autistic children may have delayed speech, and some remain silent for much of their lives. Look out for non-verbal cues. Look at their facial expressions to determine their mood. Look out for body language, their gestures, and their responses to food, toys, and other activities. If they are not looking at you, turn their head to look at your face. Use a combination of visual and auditory clues to communicate, supplemented by your supplying the words to describe the activities or objects.

Try not to spend too much time watching television, playing with the mobile phone, or computer. Anecdotal evidence suggests that such activities may not stimulate communication or speech.

7. How to optimise learning?
Approach: Find out their strengths and weaknesses. What do they enjoy? Do they enjoy certain activities like drawing, playing the piano, or constructing objects with construction blocks? Make playtime fun, but cap the time devoted to any particular activity, so it does not become obsessional.

8. How to tackle undesired behaviours?
Approach: Some autistic children indulge in prolonged repetitive behaviours, like clapping, flapping hands, rocking, and even self-injurious activities. They may make unusually loud noises or scream continuously. One approach is to distract them and try to persuade them to take part in another activity or play with another toy. Try to discover if there may be some recognisable triggers for these behaviours. For example, is it in response to your refusal to give them what they want? Maybe you do not

realise what they really want, and they are unable to express themselves in words. So, in frustration, they start screaming.

In the case of self-injurious or dangerous behaviours like head-banging, biting, pushing, or scratching, you need to stop these activities immediately. If necessary, make an appointment to consult a doctor.

9. Should we engage in special therapies?

Approach: The special therapies referred to include speech and communication therapy, occupational therapy, physiotherapy, as well as music and art therapy. Most special needs schools, nurseries and kindergartens with interest in autistic children should be able to provide some of these therapies. When you have identified those areas that you think your child might need extra encouragement and help, you might like to discuss if they are really beneficial, and where to find these therapies.

10. What is our child's future?

Approach: Different stages of the autistic individual's life will require different approaches. The young autistic child may need early intervention centres that help in several ways, including giving family support, and providing speech therapy, occupational therapy, and special needs education. Opportunities for socialising needs to be organised, so the child can mix with other children, be given opportunities to engage in art, music, sports, and outdoor activities. The long-term future may require drawing up a will, and setting aside some funds in the event that the individuals are unable to take care of themselves, especially after the parents have passed on.

11. How can we not be overwhelmed by too much information on the internet?

Approach: It is a typical response for parents to be over enthusiastic in seeking (too much) information for the sake of their child on the world wide web. The internet is a vast storehouse of information, but unfortunately, not all the information is accurate. It is important to check the facts to verify whether they are reliable. Also, discuss the data with other professionals to evaluate its accuracy and relevance.

12. How should I manage the strain on our marriage?

Approach: Looking after an autistic child can cause a heavy strain on one's marriage. Sometimes, getting relatives and friends to help out can alleviate the problem. If not, one may have to look to marital or family counselling for help.

13. Who would be best to confirm a diagnosis of autism?

Approach: The diagnosis of autism spectrum disorder should be given by an experienced paediatrician, psychiatrist, or psychologist familiar with autism. A teacher or a general practitioner, or another parent, should also be able to guide you. You can also search the Internet for websites that can lead you to resource centres, special needs schools, and government websites dealing with autism. These websites may be able to provide information and advice, and direct you to the appropriate psychologists and medical specialists to obtain a diagnosis.

The Autism Resource Centre (ARC) was set up specifically to focus on the education of autism for families and autistic individuals. ARC has also been running Certificate and Diploma in Autism courses for educators from both mainstream and special needs education institutions. They also run parent training workshops for parents and the public.

14. Which preschools and schools to choose from?

Approach: There are several factors to consider. This includes which end of the autistic spectrum your child falls under. Are there any co-morbid problems, like attention deficit hyperactivity disorder, epilepsy, aggressive behaviours, etc.? How far is the school from where you live, and is transport provided? It's best to visit the schools and discuss your child with the teachers, principals and other parents.

15. Where can we find financial support?

Approach: Some children with autism require special needs education, early intervention, and other therapies, but these can be quite costly. What kind of help is available for low-income families who are raising children with autism? Fortunately, there are government organisations and charitable foundations that can give a helping hand. The Resources section provides a list.

16. Is autism a "disorder"?

In an ideal world, everyone is accepted as they are, and treated equally. We change our environment and our mindset to embrace everyone, and we do not label them. We support this sentiment. But at the present time, we are not living in an ideal world. People on the autism spectrum face many difficulties in our current society. They may need more individualised teaching, as well as help with their education, speech and communication, and coping with their anxieties, depression, and self-injurious behaviours. We try not to place negative labels on people, and we treat each one as a unique individual. We strive for inclusivity. That is our philosophy.

CONCLUSIONS

Teamwork is the foundation of coping with autism. The good news is that there are now quite a number of organisations, schools, psychological and medical services that can help. The problem is trying to find what the best option for your child and family. The internet can overwhelm you with too much information, and the most attractive site may not offer the best advice or therapy. Discuss it with as many people as possible, including teachers, psychologists, doctors, and other parents.

Final advice: Love your child and don't give up!

RESOURCES

Malacca Malaysia http://www.wingsmelaka.org.my/
Malaysia Autism Link https://www.autism.my/
Singapore Autism Resource Centre https://www.autism.org.sg/
Singapore St. Andrew's Autism Centre https://www.saac.org.sg/
Singapore Rainbow Centre https://www.rainbowcentre.org.sg/
UK National Autistic Society https://www.autism.org.uk/

Free online courses:
• Autism Society Online Courses and Tutorials http://www.autism-society.org/living-with-autism/how-the-autism-society-can-help/online-courses-and-tutorials/

- Floortime DVD Autism Training https://www.amazon.com/Floortime-DVD-Training-Basics-Communicating/dp/B0009XZITG

Online screening tools:
- 0–2 years: ASDetect http://asdetect.org/
- 18 months: Checklist for Autism in Toddlers https://www.rch.org.au/genmed/clinical_resources/CHecklist_for_Autism_in_Toddlers_CHAT/
- 4–11 years: Childhood Asperger Syndrome Test https://www.autism researchcentre.com/project_9_cast

12 Autistic Savants

Kenneth Lyen

INTRODUCTION[1,2]

The most amazing paradoxes associated with autism is the savant syndrome.

A savant is an outlier with an incredible ability to perform tasks far beyond what most of us can achieve. And this takes place despite having a mental disability such as autism or other neurological deficits. Examples of extraordinary accomplishments include having a prodigious memory, being capable of brilliant mathematical calculations, and having phenomenal abilities in music, art or language. Most savants are only able to display an outstanding skill in one major domain, but there are some exceptions.

There may be some restrictions in the savant's abilities. For example, some of them are excessively focused on one skillset only, while others may be prone to repetitive compulsive behaviours, and yet others may have a problem finding functional applications for their abilities.

The prevalence of savant syndrome is about 1 in one million, and the ratio of males to females is around 6 to 1. Up to 50% of savants are said to be autistic. Looking at it from another angle, the number of savants observed in autistic people ranges from 1 in 10 to 1 in 200.

It is very easy to point to famous historical figures and designating them to be autistic savants. These might include Michelangelo, Isaac Newton, Charles Darwin, Albert Einstein and countless others. However, the burden of proof is diabolical. How can you diagnose autism centuries after the departure of these personalities? You are unable to verify their diagnosis of autism on any of the diagnostic scales today. Even if they were alive today, you might still have difficulty diagnosing them!

It should be pointed out that many savants are not autistic, but have some other disabilities. For example, there is Nobuyuki Tsujii who was born blind, but won several international piano competitions[3]. John Nash, featured in the movie "A Beautiful Mind", suffered from schizophrenia and won the Nobel Prize for his mathematical game theory[4]. Vincent Van Gogh is said to have suffered from bipolar disorder and produced some really beautiful paintings[5].

SAVANT SKILLS

There are some contemporary autistic savants whom we can explore and from whom we can obtain a more accurate diagnosis of autism. In the film "Rain Man", Dustin Hoffman plays the role of an autistic savant showing his phenomenal memory and amazing powers of calculation, enabling him to keep on winning at blackjack in Las Vegas. His character is based on real life autistic savants, including Kim Peek[6].

The following section details some savant skills displayed by prominent autistic individuals:

(a) Calculations

Daniel Tammet's genius lies is his ability to figure out complex mathematical calculations quicker than a calculator. He can recall pi (π) to 22,514 decimal places. When Tammet is multiplying large numbers with each other, he arrives at the answer almost instantaneously and effortlessly. After an epileptic fit, he suffered from synaesthesia, and started to see numbers as shapes, colours and textures, and he views the number two as a motion, and the number five as a clap of thunder. He said "When I multiply numbers together, I see two shapes. The image starts to change and evolve, and a third shape emerges. That's the answer. It's mental imagery. It's like maths without having to think."[7]

(b) Prodigious Memory

Kim Peek, featured in the movie "Rain Man" had an elephantine memory. He was born with a large head, damaged cerebellum and agenesis of the corpus callosum. His motor development was delayed, he did not walk until he was four years old, and he could not button up his shirts. However, he could speed-read both pages of a book simultaneously, and remember the contents of at least 12,000 books that he had read[6].

(c) Calendar Savant
In addition to having a prodigious memory, Kim Peek also possessed the ability to know the day of the week when given a date. This ability is probably the most common skill of autistic savants. They do so effortlessly[6,8].

(d) Music
There appears to be quite a number of autistic music savants, with some of them having another disability, such as blindness. Music savants have the ability of picking up music, like learning to play the piano, at an extraordinary rate. They may have a brilliant memory and can play a piece of music after having heard it only once. There is one other interesting observation, and that is many autistic music savants possess absolute or perfect pitch. Derek Paravicini is a blind autistic savant who has given many public concerts, and been featured on several television programmes.[9]

(e) Art
Artistic savants can often draw from memory extremely accurately. Stephen Wiltshire is an artistic savant who was diagnosed to have autism at the age of three. He drew many cities, including Singapore, after flying over them just once[10].

(f) Hyperlexia
Hyperlexia are autistic people who read voraciously and are able to remember everything they have read. Rain Man's Kim Peek also has this ability[6].

AUTISTIC COMORBIDITIES

Autism is often associated with several other conditions, such as those listed below.

Attention deficit hyperactivity disorder

Some 30% of autistic individuals also display attention deficit hyperactivity disorder (ADHD). Famous entertainers like Woody Allen and Johnny Depp have self-diagnosed themselves as mildly autistic plus ADHD. The hyperactive brain tends to skip around, and are thus more likely to encounter novel ideas. Autistic individuals are often obsessionally focused on a narrow range of interests. The correct balance of these two traits may enhance creativity.

Bipolar disorder

A number of autistic people are also known to ricochet like a roller coaster from mania to depression and back up again — a condition known as bipolar disorder. These mood swings can engender creative thoughts during the manic phase. Famous people thought to have bipolar disorder, but probably not on the autism spectrum, include Edgar Allan Poe, Sylvia Plath, Robert Schumann, Vincent Van Gogh, Tim Burton and Francis Ford Coppola.

Obsessive compulsive disorder

Autistic people may have obsessional repetitive behaviours. It is sometimes difficult to differentiate obsessive compulsive disorder (OCD), the psychiatric condition characterised by obsessive thoughts and compulsive behaviour, from autism. Famous persons who have displayed obsessive compulsive tendencies include inventor Nicola Tesla, film and airline magnate Howard Hughes, and entertainer Marc Summers.

Epilepsy

Many autistic persons are also epileptic. Many brilliant people have a history of epilepsy, and because it is a brain condition, it is relevant when discussing brain functioning and creativity. There are at least two theoretical possibilities why epilepsy may have a beneficial effect on one's thinking. Firstly, the electric discharges that occur during an epileptic fit may cause flashes of new ideas. Secondly, recurrent epilepsy or the transient hypoxia it can engender might fortuitously cause minor damage to those areas of the brain that inhibit thinking, and this disinhibition of thought processes may enhance creative thinking. Famous people who might have suffered from epilepsy include Julius Caesar, Alexander the Great, Napoleon Bonaparte, Pyotr Tchaikovsky, Charles Dickens, George Handel and Hector Berlioz.

Schizophrenia

Autism and schizophrenia have a long and tangled history. In fact, autism used to be called childhood schizophrenia, and indeed, there are some overlapping symptoms. Schizophrenia is a severe psychiatric disorder characterised by hallucinations, delusions, blunted emotions, disordered thinking, detachment from reality and withdrawal into the self. It affects males and females equally. There is a strong genetic component. While the aetiology is still not fully established, the current favourite biochemical theory revolves around disordered dopamine metabolism affecting certain areas of the brain. The most prominent example of a genius affected by schizophrenia is John Nash. Interestingly, Nash is quoted by biographer Sylvia Nasar as saying that he often refused to take medication for schizophrenia because it blunted his creative thinking[11]. This sentiment is reflected by a number of artists and scientists suffering from other psychological conditions, such as bipolar disorder. The medical profession is therefore faced with a dilemma of deciding whether or not to treat mild mental afflictions knowing that medical treatment may smother creativity.

HOW DOES AUTISM CREATE GENIUSES?

Compensatory adaptation

Just as the blind have a heightened sense of hearing and touch, and the deaf have increased sharpness of vision, certain types of mental disability may cause compensatory adaptation. The best candidate for this is dyslexia. If dyslexics have difficulty with language, then they compensate by increasing their powers of visual perception.

Neural connections

Recent advances in the neurophysiology of the autistic brain have shown that long-distance nervous connections are reduced, while short-distance local connections are increased. This local concentration of nerve networks is hypothesised to correlate with the obsessional focus of thoughts, and because the connections are close to one another, the speed of thinking is accelerated.

Direct effects of mood swings

As mentioned above, autism may be co-morbidly associated with bipolar disorder. Mild mania could have some benefits. It is associated with quicker thinking, greater verbal fluency, play on words, increased self-confidence, and greater optimism. Severe mania, on the other hand, can be counter-productive and may result in loss of concentration and wild behaviour. Mild depression can act as a sort of editor to prune the excesses of mania, but severe depression can dampen all activities and thinking. Once again, having an optimal balance of autism and manic depression might lead to exceptional abilities.

Knight's move thinking

Certain mental disorders like ADHD, bipolar disorder, and schizophrenia are characterised by sudden jumps in one's thinking. These leaps from one idea to another can be quite unexpected and illogical, and are referred to as the "Knight's Move" thinking, the term taken from the game of chess. This way of thinking is important creatively speaking because it enables a person to make innovative leaps without being anchored by preconceived ideas or be imprisoned by one's sense of logic.

Famous people in history who may have had autism[12]

Although unproven, it is always very tempting to try to diagnose autism in famous outstanding individuals. Here is a list of some of the more famous "savants".

- Hans Christian Andersen — Author of children's books
- Lewis Carroll — Author of "Alice in Wonderland"
- Henry Cavendish — Scientist
- Charles Darwin — Naturalist, Geologist, and Biologist

- Emily Dickinson — Poet
- Paul Dirac — Physicist
- Albert Einstein — Scientist and Mathematician
- Bobby Fischer — Chess Grandmaster
- Bill Gates — Co-founder of the Microsoft Corporation
- Temple Grandin — Animal Scientist
- Steve Jobs — Former CEO of Apple
- James Joyce — Author of "Ulysses"
- Barbara McClintock — Scientist and Cytogeneticist
- Michelangelo — Sculptor, Painter, Architect, and Poet
- Wolfgang Amadeus Mozart — Classical Composer
- Isaac Newton — Mathematician, Astronomer, and Physicist
- Satoshi Tajiri — Creator of Nintendo's Pokémon
- Nikola Tesla — Inventor
- Ludwig Wittgenstein — Philosopher
- William Butler Yeats — Poet

FINAL THOUGHTS

Unanswered questions

Several questions immediately pop up when probing autistic savants. Are we too restrictive in only looking out for a few talents, such as memory, mathematics, calendar calculations, music and art? What about other skills such as cooking, gardening, architecture and fashion design? Recently, entrepreneur Elon Musk claimed that he has mild autism or Asperger Syndrome[13,14]. Should he be considered a savant? What about cartoonists? Satoshi Tajiri, the creator of Pokémon, was diagnosed to have childhood autism[15]. How wide should we expand our outstretched arms to embrace these other domains of achievements?

If you carried the conventional picture of an autistic person in your mind, perhaps someone with a speech impairment, often isolated and not mixing with others, and obsessed with flapping or rocking motions, someone who usually requires special education, you would be surprised if you discovered that the person has hidden talents. Not simply a mild talent, but incredibly prodigiously ultra-talented. A person who is able to multiply large numbers faster than you can enter them into a calculator, or someone who on hearing a piece of music once can play it back flawlessly, or someone who can draw a major city with the number of windows of a multi-storey building drawn absolutely correctly. You would be stupefied, your mouth wide open. And that's the paradox of the autistic savant.

Yes, we know there is a link between genius and autism. But it is a complex one. It appears to be the result of a fortuitous convergence of a number of factors, including a minimum level of intelligence, the ability to join ideas from different domains, the skill in generating novel ideas, to be able to think independently and flexibly, to focus one's mind, to apply self-discipline, perseverance, and to establish the right social and cultural environment. All these factors need to converge to create a savant.

This raises the tantalising question whether we can create that perfect physical, emotional and educational environment to produce a genius. By studying the mechanisms — both biochemical and educational — that link mental disorders and genius, one may gain insight into factors that can engender creativity and kindle future potential geniuses[16,17].

In his book "Islands of Genius", Daniel Treffert describes savants that sometimes appear unexpectedly after a head injury or a stroke. He asks the provocative question, "Are all of us potential savants?" If we can wake our dormant brains up, perhaps all of us can become geniuses[18].

To sum up, here is a modified quote, "You don't have to be mad to be a genius… but it helps."

REFERENCES

1. Treffert, D. A. (2009). The savant syndrome: an extraordinary condition. A synopsis: Past, present, future. *Philosophical Transactions of The Royal Society B, 364*(1522). 1351–1357. https://www.ncbi.nlm.nih.gov/pmc/articles/PMC2677584/

2. Wikipedia. Savant syndrome. https://en.wikipedia.org/wiki/Savant_syndrome

3. Wikipedia. Nobuyuki Tsujii. https://en.wikipedia.org/wiki/Nobuyuki_Tsujii

4. StudyCorgi. (2021). *Nash's Schizophrenia in "A Beautiful Mind" Film.* https://studycorgi.com/nashs-schizophrenia-in-a-beautiful-mind-film/

5. Nolen, W. A., van Meekeren, E., Voskuil, P., & van Tilburg, W. (2020). New vision on the mental problems of Vincent van Gogh; results from a bottom-up approach using (semi-)structured diagnostic interviews. *International*

Journal of Bipolar Disorders, 8. Article 30. https://journalbipolardisorders. springeropen.com/articles/10.1186/s40345-020-00196-z

6. Wikipedia. Kim Peek. https://en.wikipedia.org/wiki/Kim_Peek

7. Johnson, R. (2005, February 12). A genius explains: Daniel Tammet. *The Guardian*. https://www.theguardian.com/theguardian/2005/feb/12/weekend7. weekend2

8. Olson, I. R., Berryhill, M. E., Drowos, D. B., Brown, L., & Chatterjee, A. (2010). A Calendar Savant with Episodic Memory Impairments. *Neurocase*, *16*(3). 208–218. https://www.ncbi.nlm.nih.gov/pmc/articles/PMC2917639/

9. Wikipedia. Derek Paravicini. https://en.wikipedia.org/wiki/Derek_Paravicini

10. Wikipedia. Stephen Wiltshire. https://en.wikipedia.org/wiki/Stephen_ Wiltshire

11. Nasar, S. (2001). *A Beautiful Mind*. Touchstone Books.

12. Applied Behavior Analysis Programs Guide. History's 30 Most Famous People with Autism. https://www.appliedbehavioranalysisprograms.com/historys-30-most-inspiring-people-on-the-autism-spectrum/

13. BBC. (2021, May 9). Elon Musk reveals he has Asperger's on Saturday Night Live. *BBC*. https://www.bbc.com/news/world-us-canada-57045770

14. Malone, C. (2021). Elon Musk Isn't the First 'SNL' host with Asperger's. *Showbiz Cheatsheet*. https://www.cheatsheet.com/entertainment/elon-musk-snl-aspergers.html/

15. Verbal Behaviour Associates. (2020). Famous People On The Spectrum — Satoshi Tajiri. *Verbal Behaviour Associates*. https://vbacalifornia.com/famous-people-on-the-spectrum-satoshi-tajiri/

16. Takahata, K., & Kato, M. (2008). Neural mechanism underlying autistic savant and acquired savant syndrome. *Brain Nerve*, *60*(7). 861–869. https://pubmed. ncbi.nlm.nih.gov/18646626/

17. Lyons, V., & Fitzgerald, M. (2013). Critical Evaluation of the Concept of Autistic Creativity. In M. Fitzgerald (Ed.), *Recent Advances in Autism Spectrum Disorders* — Volume I. IntechOpen. https://doi.org/10.5772/54465

18. Treffert, D. A. (2011). *Islands of Genius*. Jessica Kingsley Publishers. https://www.amazon.com/Islands-Genius-Bountiful-Autistic-Acquired/dp/1849058733

13 Myths About Autism

Kenneth Lyen

INTRODUCTION

Autism awareness campaigns have largely been successful — more people know what it is, how to recognise the signs, and diagnosticians are better equipped to identify and properly diagnose the condition. With the worldwide connection on the internet, there is an increasing amount of good reliable information. Unfortunately, there is a burgeoning amount of false information or "fake news". This often fuels some people's strongly held distorted beliefs about autism. The trouble is that it is often difficult to separate truth from lies or partial truths. We will sift through some of the prevailing myths about autism, and try to determine which ones we think are true, partially true, or outright false.

THE MYTHS

1. Myth: People with autism don't want to make friends.[1]
Answer: This is untrue in most cases. What is true is that they have difficulty making friends as they may not have the repertoire of social or communication skills to be able to do so. However, they can be taught to socialise and communicate. Most persons with autism do want to make friends and can love as deeply as any other person. They form close relationships with people whom they are familiar with, such as relatives and caretakers. Over time, they bond with their peers, teachers and therapists whom they frequently interact with.

2.   Myth: People with autism can't feel or express any emotion — happy or sad.[2]

Answer: It is not that autistic individuals cannot feel or express emotions, but that they do so in a different or less expressive way. They do show a degree of empathy, and can recognise happy or sad faces. But, when it comes to more subtle emotions, such as anger, fear or irony, they may have a harder time. Autistic people may have a more muted, less expressive way of displaying their emotions. Some get angry very quickly, while others may misread a situation and respond inappropriately; for example, when they see someone fall down, they may laugh because they are not aware that the person may be hurt.

3.   Myth: People with autism are intellectually disabled.[3]

Answer: Autistic individuals, like the rest of the general population, have a wide range of abilities. Many have difficulty with speech and language, and this may give the mistaken impression that they are intellectually challenged. When it comes to cognitive abilities, like people, there will be autistic subjects with intellectual difficulties. On the other hand, there are some who display outstanding prowess in mathematics, art, music, and other areas.

4.   Myth: Individuals on the autism spectrum cannot lead independent and successful lives.[4]

Answer: This is not necessarily true. Those who are more severely affected with limited language skills may have difficulty navigating our rather complex modern society without help. Those on the milder end of the spectrum can learn skills that enable them to get jobs, enter mainstream education, and lead independent lives. Training and special needs education can be very beneficial for autistic individuals, and this is highly encouraged. We know of several people across a variety of professions who are highly successful despite being on the autism spectrum.

5.   Myth: Autism can be cured.[5]

Answer: The majority of autistic persons remain so all their life. They can make significant progress with early intervention, special needs education, and vocational training that have been specially tailored for their individual needs. At the moment, many medicines have been used in a bid to reduce the manifestations of autism, but to date, none of them are completely effective.

6. Myth: Autism is caused by bad parenting.[6]

Answer: The theory that autism is caused by bad parenting, or mothers who lack emotional warmth ("refrigerator mothers"), has been disproven. When parents try to better understand and learn to connect with their children, they can help them flourish.

7. Myth: Autism is caused by vaccines.[7]

Answer: There have been many large-scale epidemiological studies that have shown conclusively that there is no scientific evidence to support any causal link between vaccination and autism.

8. Myth: Autism is caused by food allergies.[8]

Answer: There has been isolated anecdotal evidence that some children's autistic manifestations seem to worsen with certain foods, such as gluten (wheat), casein (milk), eggs, tomatoes, eggplant, avocado, red peppers, etc. However, there have been no large-scale studies to confirm these findings. For the time being, one needs to maintain a healthy scepticism linking autism with food allergies. Thus, at this stage, one should not restrict the autistic child's diet.

9. Myth: Autism is becoming epidemic.[9]

Answer: The prevalence of autism in Singapore is 1 in 150, which is close to the worldwide statistics given by the World Health Organization. There has been an increase in the number of cases being referred with a diagnosis of autism in the past 30 years, leading to an increase in the numbers diagnosed. In the US for the year 2000, the prevalence of autism was 1 in 150, but in 2017, the prevalence more than doubled to 1 in 68. How much of this is a real increase in the number of new cases is controversial. Some experts claim that most of the increase of cases stem from a growing awareness of autism and changes to the diagnostic or classification criteria, especially the Diagnostic and Statistical Manual 5th Edition (DSM-5).[17]

10. **Myth: Most autistic individuals have special gifts or savant abilities.**[10]

Answer: The prevalence of special abilities or savant skills in autistic individuals ranges from 0.5% to 10%. Famous examples include Stephen Wiltshire who has a photographic memory and can draw a city like Singapore after flying over it just once. Temple Grandin is the professor of animal science and a famous author. Kim Peek has read 12,000 books and remembers everything about them. Leslie Lemke can play the Tchaikovsky piano concerto after listening to it only once. It is postulated that if one has a disability in one area, then the body compensates by developing expertise in another area.

11. **Myth: Autism is not a "disease".**[11]

Answer: Is autism a "disease", a "disability", a "disorder", a "condition", or simply a "difference"? The difficulty in trying to see which one of these different terms best fits autism is due to the wide spectrum of this condition. If one takes the severest cases, where the child is profoundly speech delayed, is totally isolated and alone, and flaps their hands or rocks their body endlessly, such actions continuing intermittently over many years, then it would be amiss of us to downplay the condition by dismissing it being "different". This does not help the child or family. At the other end of the spectrum, however, where autistic individuals can lead a fairly normal life, then it would be fair to say that autism is not a disease. If the problem were purely that of labelling, then it would be politically correct to substitute the word "disease" and consider autism as a "disability", a "disorder", or a "condition". As long autism is recognised as a potential problem and that the child and their family are provided with the help and support they need, then it's fine to use whichever term one is comfortable with. The hope is that society will not negatively label autism, but embrace and integrate them as being different but still part of humanity.

12. **Myth: The goal of treatment is to make autistic children "indistinguishable from their peers".**[12]

Answer: Currently, most therapies aim to improve social and communication skills, and reduce the restrictive repetitive movements of autistic individuals. There is a school of thought that suggests that hand-flapping, verbal echoing, and not engaging in social interaction are not pathological, but an adaptive strategy for that person to cope with a world that seems confusing, disordered, uncertain, and overwhelming. The solution is to dig deeper into the reasons for the behaviours, and to modify the environment. For example, if the autistic person is hypersensitive to noise or buzzing fluorescent light, or uncomfortable clothing, then the intervention is to change these environmental factors. There are no right or wrong answers, and one can probably try both paths and see which one works better. Currently, most parents choose to modify their autistic child to fit into conventional norms.

13. Myth: We're just over-diagnosing quirky kids with a trendy disorder.[13]

Answer: When Elon Musk claims to be on the autistic spectrum, or we place the label on Steve Jobs or Woody Allen, many of us raise our eyebrows. Are we too trigger-happy and over-diagnosing autism? Most of us "normal" or "neurotypical" individuals probably share some autistic symptoms, such as having obsessional habits or hobbies, we may withdraw into a world of our own occasionally, or we cannot tolerate certain people, foods or clothing. So are we over-diagnosing autism especially at the milder end of the spectrum? The problem is that there is no clear cut-off point between normal and mild autism. Until we find an objective blood test or brain scan to confirm the diagnosis, we are likely to over-diagnose mild autism.

14. Myth: Autism is caused entirely by genetics.[14]

Answer: There is certainly strong evidence of the role of genes as a contributing cause of autism. Identical twins have a 70% chance of both being diagnosed with autism. In contrast, non-identical twins only have a 30% chance, and the general population has a less than 2% probability. If genetics were the sole cause of autism, the concordance rate for identical twins should be 100%. The shortfall suggests that another factor must play a role, and the most likely candidate for that is environmental.

15. Myth: Only boys get autism[15]

Answer: The ratio of boys to girls on the autism spectrum is 3 to 1. Is it because girls are under-diagnosed? Or is there a real difference in the ratio? If so, the reasons are still unknown.

16. Myth: Autistic individuals won't get into higher education or get a good job.[16]

Answer: At the mild end of the spectrum, some autistic people excel in their studies and qualify for higher education. Some of them, like Satoshi Tajiri who created Pokémon, have succeeded in their enterprise. At the severe end of the autistic spectrum, the poorly communicating, hand-flapping noisy individual who does not conform to society's behavioural norms, might well be discriminated against. Currently the unemployment rate of autistic individuals is between 50% and 85%. It is hoped that employers will learn to understand and accept the differences of autistic applicants. It is also our hope that society will create more jobs suitable for people on the spectrum.

REFERENCES

1. Denworth, L. (2020). How people with autism forge friendships. *Spectrum.* https://www.spectrumnews.org/features/deep-dive/how-people-with-autism-forge-friendships/
2. Brewer, R., & Murphy, J. (2016). People with autism can read emotions, feel empathy. *Spectrum.* https://www.spectrumnews.org/opinion/viewpoint/people-with-autism-can-read-emotions-feel-empathy/
3. Applied Behavior Analysis Edu.Org What are the extremes of intelligence seen on the autism spectrum? https://www.appliedbehavioranalysisedu.org/what-are-the-extremes-of-intelligence-seen-on-the-autism-spectrum/
4. Therapeutic Pathways. (2020). Can a person with autism spectrum disorder live an independent adult life? *Therapeutic Pathways.* https://www.tpathways.org/faqs/can-a-person-with-autism-spectrum-disorder-live-an-independent-adult-life/
5. WebMD. (2020). What Are the Treatments for Autism? *WebMD.* https://www.webmd.com/brain/autism/understanding-autism-treatment
6. Crowell, J. A., Keluskar, J., & Gorecki, A. (2019). Parenting behavior and the development of children with autism spectrum disorder. *Comprehensive Psychiatry*, *90.* 21–29. https://www.sciencedirect.com/science/article/pii/S0010440X18301925
7. American Academy of Pediatrics. (2018). Vaccine Safety: Examine the Evidence. *American Academy of Pediatrics.* https://www.healthychildren.org/English/safety-prevention/immunizations/Pages/Vaccine-Studies-Examine-the-Evidence.aspx

8. Inserro, A. (2018). Is There a Link Between Autism, Food Allergies? Study Offers Hint But No Answers. *American Journal of Managed Care*. https://www.ajmc.com/view/is-there-a-link-between-autism-food-allergies-study-offers-hint-but-no-answers

9. Hess, P. (2019). Apparent new rise in autism may not reflect true prevalence. *Spectrum*. https://www.spectrumnews.org/news/apparent-new-rise-in-autism-may-not-reflect-true-prevalence/

10. Treffert, D. A. (2019). The savant syndrome: an extraordinary condition. A synopsis: past, present, future. *Philosophical Transactions of The Royal Society B*. https://www.ncbi.nlm.nih.gov/pmc/articles/PMC2677584/

11. Stevenson, N. (2015, July 16). Autism doesn't have to be viewed as a disability or disorder. *The Guardian*. https://www.theguardian.com/science/blog/2015/jul/16/autism-doesnt-have-to-be-viewed-as-a-disability-or-disorder

12. WebMD. (2020). Parenting a child with autism. *WebMD*. https://www.webmd.com/brain/autism/children-with-autism-coping-skills-for-parents

13. Curley, B. (2019). Are We Overdiagnosing Autism? *Healthline*. https://www.healthline.com/health-news/are-we-over-diagnosing-autism#Better-diagnosis-or-overdiagnosis?

14. Mundell, E. J. (2019). Autism Largely Caused by Genetics, Not Environment. *WebMD*. https://www.webmd.com/brain/autism/news/20190717/autism-largely-caused-by-genetics-not-environment-study

15. Loomes, R., Hull, L., & Mandy, W. P. L. What Is the Male-to-Female Ratio in Autism Spectrum Disorder? A Systematic Review and Meta-Analysis. *Journal of the American Academy of Child & Adolescent Psychiatry*, 56(6). 466–474. https://www.sciencedirect.com/science/article/abs/pii/S0890856717301521

16. Rosa, S. D. R. (2018).Why is the autistic unemployment rate so high? Thinking Person's Guide to Autism. https://thinkingautismguide.com/2018/02/why-is-autistic-unemployment-rate-so.html

17. American Psychiatric Association (2013). *Diagnostic and Statistical Manual of Mental Disorders, Text Revision Dsm-5-tr* (5th ed.).

Section 4

Supporting our Clients

This final section covers Rainbow Centre's efforts in making learning accessible and maximizing potential of our clients, teaming round the client and partnerships with families and the community towards achieving quality of life.

4A   Removing Barriers

14 Augmentative and Alternative Communication

Trina Liew, Tan Seok Hui and Eileen Soh

INTRODUCTION

Children who are minimally verbal need Augmentative and Alternative Communication (AAC) to communicate their needs and wants, express their thoughts and feelings, and establish, develop and maintain relationships through social interactions.

AAC refers to all forms of communication that enhance or replace spoken and written language. An AAC is *augmentative* when it enhances speech, but *alternative* when it replaces spoken language[1]. Among the many types of AAC, written sentence strips are an example of an augmentative AAC, while picture symbol systems such as Picture Exchange Communication System (PECS), core word boards, Pragmatic Organisation Dynamic Display (PODD), and speech generating devices such as GoTalk and Proloquo2Go are examples of an alternative AAC.

AAC is divided into three categories:

(a) **No-Tech / Low-Tech** (*systems that do not require batteries*)
- using gestures and facial expressions
- drawing a picture
- by writing
- pointing to letters to spell a word
- pointing to a picture or a photograph with written words

No-Tech / Low-tech: Pointing communication board

(b) **Mid-Tech** (*systems that require batteries*)
- tapping a switch/button to generate speech via a voice output device
- activating a speech-generating device via motion sensor using a part of the body (e.g. head, hand, arm)

Mid-Tech: Big Mack

(c) **High-Tech** (*electronic, computerised voice output systems*)
- touching the icons on a communication app on a mobile device, computer tablet or dedicated communication device

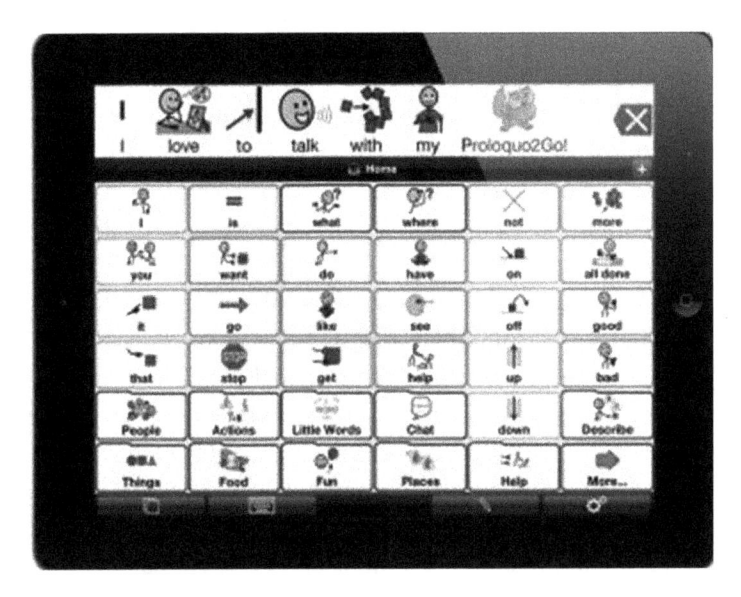

High-tech: Proloquo2go on an iPad

It is worth noting that the use of AAC may change with age, personality and individual differences. Children may need different types of AAC at different stages of development, as their communication needs evolve, and their AAC system is iteratively assessed and reviewed as their needs change.

Some children may be able to verbally request their basic needs and wants using single words like "hotdog", or short phrases like "want puzzle". However, they may still require support and modelling in the form of AAC to expand and vary their sentences, as well as express more complex concepts such as feelings of frustration or discomfort.

INTRODUCING A STUDENT

To illustrate, let's consider a young man named Skye (we changed his name and those of other students for anonymity). Diagnosed with autism spectrum condition at an early age, he started attending the Early Intervention Programme at Rainbow Centre when he was three years old. His parents observed that he would vocalise and pull an adult towards the shelves to get his favourite toys; he would also use his hands to push the adult away when it was time to keep them. His teachers also observed these behaviours at school. An *alternative* AAC in the form of picture symbols was thus introduced to help him request for items of interest: he would give his teacher a visual in exchange for a preferred toy. He also learnt to make the gesture for "more" in order to request for more pieces of a toy such as Lego or for more time with a toy. At the same time, a simple visual schedule was introduced to provide predictability in his daily routine and to help him understand the *first-then* concept: he would have to do another activity first, before he could play with a toy he liked.

When he turned seven years of age, he transitioned to the Special Education Programme at Rainbow Centre. Using single words, he could verbally request things of interest — food, toys, and favourite songs — but would rely on facial expression, body language, and gestures to protest and reject things he did not like or did not want to do. An *augmentative* AAC in the form of a pointing picture communication board was thus introduced to support the development of his language and communication skills, which in turn would help him express his thoughts and feelings. Using a communication board of core words (verbs, adjectives, prepositions, and pronouns) and fringe words (typically nouns), his teachers created opportunities for him to combine a variety of words together to make comments and requests, as well as ask questions. Skye would point to the pictures on his communication board and speak at the same time when making comments such as "Skye hungry" or "big biscuit" at snack time, and "I like" when eating chicken rice (his favourite food).

When he was 15 years of age, he entered the vocational track at Rainbow Centre, where he was given training and internship opportunities based on his vocational profile, interests and needs. Training was provided to systematically develop the necessary knowledge and skills needed to support suitable employment opportunities.

By this age, he was able to use three- and four-word phrases to make requests, comment, and answer simple questions. However, he had difficulties doing so spontaneously, particularly with unfamiliar people and in unfamiliar settings, beyond the familiar environment of home and school. Conversational scripts and role play were strategies used to teach Skye how to respond and problem solve in social interactions with others in the vocational setting. Role play along with the use of written scripts — an *augmentative* AAC — allowed Skye to become more practised at introducing himself and at requesting for his supervisor's help in the vocational setting.

At the age of 18 years, he entered his student placement at a restaurant. Using the written scripts of "Hello, I am..." and "I need help" he had learnt, he was able to engage in simple interactions when handling customers and to seek help when he needed it in the work environment, giving him confidence to manage in the work environment. In addition to learning to travel independently, he learnt how to use his phone to text his mother. He would text her the message "Here" when he arrived at work and "Go home" when he left work. Of course, not everything went smoothly all the time; he got lost once and was unable to ask for help or relate what happened when his parents found him a few hours later. Nevertheless, the restaurant manager was pleased with his performance and offered him employment as a waiter upon his graduation.

He is now 22 years of age and is still working at the same restaurant. He is a punctual employee, arriving two hours before work every day, and is a model employee, regularly receiving words of affirmation from his colleagues for being helpful. He manages to eat a balanced diet on most days and goes for walks with his parents on the weekends. From our perspective, he seems to have a fairly good life, being meaningfully engaged in work and independent when going about his daily activities. But perhaps we can ask ourselves if our students like Skye are truly *engaged* and *independent*. His parents remain his main social circle, and they still continue to worry about his safety and overall well-being. He keeps in touch with his teachers by calling or texting, "Hello Teacher, when is your birthday?" When they ask, "How are you, Skye?", he replies "Good!" However, he neither socialises with people outside his family nor does he participate in recreational activities without his parents. Are the limitations in his communication skills an obstacle to him making friends and allowing him to be fully *included* and *heard*?

What helps students like Skye communicate? Are there barriers or factors which facilitate communication success? One way in which we can conceptualise the process of achieving successful communication is by considering participation barriers outlined in Beukelman and Mirenda's (2013) Participation Model.[2]

Opportunity Barriers				
Policy	Practice	Facilitator skill	Facilitator knowledge	Attitude

Access Barriers		
Natural ability	Environmental adaptations	Utilisation of AAC system (Motor, Cognitive, Linguistic, Literacy, Sensory/ Perceptual abilities)

Beukelman and Mirenda's (2013) Participation Model

Illustrated in the figure above, the model provides a framework to guide assessments and interventions for people using AAC. Specifically, team members including speech language therapists, teachers and educators, parents and caregivers, and assistive technology specialists identify participation barriers of AAC users by using the functional participation requirements of same-age peers without disabilities as a reference. Using our student Skye as an example to illustrate, we would identify factors which help or hinder Skye from using his AAC, with the expectation that he should be able to perform the communication functions of his peers using his AAC, such as asking for help at his workplace.

BARRIERS TO COMMUNICATION

As shown in the figure above, the model identifies two types of participation barriers — access barriers and opportunity barriers, which affect the active participation of an AAC user.

(a) Cognitive and Language Abilities

Access barriers are factors which relate to the person using AAC. One access barrier is the student's *cognitive and language abilities*, meaning we need to consider the student's understanding of cause-and-effect, object permanence, and their ability to engage in joint attention, among other prelinguistic skills. We should also consider whether the student is able to use single words, two-word combinations, or simple sentences, and whether the student is only requesting and rejecting things they like or do not like, or are able to express their thoughts and feelings. Using our earlier example, when Skye was using motoric actions instead of symbolic language to request for a toy, an alternative AAC in the form of picture exchange was used to help him request appropriately for his preferred items. When he had learnt to read and was using longer phrases to verbally express his thoughts and request for help, an augmentative AAC in the form of written sentence strips was used to help him request for assistance in different settings and with more spontaneity.

(b) Motor and Sensory-Perceptual Abilities

Proximity switch (left); Big Mack (right)

Another access barrier is the student's *motor and sensory-perceptual abilities*, which impact the student's ability to access AAC. Students with motor difficulties may be unable to use a pointing picture communication board or picture exchange communication system. However, they may be able to press a switch such as the Big Mack which then plays a pre-recorded message. Students who are unable to activate a switch manually may be able to turn their head to activate a proximity switch, which then plays a pre-recorded message.

High technology — Eye gaze system

Students with limited motor movements may still be able to access AAC systems via other means such as eye-gaze.

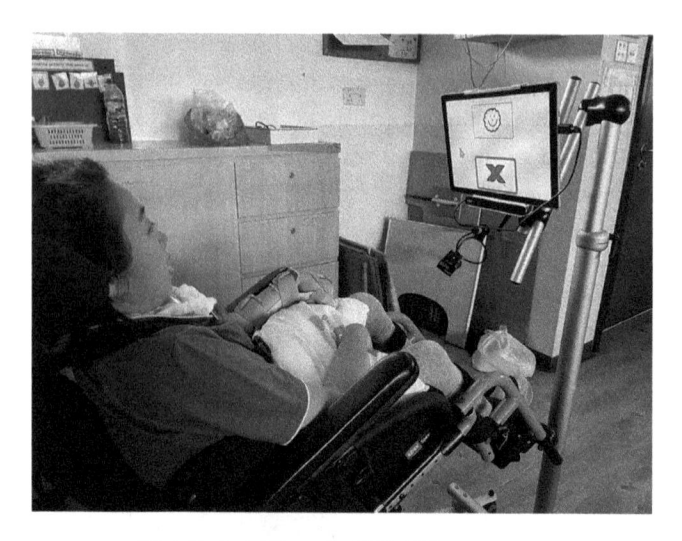

High-Tech AAC — the TOBII iGaze system

Wendy (not her real name) is a student who harnesses a high-tech communication system via eye gaze to communicate. This allows the student to participate in leisure and learning activities within the classroom. Her favourite game on the system is "Killer Bee", where she uses her eyes to track the movement of the bees and "catch" them by sustaining her eye gaze (dwelling) on the bee. Wendy smiles with pride whenever she catches the bee. In class, she uses the system to participate in learning by answering questions (out of two given options), and sharing information about herself (e.g. "I like Blackpink").

The Occupational Therapist (OT) also gets Wendy to actively provide feedback using her high-tech communication system (e.g. "change position") as they make adjustments to her seating device. This helps the OT make the right clinical decisions regarding Wendy's positioning, taking into account her comfort level and ease of participation in classroom activities.

Edward (not his real name) is a student who communicates via switch access to a high-tech AAC device. The device provides visual scanning by highlighting a set choice (with red border), allowing Edward to choose his target by tapping his right hand on the switch (attached to the right side of his wheelchair). Edward uses this to answer questions, and to choose his favourite game — Wheel of Fortune — over another activity. Edward is very motivated to use the switch to select the correct target. He vocalises his excitement when he makes his choice.

When Edward does not have access to his high-tech AAC, he relies on his communication partner to do partner-assisted scanning, where his partner shows (visually) and speaks (auditory), a set of two choices. Edward relies on his understanding of the spoken labels or his ability to visually recognise the symbols in order to choose his target. He then makes a choice by moving his head left or right to activate the proximity switch (orange, attached on a bracket positioned beside his head rest). The proximity switch is connected to a speech-generating device (red Big Mack, kept under his wheelchair) that will play a pre-recorded message of his choice.

Signing systems

Signing systems which rely on hand signs and gestures is another AAC system that may be suited to students with a hearing impairment or students who are learning to communicate using a multi-modal approach, e.g. like Skye who uses both pictures and signs to convey his requests. One example of a signing system is the Key Word Sign (Singapore) which was launched on 3 December 2020, being a collaboration among Movement for the Intellectually Disabled of Singapore, Singapore Association of the Deaf, and Key Word Sign Australia. This initiative helps the signing community to identify signs that are pertinent to the local context, and supports individuals with communication difficulties via training of professionals, caregivers, and the general public.

Interpretation/ Function	Description of Sign	Photo
Eat	Combining fingers together and places them on lips	

Interpretation/ Function	Description of Sign	Photo
Toilet	Taps right 1st finger (i.e. pointer) on centre of palm	
Home	Joins right and left fingertips together in front of chest	

Examples of American Sign Language / Australian Key Word Sign System

Clara (not her real name) is a student who has a preference for using signs and hand gestures to communicate her needs and wants. A dictionary was created to provide anyone who communicates with Clara to serve as a visual reference of what the signs mean and how to produce them. Clara uses signs and gestures that were created and/or adapted from American Sign Language and Key Word Sign Australia.

OVERCOMING BARRIERS

(a) Policy and Practice

As seen in the Participation Model earlier, there are a number of opportunity barriers which impact a person's communication success. Opportunity barriers are factors which are imposed by other people. *Policy* is an opportunity barrier when the policy at school or the workplace does not allow the student to use his or her AAC, while *practice* is an opportunity barrier when there are no opportunities for the student to practise using his or her AAC. In the case of Skye, neither *policy* nor *practice* were opportunity barriers in the school context. Rainbow Centre has a campus-wide policy where teachers and therapists actively encourage students to have their AAC at hand across settings, be it the classroom, canteen, therapy rooms, community based activities or vocational training. In Skye's case, his teachers and therapists provided him with ample opportunities to make requests and express his opinions and feelings using his AAC. In comparison, *policy* and *practice* were opportunity barriers for Skye at the workplace: spoken language was the only mode of communication that was endorsed there.

(b) Knowledge

Knowledge is an opportunity barrier when persons facilitating AAC usage lack knowledge about a particular type of AAC. For example, teachers who are knowledgeable about picture exchange and pointing picture communication systems may lack the knowledge required to support a student using a Pragmatic Organisation Dynamic Display or PODD system. This speaks to the need for communication partners to actively attend training sessions to learn about different AAC systems and their appropriate communication strategies.

Pragmatic Organisation Dynamic Display (PODD)

Colin (not his real name) uses a PODD book (expanded language, 5x4) to help him communicate with others. He enjoys sharing with his peers what he did over the weekend, and his experiences of performing at piano recitals. His PODD book allows him access to a larger vocabulary, thus providing him a better way to express his personality through commenting (e.g. "On [Saturday], I perform at BMC [concert]), and asking questions ("[I'm asking a question], Where did you go on Saturday?"), and expressing his opinions (e.g. "Piano practice is [tiring] and [frustrating]. It is long but I am [good] now").

(c) Skill

After learning how a particular AAC system works, the facilitator's skill in using the AAC is another factor to consider. *Skill* is an opportunity barrier when communication partners have the knowledge but have had limited opportunities to practise using AAC. In Skye's case, his teachers and therapists were skilled at facilitating his use of PECS, but only some of his teachers were practised at facilitating his use of sentence strips. Research has demonstrated the effectiveness of communication partner instruction[3]: Coaching facilitators on how to appropriately modify their strategies improves the communication ability of the AAC user.

(d) Attitude

Attitude is yet another opportunity barrier when individuals do not believe that AAC is a valid mode of communication either as an alternative to spoken language or in an augmentative role to supplement spoken language. Despite evidence that AAC usage in the alternative or augmentative role leads to improved communication both in terms of language and communication function[4,5], caregivers and/or educators may hold beliefs to the contrary. Thinking that an AAC system such as picture exchange or a pointing communication board will impede spoken language development or is unnecessary since the student can already make requests verbally, means that the student will be unlikely to receive ample opportunities to use their AAC to communicate. This is because individuals in the facilitating role will be unlikely to create opportunities for the student to practise using his or her AAC.

Happily for Skye, this was not the case. Skye's teachers and therapists not only facilitated the use of his AAC, his parents also received support for using appropriate strategies to facilitate Skye's AAC use. Studies have shown that families also need adequate support to integrate an AAC system into their children's daily routines, without which negative attitudes may arise and the AAC system may be abandoned[6].

Parental involvement

Knowledge and *skills* are both key to facilitating children's language and communication skills using AAC. At Rainbow Centre, we value the importance of partnering parents to achieve each student's potential and we do so by working closely with parents to share and coach them on communication strategies that are used with their child in school. This allows their child to generalise communication skills acquired in school to the home setting, and helps parents create more practice opportunities for their child to develop competency in his or her AAC use.

The Hanen Centre in Canada published a book *It Takes Two to Talk*[7] to equip parents with strategies to understand and respond appropriately to their child's communication. When parents understand what their child is seeking or what their child is attempting to escape from, they can then respond appropriately, and in turn facilitate their child's communication.

The authors explain that *all* communication begins with interaction. For parents to facilitate fun and meaningful interactions with their child, we first need to let our child lead. What does this mean? It means that we need to know what our child is interested in. We can do this by observing our child's facial expressions, body language, gestures, and vocalisations. The activity that engages our child at that moment could be something as simple as jumping. It could be sand play or it could be spinning a ball. It can be anything!

To know what our child is interested in, we need to *O.W.L: **O**bserve* carefully, ***W**ait* patiently, and ***L**isten* attentively to the cues our child is giving. We then follow our child's lead by responding immediately and enthusiastically in the activity that our child is interested in. We would then join in to play with them, and show interest by imitating what they are doing and/or saying.

Some parents might ask, "What if my child is passive and doesn't initiate an interaction with me?" The following list offers a few ways in which parents can create interaction opportunities for their child:

(i)   provide choices of objects and activities of interest to the child,

(ii) present a novel item and wait to see how they respond,

(iii) present a little of something the child likes and wait to see if he or she wants more, and

(iv) place the child's favourite item within sight but out of reach, thus getting them to request for it.

Once we get the communicative interaction going, we can create multiple opportunities to model language for our child and motivate our child to communicate using their AAC. For a child who uses a switch system, he or she might press the Big Mack to request for *more* of a snack they like. For a child who gestures or signs, they might sign the request to *eat*. For a child who uses a pointing board, we can pair what we say verbally with a picture at snack time to comment, *Yummy*!

As our child develops familiarity with their AAC system, we can continue to follow our child's lead and encourage their language development in a number of ways.

Expanding

We can build on what our child says. For example, if our child is using one word "ball" as he or she plays with a ball, we can add another word to it. We can say, "Bounce ball!" if our child is bouncing it. We can say, "Big ball!" if our child chooses a big ball over a small one. Paying attention to what is most meaningful for our child to learn, and using the word in that context will enable us to add words while using our child's AAC system. It's important to keep it at a *just right* level for our child so that it is adequately engaging, but not overwhelmingly challenging for them!

Recasting

When our child says or does something that is not entirely accurate, we can rephrase it for him or her in an unobtrusive manner. We can highlight the correct information to our child without disrupting the communication exchange. For example, if our child says "wa" when requesting for water, we can provide the correct model by saying "water" while pointing to the picture, before giving the cup of water to him or her. The visual helps our child link the word "water" to the picture and the actual object, and helps him or her pay attention to the way the word is being said.

If the child needs your help to take a toy, and taps on his communication system to ask you for help, but taps on the wrong symbol such as "eat", you can model to the child the *right word* which is "help". If your child says "bubble blow", you can repeat back the correct model "blow bubble" while pointing to the pictures in the correct sequence to him/her. The concrete nature of visuals in the AAC system helps emphasise the correct word sequence to the child without stopping the natural flow of the conversation. It also provides an opportunity for them to communicate back to us!

We would want to avoid telling our child, "It's wrong! Say this…" because it breaks the flow of communication. Instead, the technique of *recasting* provides repeated opportunities to model the correct word to the child unobtrusively. This helps us avoid the situation where our child is turned off by the chore or task of communicating because it is so effortful and/or frustrating.

Community involvement

As highlighted in the example of Skye, the emphasis on spoken language as the only mode of communication in his workplace presented a barrier to his communication effectiveness. The fact that he does not have a social circle outside of his parents from home and ex-teachers from school narrows his ability to connect and form friendships beyond these settings. For individuals with communication difficulties, the community can help them be *connected*, *included* and *meaningfully engaged* in society by taking the first step — by accepting and embracing different modes of communication from all walks of life.

Some might ask, "But I don't know how to use the AAC system! What can I do?" It's a great start to be cognisant of the fact that other people communicate differently from us; they are not less able if we give them a chance to share their thoughts and feelings. But the mode in which they communicate *is* different, and they may require time and patience on our part. The following are some ways to facilitate communication with an AAC user.

1. Don't assume
We can ask the person to share how best to communicate with him or her. He or she will be happy to show you!

2. Say less and stress
We can adopt Hanen's strategies when interacting with someone using an AAC. By *saying less* we reduce clutter and confusion for the person. *Stressing* the key words helps the person focus on the main points of the conversation, and keeps the communication exchange going.

3. Go slow and show
Hanen's *4S* strategy also suggests that we can go *slow*: slowing down the speed at which we talk gives the person time to process what we are saying. We can *show* the person what we are talking about by pointing to the objects or pictures of reference. We can also point to relevant pictures in the person's communication system. It is okay if we are not knowledgeable or familiar about how to use the AAC system. The important thing is for us to show genuine intent in connecting with the person.

If the person is part of your community, you can talk to his or her caregiver or parents to learn from them. You can also get in touch with professionals to learn more about different types of communication systems and communication strategies. If you are interested in connecting with other AAC users in our local community, you can reach out to ISAAC Singapore and participate in their activities, or sign up as a volunteer! ISAAC Singapore is a local chapter of the International Society of Augmentative and Alternative Communication. They are a local, non-profit organisation led by AAC users and professionals that aims to raise awareness and build AAC communities in Singapore. With this community, they hope to achieve the bigger vision of ISAAC that AAC will be recognised, valued and used throughout the world.

4. Build connections
We all want to form friendships and develop meaningful relationships with others so that we feel connected and plugged in the community we live

and interact in. Consider joining a befrienders programme to connect with people who use an AAC. Rainbow Centre offers a Befriender Programme that coaches and matches you to individuals like Skye who are looking forward to casting their social networks wider, so that they too can lead fulfilling lives like everyone else.

REFERENCES

1. Elsahar, Y., Hu., S., Bouazza-Marouf, K., Kerr, D., & Mansor, A. (2019). Augmentative and Alternative Communication (AAC) Advances: A Review of Configurations for Individuals with a Speech Disability. *Sensors, 19*(8). 1911. DOI: 10.20944/preprints201903.0033.v1

2. Beukelman, D. R., & Mirenda, P. (2013). *Augmentative and Alternative Communication: Supporting Children and Adults with Complex Communication Needs.* Brookes.

3. Kent-Walsh, J., Murza, K. A., Malani, M. D., & Binger, C. (2015). Effects of Communication Partner Instruction on the Communication of Individuals using AAC: A Meta-Analysis. *Augmentative Alternative Communication, 31*(4). 271–284. DOI: 10.3109/07434618.2015.1052153

4. Allen, A., Schlosser, R. W., Brock, K. L., & Shane, H. C. (2017). The Effectiveness of Aided Augmented Input Techniques for Persons with Developmental Disabilities: a Systematic Review. *Augmentative Alternative Communication, 33*(3). 1–11. DOI: 10.1080/07434618.2017.1338752.

5. Zimmerman, T. O., Light, J., & Pope, L. (2018). Effects of Interventions That Include Aided Augmentative and Alternative Communication Input on the Communication of Individuals With Complex Communication Needs: A Meta-Analysis. *Journal of Speech Language and Hearing Research, 61*(3). 1–23. DOI: 10.1044/2018_jslhr-l-17-0132

6. Baxter, S., Enderby, P., Evans, P., & Judge, S. (2012). Barriers and Facilitators to the use of High-technology Augmentative and Alternative Communication Devices: A Systematic Review and Qualitative Synthesis. *International Journal of Language & Communication Disorders, 47*(2). 115–129. DOI: 10.1111/j.1460-6984.0211.00090.x

7. Girolametto, L., & Weitzman, E. (2006). It Takes Two to Talk — The Hanen Program for Parents: Early Language Intervention through Caregiver Training. In R. J. MacCauley & M. E. Fey (Eds.), *Treatment of Language Disorders in Children* (pp. 77–104). Brookes.

15 Human-centric Assistive Technology and Innovation

Koh Kheng Wah and Tan YN

REDUCING BARRIERS TO ACCESSIBILITY

Assistive technology (AT) refers to a product, equipment, software, system or service that enhances learning, working, and daily living for persons with special needs. From a broader perspective, assistive technology assists persons with disabilities to remove barriers to accessibility of education, transportation, housing, recreation, and employment, so that they can reach their full potential, live more independently, and participate more fully in mainstream society.

AT includes physical assistive products such as wheelchairs, adaptive switches and utensils, digital assistive products such as software and apps that support communication, access to information, rehabilitation, and education. It also includes physical environment adaptations, for example, portable ramps or grab rails.

The World Health Organization (WHO) and United Nations Children's Fund (UNICEF), in their joint Global Report on Assistive Technology (2022), advocate that access to assistive technology deserves greater attention now than ever before. Access to appropriate, quality assistive technology can mean the difference between enabling or denying education for a child, and participation in the workforce for an adult.[1]

Due to accessibility barriers, people with disabilities can often become excluded and isolated, thereby increasing the adverse impact of the disability on a person and their family. AT can help remove some of these barriers, thus helping them to live healthy, productive, independent, and dignified lives.

EMPATHY IS KEY

In determining what form of AT is suitable for a student with special needs, a human-centric approach is critical. One part of this approach is the 3-LENS framework (See Figure 1) to enable access for all of our students and families, with the sole purpose of creating a sense of belonging to communities and having access to things and services that matter.

A sense of belonging is an integral part of a person's worth and dignity. It involves connecting people, building interdependent relationships and forging new lenses to see each person as a unique individual. It also underlines the importance of belonging to communities and having access to things that matter.

Figure 1 illustrates the shift in the mindsets needed for us to embrace diversity and inclusion. There are three categories of stakeholders we need to reach out to allow our students and families to achieve a sense of belonging and thrive as they graduate from Rainbow Centre. The three categories are: 1. Our students and their caregivers; 2. Professionals working in the sector; 3. Our partners in the community.

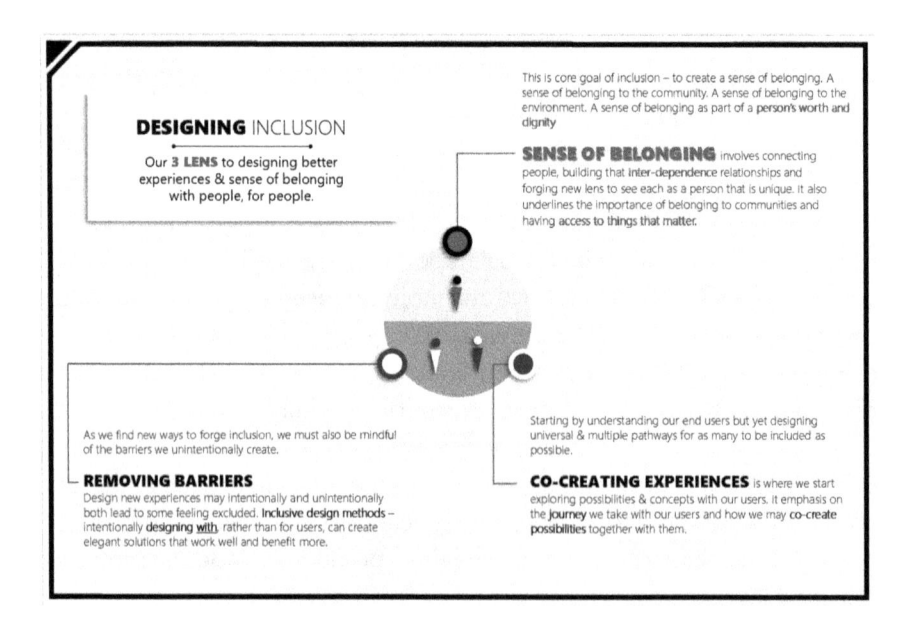

DESIGNING INCLUSION

Our **3 LENS** to designing better experiences & sense of belonging with people, for people.

This is core goal of inclusion – to create a sense of belonging. A sense of belonging to the community. A sense of belonging to the environment. A sense of belonging as part of a person's worth and dignity

SENSE OF BELONGING involves connecting people, building that inter-dependence relationships and forging new lens to see each as a person that is unique. It also underlines the importance of belonging to communities and having access to things that matter.

As we find new ways to forge inclusion, we must also be mindful of the barriers we unintentionally create.

REMOVING BARRIERS
Design new experiences may intentionally and unintentionally both lead to some feeling excluded. Inclusive design methods – intentionally designing with, rather than for users, can create elegant solutions that work well and benefit more.

Starting by understanding our end users but yet designing universal & multiple pathways for as many to be included as possible.

CO-CREATING EXPERIENCES is where we start exploring possibilities & concepts with our users. It emphasis on the journey we take with our users and how we may co-create possibilities together with them.

Figure 1.   3-LENS Framework (RCTC, 2019. unpublished material)

These three categories of stakeholders form the triangle of expertise, knowledge and understanding of our students in relation to the types of AT products available to meet their needs.

Our human-centric approach

Another part of our human-centric approach in developing AT solutions for our students is illustrated in Figure 2, which shows the key components of an agile, iterative, collaborative process. The most critical step is to start with a deep empathy and understanding of our students' needs.

With the human-centric AT evaluation approach, we consider our students' individualised education plan, the assessments made by the therapists and teachers who have interacted with the students, our students' personal preferences and their family members' wishes. For students who are above the age of 15, their Post-18 or Good Life Plan is also factored in during the consideration of the types of AT suitable.

Taking an ability-based rather than disability-based approach is important. Consider the student's strengths that can be built upon, and not merely the challenges or limitations faced by the student. For students with more complex needs, such as severe cognitive impairment or living with co-morbidities, understanding the student may take a much longer period with more iterations before we get it right. Observation will play a key

Our Human-Centric Approach

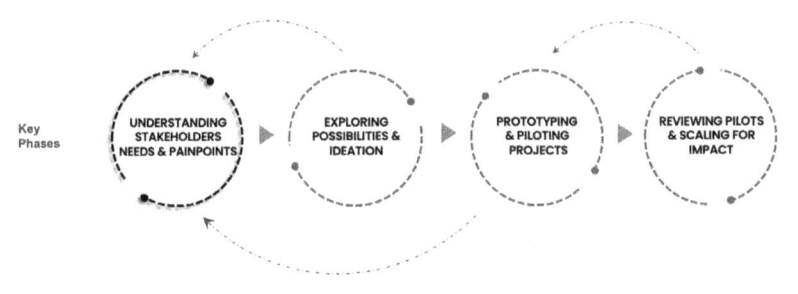

We will be adopting a **human-centric** approach to undertake this **multi-year transformative** project. Understanding the needs of our stakeholders will take centerstage in every phase, as we **co-create possibilities** to meet their needs. **Prototypes** will be built as a means to **gather feedback** and pilot trials will be implemented and reviewed before any larger scaling & deployment is done.

Figure 2.   Human-centric Approach (RCTC, 2019, unpublished material)

role in this phase, taking on perspectives from the interactions the student has with objects, the environment, routines, communication modes, etc.

Once we establish a deeper understanding of the student and their pain points, the team will explore the availability of suitable AT devices locally and overseas, or develop a prototype to test its suitability, and obtain feedback from the student and other stakeholders before working on the next iteration.

In this human-centric approach of developing AT solutions, it is important to place empathy at the core of the work we do. This allows us to connect with our students and their families in order to develop a deep understanding of their struggles, their needs and their aspirations. We need to constantly re-frame our perspectives and to tap the collective wisdom of the interdisciplinary team and partners, so as to be able to ideate and implement practical AT solutions and innovations.

ASSISTIVE TECHNOLOGY FOR AUTISM AND OTHER DEVELOPMENTAL DISABILITIES

Rainbow Centre serves a student population with multiple disabilities (MD) and autism spectrum disorder (ASD). The AT needs for students with physical disabilities and those with ASD differ. The evaluation of suitable AT is anchored on an in-depth understanding of the individual student's profile, including his or her abilities, challenges, interests and other characteristics, as well as his or her learning and living environment and ecosystem.

To evaluate what form of AT is suitable for students, we start with the human-centric approach of understanding stakeholders' needs and pain points. We rely on a shared understanding of the student from the inter-disciplinary educational team and the family. Taking an ability-based rather than disability-based approach, we consider the student's strengths that can be built upon, and not just challenges.

In exploring the types of assistive technology for our MD students, we focus on:

- Identifying alternative access to perform learning/daily living tasks limited by their physical disabilities. For example, use of switches and head/eye tracking AT to access and control computers/tablets vs the standard computer mouse and touchscreen;

- Ideating ways to redesign tasks to be engaging to support training them in mastery of the tasks. For example, an adaptive knife and cutting board which have been ergonomically designed for students with cerebral palsy to perform effective single-hand cutting so that they enjoy wider options in terms of meal preparation, with limited support from the teacher/caregiver.

Autism is often referred to as the "invisible disability". Using the human-centric approach in evaluating assistive technology for our ASD students, we focus on areas such as:

- Supporting them in coping with their invisible sensory challenges and reducing repetitive behaviours, for example, use of noise cancelling headphones for students with profound auditory sensory challenges or use of dimmable LED lighting in the classrooms to moderate visual sensory challenges;
- Augmentative or alternative ways to address receptive and expressive communication difficulties, for example, use of Augmentative and Alternative Communication (AAC) apps on iPads or printed picture cards for communication;
- Supporting them to improve their social interaction skills, for example, use of video social stories.

To illustrate the human-centric approach in AT solution development, let's take a closer look at one such area of application: Many students with autism have speech impairment, with both verbal receptive and expressive communication being their weaknesses. As many of them have difficulty in filtering irrelevant background noise, they often find it difficult to understand and follow spoken instructions.

Capitalising on their visual learning strengths, we teach students to use (low-tech) printed visual images and (high-tech) AAC apps as alternative ways for non-verbal students to visually express their needs and thoughts. For students with some speech, visual AAC is also useful for them as they may not be able to express their wants comprehensively, thereby helping to reduce frustration and resulting behavioural problems. Well-designed AAC apps can help teachers and caregivers to communicate their expectations and teach the students skills more effectively.

Visual schedules are also useful in communicating to the students the day's schedule and any changes, so that it helps them to know what to expect, thus reducing their anxiety. Visual scenes, through the use of photos and videos, can be used to augment verbal communication and narrate stories to teach social skills.

Although the visual cards system as a form of AAC has been in use for a few decades and AAC apps are not new to educators and families, there are still many speech-impaired individuals with autism who are not using any form of AAC. The issues that inhibit wider adoption of AAC are complex, with several hurdles that need to be overcome, including:

- There is a myth that the use of AAC hinders the development of verbal communication, which has resulted in hesitation on the part of some caregivers to use AAC with their children. Studies have shown that the use of AAC does not inhibit speech production. Instead, AAC may support development of speech and language.[2,3]
- We need wider public awareness of AAC and to combat social stigma relating to its use. More people have to understand that the use of AAC system, with its attendant gestures and vocalisation as a means to "converse", is an acceptable multi-modal way of communication.
- Progress in using AAC for communication may be very slow for students with profound autism; as such, caregivers and even professionals might give up too early in the process. Much patience, persistence, and training are needed to support the students as well as their caregivers.
- For a neurotypical child to develop communication and language skills, immersion in an environment where that language is widely used can speed up their fluency in using that language to express themselves. Similarly, to develop our students' ability to use AAC to express themselves effectively is not something that a Speech Language Therapist can achieve alone. There is a need to integrate the use of AAC throughout the day into various daily activities and to establish an ecosystem of teachers, allied professionals, caregivers, family, volunteers and public, all adopting the use of AAC to support the individuals with autism to develop effective use of the AAC to communicate their needs and thoughts.

REPURPOSING CONSUMER TECHNOLOGIES FOR ASSISTIVE TECHNOLOGY

There is a wide range of assistive technology available in the market developed to address various types of special needs. The cost of development and production can be high, often due to there being relatively few users of a particular type of customised AT, which results in proportionally high prices for users.

The high cost can be a barrier to users adopting certain AT that can potentially benefit them. To address the cost factor, one exciting development is adapting and repurposing consumer technology to become assistive technology. Examples of how we have repurposed consumer technology for assistive technology applications include:

- While speech-generating devices used to be the choice of high-tech communication devices for speech-impaired students, the widespread availability of iPads and a variety of AAC apps has driven us to switch to iPads as our tablet of choice. The cost is significantly lower and a focus on diversity and inclusion by Apple ensures there is a drive to constantly improve the content and support surrounding its use.
- As we have a student who is not able to project his voice audibly, we piloted the use of a throat microphone (used by the military and gamers) and voice amplifier (used by teachers and group sports instructors) for him. His voice can now be heard much more clearly; he can also share his thoughts and have conversations comfortably with his teachers, school mates, and family members. The cost is relatively low as these devices are repurposed from consumer products, and not medical grade devices.
- Apple, Google and Microsoft have developed a number of accessibility features in their software, including support for a variety of switches and user interface navigation, and these provide alternative ways to operate the devices. For example, for examples, by enabling the use of head movements and facial gestures to control the user interface.

ASSISTIVE TECHNOLOGY INNOVATIONS IN LEARNING AND DAILY LIVING

Various assistive technologies have been used in Rainbow Centre for many years in supporting students to achieve their IEP and Good Life goals. In this section, we will share some of the AT innovations we are piloting in Rainbow Centre to create enabling environments for students to learn and participate more effectively, meaningfully and actively.

Classroom environmental accommodation for students with ASD

Many individuals with profound ASD often have visual and auditory sensory processing impairment, resulting in sensitivity to environmental light and sound conditions. Teachers and allied professionals working with students with profound autism have observed that many of them get distracted by bright fluorescent lighting and sharp noises, and they often attempt to cope through repetitive behaviour like stimming. Some are affected to the extent of suffering from sensory overloading situations.

We embarked on a project, under the Accessibility-Lab Strategic Initiative, to pilot ways that classrooms can be designed to be a more conducive environment to support ASD students in learning and participation.

In understanding the stakeholders' needs and pain points, we referred to several studies in this area. ASD students with auditory sensory processing challenges often face difficulties filtering out irrelevant sound and background noise, and those with visual sensory processing challenges are negatively impacted by fluorescent lighting. When the classroom environment adds further demands on attention and sensory processing, students with ASD may experience increased difficulty in fully participating or engaging in the classroom activities.

In the first phase of the pilot, we identified two classes of students with ASD with profound visual and/or auditory sensory processing challenges. We aimed to implement environmental accommodation measures to reduce light sensitivity and noise echo in the classrooms by replacing the fluorescent lights with dimmable/tuneable indirect LED lights, and installing echo-absorption acoustic panels on the ceilings/walls.

Eight students were observed before and after installation, where both quantitative (e.g. repetitive behaviours served as behaviour indicators of their sensory dysregulation) and qualitative (e.g. observations of participation and engagement, surveys and interviews with teachers) data was collected.

With the implementation of the environmental accommodation measures, we observed promising results whereby several of the pilot students showed some reduction in repetitive behaviour, and displayed some increased engagement and attentiveness, as well as decreased anxiety.

Teachers also reported that the dimmable LED lights and reduced noise helped them feel calmer and less stressed. The tuneable indirect LED lights also allowed teachers to adjust the lighting temperature and brightness according to the needs of the lessons being conducted.

From the pilot, we also realised that based on light and sound accommodation alone, results for students with more complex (psychological, behavioural, cognitive) conditions were inconclusive. Such students were impacted by classmates' dysregulation or other issues outside the classroom. To better accommodate the students' behavioural and sensorial challenges, especially for students with more complex conditions, additional environmental accommodation and support integrated with other interventions practised in the classroom holistically would be necessary.

Road safety augmented reality training stimulator

The ability to travel independently is an important life skill for many of our students to acquire, in order that they can travel to and from home and school, to participate in community life and in post-school years to work and live an independent life.

Road safety awareness is an important aspect of independent travel training. Using the human-centric approach, our teachers designed a number of creative resources to train our students on road safety. These resources include visual instructions, videos, quizzes, real-life sized working replicas of pedestrian crossing traffic lights and zebra crossings within the school premises. These resources enable the scaffolding of road safety lessons for students, especially for those with cognitive challenges.

One of the challenges faced in the teaching of mobility training and road safety is that without actual cars, many of our students cannot visualise oncoming vehicles and do not understand the danger involved. We experimented with virtual reality headsets but found that some students were uncomfortable with its use, due to their tactile and visual sensory processing difficulties. We then explored other potential solutions with the project team, prototyping using three TV screens and augmented reality (AR) software to develop and trial prototypes with teachers and students iteratively.

Eventually, the team was able to develop engaging lessons with realistic AR stimulation of real-life pedestrian traffic crossings. Students are able to see AR simulations of oncoming vehicles, learn how to judge the stopping of vehicles and interact with real-life-like scenarios. With the AR software, we were also able to simulate an accident scene when a student crossed the road when it was unsafe, thus helping to teach in a concrete way the danger of traffic accidents. By prototyping and piloting in an agile way, we are able to keep the risk of high-cost failure low, and scale up innovations only after we had tested that the solutions work for our students.

THE IMPACT OF ASSISTIVE TECHNOLOGY

Assistive technology in the form of assistive products as well as environmental adaptations, when integrated well into lesson plans and therapy programmes, can support innovation and the efficiency of teachers and allied professionals in their delivery of lessons and therapy.

The successful implementation of assistive technology solutions requires a deep empathy and understanding of the students' needs, and an agile, iterative, collaborative approach involving various stakeholders, which includes caregivers. We are hopeful of its potential to positively impact the lives of individuals with special needs by improving learning and active participation in daily living activities.

REFERENCES

1. Holmes, K. (2018). *Mismatch: How Inclusion Shapes Design*. Cambridge, Massachusetts: The MIT Press.
2. Miller, D. C., Light, J. C., & Schlosser, R. W. (2006). The Impact of Augmentative and Alternative Communication Intervention on the Speech Production

of Individuals With Developmental Disabilities: A Research Review. *Journal of Speech, Language, and Hearing Research*, *49*(2), 248–264. https://doi. org/10.1044/1092-4388(2006/021).

3. Schlosser, R. W., & Wendt, O. (2008). Effects of Augmentative and Alternative Communication Intervention on Speech Production in Children With Autism: A Systematic Review. *American Journal of Speech-Language Pathology*, *17*(3), 212–232. https://doi.org/10.1044/1058-0360(2008/021)

4. World Health Organization and the United Nations Children's Fund (UNICEF). (2022). Global report on assistive technology. https://www.unicef. org/media/120836/file/%20Global%20Report%20on%20Assistive%20 Technology%20.pdf

4B Teaming Around the Client

16 Collaborative and Interdisciplinary Approach to Managing Children with Autism and Multiple Disabilities

Manoj Pathnapuram

INTRODUCTION

Case management is a complex concept for which diverse definitions exist. One definition states that case management is a delivery model for providing client-focused care. Interdisciplinary case management is required when clients present problems that do not fall within the purview of any one discipline. The interdisciplinary approach entails the participation of professional and support staff, along with the client and his or her family, in diagnosis, individual programme planning, implementation, and evaluation. For effective case management, it is important that teams work in a collaborative manner.

Collaboration is a way of interacting and working together. Collaboration conveys how a process, task or activity is occurring and how individuals are communicating and interacting with one another. These interactions occur both formally and informally. For example, school leadership teams, programme teams, cohort teaching teams, and Individual Education Plan (IEP) team meetings are some of the formal structures in school that rely on collaboration for student success. Meetings between teachers and allied professionals (APs) to respond to immediate student needs, corridor conversations, as well as phone calls to parents are examples of informal collaboration. Informal collaboration will always take place as relationships between individuals develop and grow; however, effective formal collaboration requires school structures and processes in the context of a collaborative school culture (Friend & Cook, 2014).

This chapter aims to highlight the importance of collaboration and collaborative processes in interdisciplinary and transdisciplinary case management of students with autism and multiple disabilities by teams of educators, allied professionals, families, caregivers and other relevant stakeholders, in the context of the Rainbow Centre schools and programmes.

UNDERSTANDING COLLABORATION

Collaboration does not come naturally. It is more complex than it appears; to be successful in this way of interacting and to form effective partnerships with colleagues, a comprehensive understanding of collaboration is needed.

Friend and Cook (2014) identified six core characteristics of collaboration.

1. Collaboration is a voluntary relationship: It is not possible to insist that people interact in a certain way. If, however, individuals can see the benefits of a collaborative way of interacting, then they are more likely to think about trying it.
2. Collaboration is based on equality among team members: Everyone's contribution and perspective is equally valued.
3. Collaboration is based on shared goals: There must be an agreement around shared goals for a student and the goals for a team. This guides discussion, problem solving and action planning.
4. Collaboration requires shared responsibility for key decisions: Although team members may take individual responsibility for completing individual tasks, the team shares responsibility for the decisions on which actions and plans are based.
5. Collaboration requires team members to share resources: Everyone is responsible for sharing knowledge, skills, information, equipment, materials, thoughts, ideas, and time.
6. Collaboration requires shared accountability for outcomes: Successes and failures are shared by everyone in the team. When teams take time to acknowledge success, they are celebrating their connectedness

and when they reflect upon what has not worked, they are taking time to proactively seek solutions to improve their practice (Friend & Cook, 2014).

In addition to these six core characteristics, there are emergent characteristics of collaboration that happen as collaborative relationships begin to take shape. Over time, as teams practise using a collaborative approach, positive perspectives grow. As collaborative relationships form, trust and subsequently respect begin to establish in a team. A sense of community develops from collaborative practice and, what is increasingly seen, is that the development of a sense of professional community leads to better outcomes for students as well as satisfaction and support for educators (Conoley & Conoley as cited in Friend & Cook, 2014).

In Rainbow Centre, the teaming around a child or student is based on the principles of collaboration described by Friend and Cook (2014). The educators, allied professionals and caregivers bring to the table their knowledge, expertise and perspectives thus levelling the playing field. The individualised education plan with contributions from all parties serves as the foundation for this collaboration. The decision on learning outcomes for the student is done collaboratively with each professional, who, firstly, contribute from their areas of expertise through the process of assessment, intervention and evaluation and secondly, integrate this process with the rest of the members' contributions to prioritise the learning areas for each student. What emerges from this collaborative process is a sense of community and opportunities for learning beyond trained areas of expertise.

COMMON MISUNDERSTANDINGS ABOUT COLLABORATION

Collaboration is often misunderstood; it is time consuming and requires different skills from working independently within one's profession. Working together in an organised manner is essential to the practice of supporting children and young people who have complex disabilities and needs; however, this is not always easy to achieve. Collaboration is one of the most advanced ways of working together based on sharing, joint purpose, mutual trust and support (Lacey et al., 2015).

Collaboration takes time and effort and with this in mind, schools need to prioritise what needs collaboration to ensure effort is best placed to achieve successful outcomes for students. Getting on well with colleagues is no guarantee of achieving collaborative and interdisciplinary practice. Focus and training need to be proactively placed on understanding and practising the core characteristics of collaboration.

THE APPROACHES OF WORKING TOGETHER

There are a multitude of terms referring to professionals working together. These terms are at times used interchangeably and can easily produce misunderstanding about what collaborative teaming means. Considering the words that we use as well as giving thought to definitions and what we mean inform effective communication and collaboration. Assumptions should not be made; the process of forming definitions or descriptions requires careful attention because meanings can vary from person to person and context to context (Knackendoffel *et al.*, 2018).

It is important that context, detail and explanation are offered during communication and discussion in teams. Taking the time to do this ensures that all team members have the same information and understand the current issues and concerns for a student. The discussion can then be more comprehensive and constructive which in turn informs creative problem solving and solutions going forward.

The collaborative teaming model has roots in an educational context and is based on a team sharing their knowledge, skills and resources for the benefit of students and successful educational outcomes (Orelove *et al.*, 2017). There has been a move away from professionals and other consultants offering an expert role (multidisciplinary) to the use of a more collaborative orientation for consultation (interdisciplinary).

INTERDISCIPLINARY APPROACH

In the Rainbow Centre schools, teaming of APs is done in an interdisciplinary manner where the team of APs provide specialised support in their areas of expertise while working together to achieve the individualised goals of the students. The teams are led by senior APs who can come from the disciplines of therapy, social work or psychology. Experienced and senior APs also provide domain specific supervision, coaching and mentorship. This arrangement enables the T-shaped development of professionals, allowing them to deepen skills in their own domain and expand their understanding and skills in other domains. Teams of APs work together with the educators, caregivers and other relevant stakeholders to meet the individualised goals of the students and enable them to achieve their good life plans.

TRANSDISCIPLINARY APPROACH

Yet another approach is the transdisciplinary approach, where collaborative consultation is an interactive process that involves team problem solving and generating creative solutions that may involve role release, where one team member releases some functions of the role to another team member and when team members are open to being taught by their team colleagues. Role release requires team members to step out of their usual roles to become either a trainer of other team members or learners taught by another team member. Being a trainer of another team member means sharing the knowledge and expertise of one's position as a teacher, AP, parent, or other.

The transdisciplinary approach adopted by the Rainbow Centre Early Intervention Programmes begins with prioritising the goals which parents/caregivers have for their children. They are involved in the goal setting and progress monitoring together with the APs and early intervention teachers. Team members meet regularly to make assessment and intervention decisions. The IEP document serves as a collaboration tool that reflects the team's assessment and intervention plans, visions and goals for the student and family. Since the team comprises different professionals, the intervention strategies are not delivered in isolation but across team members. A key worker, usually the early intervention teacher, is identified to be the main liaison for the family. A key therapist is identified depending on the student's most salient area of needs at that point in time. The key worker and key therapist are the two main team members involved in the engagement of the family and the intervention of the child.

In an integrated teaching and allied professional approach, there may be a few highly specialised procedures for evaluation or intervention that should only be performed by specifically designated and trained individuals based on their judgement and profession. Another team member should only be expected to learn and perform procedures and strategies that are appropriate for them with the assurance that statutory required supervision by registered or certified professionals is regularly scheduled.

COLLABORATION AND TEAMS

Teaming is the most frequently advocated structure for implementing school initiatives that address school improvement, planning, curriculum design, student progress and achievement, as well as school-wide initiatives e.g. school-wide positive behaviour support, school governance, professional development, resources management, etc. (Friend & Cook, 2014). Simply put, the overall purpose of a collaborative team is to "promote student learning and success in school" (King-Sears et al., 2015). All professionals participating in an IEP team bring unique and valuable perspectives that enhance problem solving, planning and implementation of creative solutions. The perspective of a student and his/her parents is equally important; collaboration positions students and parents on a par with other team members (Olivos, Gallagher & Aguiler as cited in Friend & Cook, 2014).

In summary, collaborative teams require structures that provide sufficient time, resources, places to meet, efficient schedules, planning, and interactive processes for effective and efficient functioning.

RECOGNISING THE CHALLENGES OF COLLABORATION

Despite the clear importance of collaboration and its increasing emphasis in education, there are several challenges that may arise when teachers, APs, students, families and others attempt to establish collaborative relationships and practice (Knackendoffel et al., 2018). Research focuses on the competencies and skills needed for working collaboratively and the perceived benefits and challenges to working in this way for team members. The effects of collaboration and positive outcomes for teachers are more widely documented; however, the benefits of collaboration for students and successful educational outcomes are less so (Dobson & Gifford-Bryan, 2014).

A significant challenge for studying the effects of collaboration is the lack of a theoretical framework for understanding the relationship between collaborative interactions and outcomes. Whilst there is limited quantitative research demonstrating that collaboration improves outcomes for students, it is reported that sustained interaction and collaboration between professionals enables them to inform and re-configure their existing knowledge, and that this, in turn, results in more creative solutions to problems (Villeneuve & Hutchinson, 2012).

Anticipating some of the challenges of logistics and difficulties that arise due to the lack of understanding and personal experience with collaboration can be alleviated with proactive planning and preparation. Whilst collaboration can be an effective approach to achieving successful outcomes for students, an awareness and understanding of the potential sources of stress and having strategies in place and the means to address them is documented in the literature (Friend & Cook, 2014; Orelove et al., 2017). These challenges are:

1. **Professional challenges:** Team members from different disciplines often approach teaching and therapy differently. Some people may not be familiar sharing part of their professional role. Professional perspectives can be influenced by traditions and conventions that are carried out through habit or convenience (Knackendoffel et al., 2018). Professionals often work in isolation from one another and are not aware of what each of them can offer. Team members may also have difficulty deciding and coming to an agreement on who is best positioned to provide an intervention for a student.

2. **Personal challenges**: People from all walks of life bring their own perspectives and preferences to work. Given that collaboration involves reflecting on your personal commitment to this approach, it might not be an individual's choice to interact in this way. This is when strong organisational support for collaboration is important. Sharing one's expertise is a matter of trust for some individuals as this places a team member's skills in the spotlight. A lack of clarity for team roles and responsibilities can be a source of interpersonal challenge particularly in the absence of a set of team ground rules that are agreed by all.

3. **Logistics**: Collaboration in schools is often constrained when time, space, resources and other logistics are not adequately considered.

The most often cited difficulty of working together in any way, shape or form, is time. We all use time differently; teachers are tied to time in the classroom, APs manage time across classes and programmes, etc. Challenges arise when trying to run these together as they lead to very few compatible moments for meeting. Finding such time is essential; it is impossible to be a team without time to talk. Time needs to be allocated to supporting how teams are defined and established. For time to be used efficiently, robust structures and processes for collaborative teaming need to be in place.

Interdisciplinary and transdisciplinary teaming in Rainbow Centre is not immune to the challenges described above. Challenges to teaming and collaborative engagement can be summarised under the areas of individual and collective competencies, opportunities for sustained interaction and engagement between team members, logistical and scheduling issues, common framework for alignment and role release, individual personality differences and preferences, clarity of roles, as well as accountability and responsibility, etc., to name a few.

However, given the complex nature of the needs of students supported in Rainbow Centre, it is pertinent that the teams are given the opportunity to work collaboratively with appropriate structure, processes, competencies and leadership in place to support such collaborative practice. Following are some ways in which Rainbow Centre staff work together to alleviate the challenges.

Structurally, teams are organised in an interdisciplinary manner under a team leader (lead AP) who can be from the discipline of therapy, psychology or social work. The Lead AP plays a key role in overseeing the case management of the AP team to ensure that clients receive effective and coordinated intervention services based on best practices for quality outcomes, in collaboration with the teaching team and other key stakeholders like families. The IEP is a document that captures the goals, intervention plans, roles and responsibilities of individual members and the team collectively. Regular IEP discussions are scheduled to monitor the progress of the student's goals.

The prioritisation of learning areas is determined through a process of individualised and team assessments. Priority for individualised, group or classroom based support is also determined by the team in this assessment process. In addition to this regular structure and process to meet students' learning needs, case escalation is also practised where teachers can highlight unique and sporadic learning or behavioural needs of the students through a process of referral to the IEP teams.

In addition to regular and scheduled IEP meetings, fortnightly case discussions are conducted where teams present and discuss complex cases in the presence of their peers and leaders. These case discussions serve as a platform for competency development and where new areas of assessment and intervention are explored through rigorous case analysis. These opportunities, together with the structured supervision, ensure that the team members continue to stay current in their domain knowledge, thus contributing to the overall team skills. These platforms also help team members to go beyond their domain-specific knowledge to develop competencies to support the holistic development of the students they support. The interdisciplinary and transdisciplinary arrangement of teams also facilitates the development of soft skills such as active listening, conflict resolution, etc. which are essential for looking beyond individual differences and abilities to contribute fully to the team. Collaborative teaming depends on each team member sharing their own perspectives whilst being open to these being shaped and changed as they work with others.

CONCLUSION

Collaboration is an increasingly significant approach in school reform and more generally in society today (Friend & Cook, 2014). However, it is not simple or straightforward and is in fact, one of the most advanced ways of people working together. It requires professionals to recognise and acknowledge the differences and diversity of colleagues and others, as well as to be curious about and respectful of what everyone can offer to support a student to access learning, achieve his/her learning outcomes and participate and enjoy the Good Life that he/she chooses. A student and his/her family are at the centre of all that we do — this is the premise of the person-centred approach, that the person is at the centre of any given effort. The time and effort necessary to effectively support a student and his/her family through the stages of life in school and beyond, are often underestimated. Everything we do is relational and it is the way in which we work with one another that will have an impact on how successful and positive the outcomes will be for students.

For collaboration to be effective, structures and processes need to be in place; the skills for effective collaboration need to be acknowledged, understood and acquired; and realistic amounts of time need to be allocated for this. For structures and processes to work well and for skills to be confidently and competently practised, they need to be positioned in the context of an organisational culture of support for collaboration and collaborative practice.

REFERENCES

Carpenter, B., Egerton, J., Cockbill, B., Bloom, T., Fotheringham, J., Rawson, H. & Thistlethwaite, J. (2015). *Engaging Learners with Complex Learning Difficulties and Disabilities — A resource book for teachers and teaching assistants.* Routledge.

Conroy, P.W. (2012). Collaborating with culturally and linguistically diverse families of students in rural schools who receive special education services. *Rural Special Education Quarterly, 31*(3), 20–24.

Conoley, J., & Conoley, C. (2010). Why does collaboration work? Linking positive psychology and collaboration. *Journal of Educational and Psychological Consultation, 20*, 75–82.

Dettmer, P., Thurston, L., & Dyck, N. (2005). *Consultation, Collaboration, and teamwork for students with special needs.* (5th ed.). Chapter 2. USA: Pearson Longman. Retrieved from http://www.ablongman.com/html/productinfo/dettmer5e/0205435238_ch2.pdf

Dobson, E., & Gifford-Bryan, J. (2014). Collaborative-Consultation: A Pathway for Transition. *KAIRARANGA Weaving Educational Threads. Weaving Educational Practice, 15*(1), 11–18. Retrieved from https://files.eric.ed.gov/fulltext/EJ1040125.pdf

Filbey, L. (2017). 'The most valuable resource you have is other people's ideas': The role of informal knowledge sharing and collaboration in supporting teachers working in a special school. *The SLD Experience, 76*(1), 26–30.

Friend, M. (2000). Myths and misunderstandings about professional collaboration [electronic version]. *Remedial and Special Education, 21*(3), 130–132.

Friend, M., & Cook, L. (2014). *Interactions: Collaboration skills for school professionals* (7th ed.). Upper Saddle River, NJ: Pearson Education.

Hill, S. (2020) Rainbow Centre Pedagogy Guide Chapter 5 Collaboration. (c) Rainbow Centre

King-Sears, M. E., Janney, R., & Snell, M. E. (2015). *Collaborative Teaming* (3rd ed.). Paul. H. Brookes Publishing Co.

Knackendoffel, A., Dettmer, P., & Thurston, L. (2018). *Collaborating, Consulting and Working in Teams for Students with Special Needs.* Pearson.

Lacey, P., Ashdown, R., Jones, P., Lawson, H., & Pipe, M. (Eds.). (2015). *The Routledge Companion to Severe, Profound and Multiple Learning Difficulties.* Routledge.

Lacey, P., & Ouvry, C. (2012). *People with Profound and Multiple Learning Disabilities — A Collaborative Approach to Meeting Complex Needs.* David Fulton.

Olivos, E. M., Gallagher, R. J., & Aguilar, J. (2010). Fostering collaboration with culturally and linguistically diverse families of children with moderate to severe disabilities. *Journal of Educational and Psychological Consultation, 20*(1), 28-40.

Orelove, F. P., Sobsey, D., & Gilles, D. L. (Eds.). (2017). *Educating Students with Severe and Multiple Disabilities — A Collaborative Approach* (5th ed). Brookes Publishing.

Raiff, N. R., & Shore, B. K. (1993). *Advanced Case Management: New Strategies for the Nineties.* Newbury Park, CA: Sage Publications.

Villeneuve, M. (2009). A critical examination of school-based occupational therapy collaborative consultation. *Canadian Journal of Occupational Therapy, 76*, 206–218.

Villeneuve, M., & Hutchinson, N. (2012). Enabling Outcomes for Students with Developmental Disabilities through Collaborative Consultation. *The Qualitative Report 2012, 17*(49), 1–29. Retrieved from https://files.eric.ed.gov/fulltext/EJ990028.pdf

17 Teaching and Engaging Students with Autism

Lynette Gomez and Eileen Oh Kai Ling

"Just because a child with special needs is not learning all the time, does not mean he cannot learn. In a school with teachers who care enough to be curious and brave enough to be present, the child then has a chance to learn. Education for children with special needs is not giving everyone the same thing but giving each one what they need to succeed."

Jessica Wee, Principal
Rainbow Centre, Yishun Park School

As an educator, it is essential to understand the characteristics of autism and know how to cater to these characteristics in order to maximise engagement and learning. Even more critically, by understanding these features, the special educators at Rainbow Centre's are enabling our students to feel secure and comfortable, ready to learn and interact with others, and to be respected.

As the main aim in the classroom for the Rainbow Centre Educator is to enable access to learning and maximise students' participation in all activities, our educators pay close attention to these characteristics and apply their understanding to the learning environment, the learning climate, behaviour management practices, and teacher-student relationship.

Structures and routines are key features in teaching and engaging students with autism[1]. It is important to structure both the physical and visual environments to create predictability. This predictability, together with routines, helps to create a sense that the world around them is organised, safe and stable. Using schedules and developing a work system for each student therefore serves as a good form of support for the students. At Rainbow Centre, we find that this approach works for all our students, including those with other developmental challenges.

The beautiful thing about special education is the importance of understanding the individual child and supporting the child based on his or her strengths, preferences, interests and needs (SPIN), or, what we at Rainbow Centre fondly refer to as the student's SPIN. The student's SPIN offers important information and considerations for the teacher when organising the learning environment, developing the teacher-student relationship, as well as helping the student to manage his behaviour and developing critical self-management skills.

To understand this better, let's look at each key aspect of teaching our students.

THE LEARNING ENVIRONMENT

"We need to be sensitive to the needs of our students and consider elements such as temperature, lighting, sound and movement within the space. The learning environment has to feel safe and secure, going beyond organising furniture in a physical space."

Michelle Soon, Senior Teacher
Rainbow Centre Margaret Drive School (RCMDS)

Classroom organisation

In considering the learning environment, we first need to look at the organisation of the physical structure of our classrooms and of its visual environment. A conducive learning environment has to be clutter-free, tidy and safe for the students. The arrangement of the furniture and learning materials or resources must be able to enable students to have access to them, allowing them to be on task with minimal distractions. Ensuring that the physical environment allows for the student to be able to have the right ergonomics when seated, i.e. having both feet firmly on the ground, and ensuring stability in balance, will also enhance their readiness to learn.

Each student's learning space must meet the student's sensory needs or ensure that over-stimulation of the senses is minimised or eliminated. To do this, the students' sensory needs must be known and understood, as well as the individual student's needs and preferences, with reference made to the student's SPIN.

At the Rainbow Centre schools, teachers create individual work areas to enable a student to develop independence in learning, staying on task, and engaging in activities. The work areas also cater for group or paired learning where possible. The classrooms are also divided into specific areas that are clearly demarcated for use for other activities like sensory play, quiet time or group engagement. Students are taught to use these areas through visual cues and aids, understand the rules of each space, and how to keep safe when they are in the spaces.

Picture A

Picture B

As seen in Picture A, individual work spaces are created for each student and appropriately labelled with a visual to identify the area and also to indicate what is expected to be done at that space. Students are also taught how to use the space properly, respecting the property and others in that space. Other types of spaces are created within the classroom as well, such as Play Corner, Break (Rest) Area, and Calm Corner. In teaching our students to use the spaces in a classroom, teachers also make sure to teach our students how to communicate their requests to use the Break Area or Calm Corner, as well as the individualised calming strategies that they can use within the space when they need them. The rules of use are presented in these spaces visually.

At Rainbow Centre, we believe that a well-structured classroom can play the role of the third teacher, empowering students to transit around the room independently, introducing familiarity, reducing anxiety[2]. These strategies enable the student to be successful in learning and participating in the lessons.

The visual environment

"In my pursuit to deliver effective lessons and teach skills that are functional and meaningful to children with autism, I've discovered the power of visuals — utilisation of visual aids in our classrooms recognises and capitalises on students' strengths, fosters learning, and creates conditions and climates that respect the culture of autism. It empowers our children with the ability to find their own independence and self- worth. As I continue on in my journey in SPED, I aspire to share this belief with colleagues to bring about success and empowerment in their teaching, at the same time upholding the dignity of and respect for our students."

Eileen Oh Kai Ling, Lead Teacher
Rainbow Centre, Admiral Hill School (RCAHS)

Being predominantly visual learners, students with autism and also those with multiple challenges benefit from having visual aids and support structures within their learning environments. A clear visual aid and structure provides much needed predictability and clarity, so they know what to expect either for the day, the planned activity, or when using the classroom space. This predictability and clarity reduces anxiety and enables our students to anticipate and understand what will be happening next.

At Rainbow Centre, we place a great emphasis on the usage of visual aids with teachers creating and using visuals regularly with their students. The pictures below show the visual schedules for each student. Depending on the needs of the student, some schedules can be longer while others are shorter. The visual schedules inform a student of what he needs to do first, and what comes next. Teachers also teach the students to use the schedule in order to enable a certain level of independence when they are ready. The development of visual schedules requires the teacher to understand the student, with careful consideration for the student's needs. Some students may need to start with simple schedules before moving on to more a complex ones. Our teachers also ensure that the schedules are functional and meaningful for the student. thereby helping them to increase their independence.

These pictures our students' schedules. Depending on the level of visual representation of our students, the student's visual schedules can be in the form of words or pictures.

In addition to visual schedules, teachers use other forms of visual information as well, both within the classroom and in other parts of the learning environment. Information paired with visuals enables our students to better understand what is expected of them. Our teachers also ensure that there are visuals that are used to provide information, visuals that might be used for learning support and accommodations where these play a visual instruction role. These visuals are included in instructional materials to add clarity to and support understanding of a concept being taught or information imparted. There are also instances when visuals are used as the primary instructional cue as there may be more anxiety when verbal instructions are given.

Visuals such as the ones below are examples of how, when our students are taught to understand these symbols through frequent reference and use, they might be able to then perform these actions independently, with these visuals being withdrawn, upon mastery.

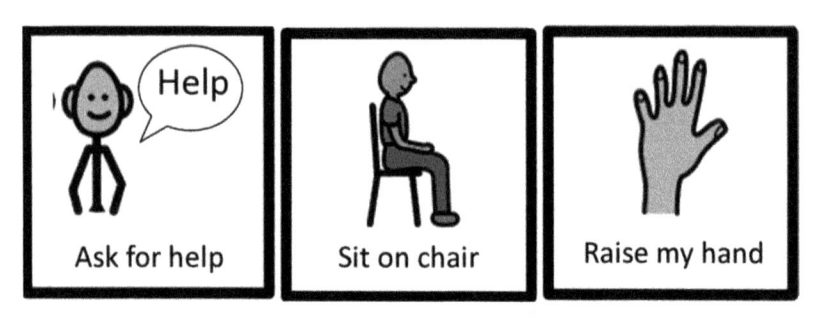

Visuals can also help our students in managing transitions. Teachers use the schedules to introduce what's coming next and even change activities. This helps to prepare students for changes that may occur in the student's routines. When students are more familiar with using these schedules, teachers introduce choices to their routines, to develop skills in making choices.

Using work systems

The teachers at Rainbow Centre are also trained to create work systems for their students. A work system is a strategy used for structuring tasks for the student systematically, giving the student clarity on the task that the student is meant to complete. A good work system addresses the following four questions for a student: "What work do I do?", "How much work do I do?", "When will the work be completed?" and "What do I do next?" Teachers create work systems as a way to structure the various activities that the student is required to complete for the lesson. It is a strategy that is also used to help our students complete their tasks and learn work behaviour concepts such as completing tasks, staying on task and finishing.

Teachers conduct assessments with every student to determine the student's individual work system format and length. There can be several formats. Examples include a 'Tick Off' work system where the students check off a box that indicates "Finish", and a 'Left to Right' work system in which the students start off working on a task from the left and completing it by moving to the right, and when the task on the right is completed, his work is "finished". These tasks can be placed in a 'Finish' box. In this way, students also learn the concept of 'finish' or completing tasks.

Individualised work systems help to develop independent work skills, thereby increasing their level of independence in various tasks and activities.

THE LEARNING CLIMATE

"The world our children see may be different, but like all of us, a positive learning climate where we feel safe and valued is crucial for growth."

Michelle Ong, Principal
Rainbow Centre, Margaret Drive School

A positive learning climate begins with understanding the student and developing rapport with the student. This will create a sense of belonging, leading to a sense of security, thus helping the student to be better prepared to learn.

Home-school partnership

At Rainbow Centre, we do this by engaging with parents and caregivers in the first year of each cohort, to develop useful information for a student's SPIN. This information enables teachers to suggest areas of development that need to be prioritised, decide with parents and then select the appropriate learning objectives from the curriculum. Parents and caregivers will then confirm the selected learning objectives for the year. While this reflects our person-centred approach, it also highlights the important and active relationship between the school and home. In educating students with autism, all Rainbow Centre Educators believe and agree that a positive and collaborative relationship with our student's families will take our students further.

Teachers provide weekly updates to parents. They share strategies used in the school that parents can also apply at home. This is to support the transfer or generalisation of communication, self-regulation and other skills development, in the natural context of the home and in the community. To encourage two-way communication and collaboration, parents are also asked to share their thoughts, concerns and challenges. This positive and collaborative relationship forms part of a positive learning climate in our schools.

Building teacher-student rapport

> "When I think of teacher-student rapport, I think of the times our students communicate in unique ways that are not comprehensible to most people, and yet as teachers, we are immediately able to understand what they are trying to say. This is the importance of building a strong relationship with our students, such that even the slightest gesture or the softest word spoken is not brushed aside, but acknowledged and built on, paving the way for more successful instances of communication."

Thiong Kai Teng, Teacher
Rainbow Centre, Admiral Hill School (RCAHS)

Our Rainbow Centre teachers would also incorporate the student's strengths, preferences and interests into daily engagement with the student, as well as lesson activities and tasks.

The teacher begins by building on the strengths of the student. Keen observations are recorded and verified with parents and caregivers. These observations enable the teacher to understand the student more deeply. The connections or bonds that are developed between the teacher and the student sometimes manifest during the most trying of times, when a lesson is not going very well, or when a student is having an outburst or meltdown or when a student is simply having an 'off' day.

Teachers will include the students interests when creating opportunities for interacting with the students developing their work systems, as well as helping them start a task, stay on task or complete a task. We usually refer to this as using high-interest activities to draw the students towards engaging with the teacher. This rapport building is critical as it sets the tone for trust and a sense of security on the part of the student, as well as easing the anxiety of both students and teachers.

Teachers also have to observe and find out more about the sensory needs of the student, the preferred mode of communication, the triggers that may affect the student's state of calm, as well as the strategies that might help the student regain his state of calm. At Rainbow Centre, all of this is translated into a one-page snapshot of the student, known as the Student Passport.

An example of a student's passport is shown below.

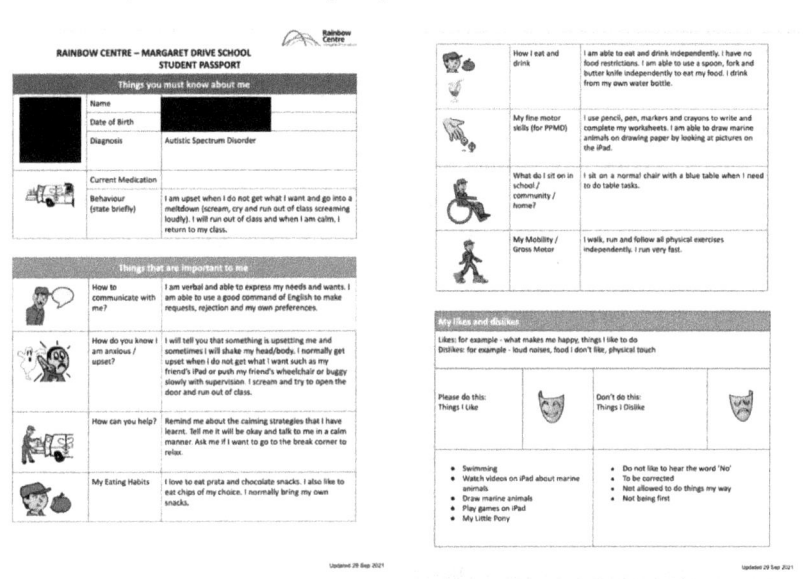

As apparent from the information captured, it is a useful tool that enables anyone who needs to work with the student to get a snapshot of the important information on the student. The Student Passport is updated regularly and kept in classrooms for easy and convenient access.

As part of encouraging a positive learning climate, teachers in our classrooms practise mindfulness in class. Body language, tone of voice, and language use are respect each student and exude a warm and caring atmosphere in class.

Strong teacher-student rapport also helps teachers to manage challenging behaviours in class. Behaviour management is an important part of teaching students with autism. When students exhibit challenging behaviour, it can be a struggle to ensure quality teaching and learning for the student. To address behaviour issues, teaching and developing self-regulation and behaviour management skills are key might not be handled so effectively.

THE CURRICULUM

One of the most important intents of teaching our students a skill, is to impart to them the ability to generalise the skill across different contexts such as school, home and the community, and being able to use the skills learnt with different people. Generalisation is emphasised when teaching students with autism and multiple challenges, because this is something that they can find challenging to do. For such students, skills can be learnt but may only be applied in familiar contexts and with familiar people. However, it is vital that these skills be translated into actions that the actions that students can perform in various contexts, so that they can be as independent as possible and participate in the community.

The Rainbow Centre SPED Curriculum emphasises the need to generalise the skills taught, with teachers being required to create a variety of contexts and opportunities for the student to generalise. In addition to generalisation, the student must be able to perform the skills across a period of time to ensure their mastery. Hence, our teachers will observe our students over an extended period to assess their mastery of the skills that they have been taught.

To do this, the learning objectives from the curriculum cannot be taught in silos but holistically. While teachers start with explicit teaching of skills, they also transit the student's learning towards their application in relevant real-life contexts which includes grouping of the skills where applicable. The Rainbow Centre SPED curriculum has six domains, namely, Daily Living, Language and Communication, Numeracy, Social Emotional, Physical Development and Vocational Education.

All six domains are taught in a functional context, that is, the contexts are applicable in the real world. It goes without saying that these six domains are critical areas of one's development, allowing them to participate in their community and live as independently as they can. At Rainbow Centre, the teachers use the "I Do We Do You Do" approach. This is when the teacher first models a skill (I Do), then doing/practising the skill together with the students (We Do), before getting the students perform the skill independently (You Do). The skills are also broken down into smaller skill steps and organised in a sequential manner. This is known as Task Analysis and is used for functional tasks like using the toilet, tooth brushing, etc.

Regular and on-going assessments are done every day to assess the level of skills acquisition, and this is termed as formative assessments of students' learning.

One very critical aspect of teaching our students is developing their abilities to be able to interact with others, express themselves and participate in social activities.

> "Communication comes easy for most typical children but teaching students with autism to communicate even their basic needs and wants requires a whole village of help: from parents and siblings to teachers, therapists and the public at large. Each one of us needs to recognise that we play a part in helping these students to learn to communicate by whatever means available so that their wants, needs, thoughts, feelings, aspirations and dreams can be made known and understood by all."

Joanne Chua, Senior Teacher
Rainbow Centre Admiral Hill School (RCAHS)

The quality of opportunities that our students have to communicate are only as effective as the communication partners around them. These would include their family members, teachers and peers and others who come into regular contact with them. The belief that these stakeholders have in the importance and function of communication is important as some of our students rely on Augmentative and Alternative Communication Systems (AACs) in order to communicate. This would require their communication partners not only to know how to use the AAC system to communicate with the student, but also to teach the student to grow his communication skills through the use of the AAC system.

At Rainbow Centre, teachers are supported and trained in the use of different AAC systems, as well as to continuously provide opportunities to communicate, make choices and initiate communication. This is done through modelling and using high-interest activities to encourage increased use of the AAC system.

CONCLUSION

Teaching students with autism and other developmental challenges requires skills, perseverance, a dedication to improving one's practice and a positive mindset — one which sees and believes in the possibilities and potential of these students. It requires pairs of loving hands that are willing to hold and partner them and their families as they journey towards success. On top of it all, we are to be the ever calming and encouraging voice beside them, to respect and support them as they improve in their own skills, gaining empowerment to lead a good life, independently and with dignity.

REFERENCES

1. Mesibov, G., Shea, V., & Schopler, E. (2004). *The TEACCH Approach to Autism Spectrum Disorder*. New York: Springer.
2. O'Donnell Wicklund Pigozzi and Paterson, Mau, B., & Orr, D. W. (2010). *The Third Teacher: 79 Ways You Can Use Design to Transform Teaching & Learning*. New York: Abrams Books.

18 Sensory Processing — A Rainbow Journey

Jimson Tham and Hong Kai'En

INTRODUCTION

Imagine a day at the playground. Boy A sits on the swing, laughing excitedly as he gets his teacher to push him harder and higher. Boy B walks cautiously around the playground, watching his friends play as he keeps away, fearing he may trip or fall yet again. Girl C rolls around happily in the sandpit before running over to explore the grass patch, oblivious to the sand in her hair and clothes. Girl D sits on the bench as she eats some chicken nuggets and fries, the only food she enjoys. These students have their own unique personalities but they also have something in common — challenges in sensory processing.

Definition

We experience the world through our senses. As we go about our daily lives, our bodies receive sensory information from our environment and our brains process it to help us make sense of our experiences. This process happens at every moment, and it gives us both internal and external information on what is happening in our environment, with our bodies, and within our bodies. This process is known as sensory processing.

Being able to effectively make sense of and respond to sensations is essential to help us feel safe, move around, complete activities, and build relationships with others. In short, sensory processing helps us be successful in other aspects of our lives.

Our eight senses

We receive and process sensory information through our eight sensory systems. We have five 'main' senses – touch, sight, hearing, taste, and smell, as well as two other 'hidden senses' known as proprioception, our body sense, and vestibular, our sense of balance and movement. We also have an 'eighth' sense known as interoception, which refers to understanding the physiological condition of our body. Each of these eight sensory systems contributes to our overall sensory functioning.

Sensory system	Function
Tactile (Touch)	• Helps us interpret information coming into the body by the skin. • Uses receptors in the skin to receive touch sensations like pressure, vibration, movement, temperature and pain. • Provides information such as the shape, size, and texture of objects, which helps us better understand our environment and manipulate objects.
Visual (Sight)	• Helps us understand and interpret what is seen. • Uses the eyes to receive information about contrast of light and dark, colour, and movement. • Helps us to identify and interpret shapes, colours, symbols, body language, and more, which guides our movements and social interactions.
Auditory (Hearing)	• Helps us understand and interpret information that is heard. • Uses the outer and middle ear to receive noise and sound information about volume, pitch and rhythm. This helps us interpret sounds into meaningful syllables and words. • Helps us identify the quality and direction of sounds which allows us, for example, to recognise a person's voice and how far away they are.

(Continued)

Sensory system	Function
Gustatory (Taste)	• Helps us interpret information regarding taste in the mouth. • Uses the tongue to receive taste sensations, and detects the chemical makeup through the tongue to determine if the sensation is safe or harmful.
Olfactory (Smell)	• Helps us interpret smells. • Uses the nose to receive information about the chemical makeup of particles in the air to determine if the smell is safe or harmful.
Proprioception (Muscle & joint)	• Helps us interpret where our body parts are in relation to one another. • Uses information from our joints and/or muscles contracting, stretching, bending, straightening, pulling and compressing to inform us about the position and movement of our body. • This helps us identify our body's position in relation to itself and other objects.
Vestibular (Balance & movement)	• Helps us interpret information relating to movement and balance. • Uses the semi-circular canals in the inner ear to receive information about movement, change of direction, change of head position and gravitational pull. • This helps us understand how fast or slow we are moving; balance; movement from the neck, eyes and body; body position; and orientation in space.
Interoception (Physiological)	• Allows our body to perceive its internal state and helps to control the way that we feel. • Helps us identify our bodily sensations and emotions, including hunger and feeling hot/cold, and be motivated to seek comfort in a timely manner.

As depicted by the Pyramid of Learning (Williams and Shellenberger, 1996) in Figure 1, our sensory systems underpin all other functions. Each system is related and builds a foundation for learning. When we have well-integrated sensory processing, we are able to develop skills such as sensorimotor and perceptual motor skills needed at different stages of our development. These skills support our cognitive abilities such as attention, organisation and sense of purpose, which positively support learning and participation in our daily lives.

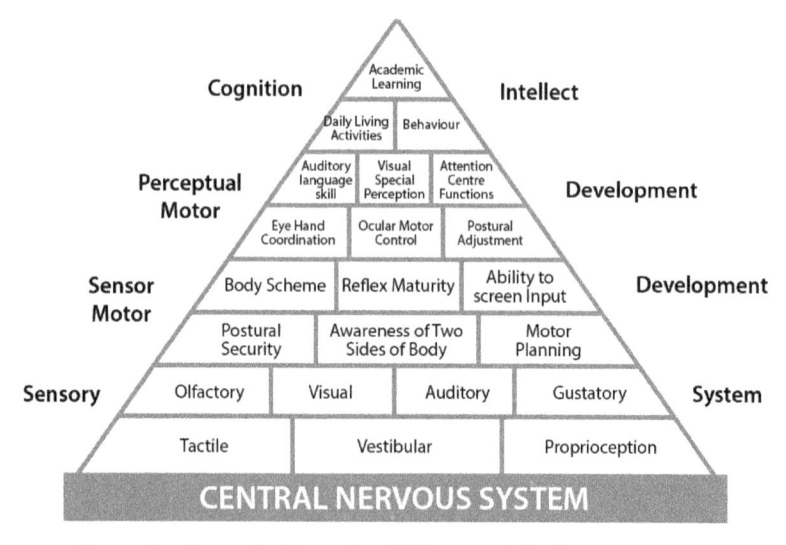

Figure 1.   Pyramid of Learning (Williams and Shellengerger 1996)

What happens when our senses are not working well?

Everyone processes and responds to sensory information differently. For some individuals, sometimes the central nervous system is unable to manage sensory information effectively to the point of it delaying acquisition of developmental skills and adversely affecting participation in daily routines. When this happens, we term this condition as Sensory Processing Disorder (SPD).

Dr Ayres likened SPD to a neurological 'traffic jam', preventing certain parts of the brain from receiving necessary sensory information for us to interpret and produce an appropriate motor response. An individual with SPD will find it difficult to process and interpret all the sensory information from their environment. For example, Boy A at the playground wants to be swung higher and higher on the swing as he needs more vestibular input to feel organised. Boy B who avoids playing catch with his peers and going onto the playground structures may not be able to feel his muscles and joints very well, and hence have a hard time coordinating his body movements. Girl C rolling in the sandpit enjoys messy play as she needs a whole lot of tactile input on her body before she can make sense of and interact with objects in her environment. Girl D who only eats chicken nuggets and fries may be so sensitive to other tastes, smells and textures that she finds it difficult to try new food.

Individuals with SPD can often present as hyperactive, withdrawn, shy, or anxious, depending on their symptoms. SPD affects one's ability to behave 'normally' as their responses to sensory experiences can be drastically different from others. These difficulties can result in challenges such as difficulties in paying attention, movement and coordination, and other developmental difficulties.

SENSORY PROCESSING IN OUR EVERYDAY LIVES

Common sensory processing challenges

We can look at sensory processing challenges through three main patterns — sensory modulation, sensory based motor disorder, and sensory discrimination. Figure 2 below shows the three major patterns and the six subtypes of SPD.

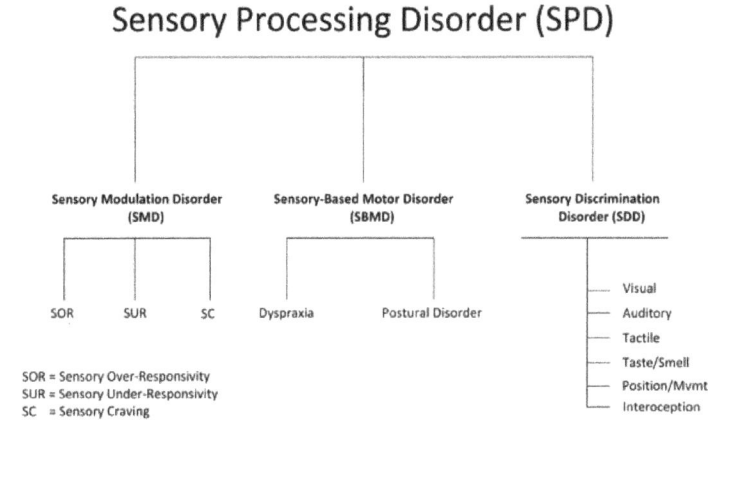

Figure 2. Subtypes of Sensory Processing Disorder

A. *Sensory modulation disorder*

Sensory modulation disorder refers to problems regulating responses to sensory input, in which an individual over or under responds to the sensory input received. This means that someone with sensory modulation problems displays disproportionately big or small responses upon receiving a sensory input compared to the typical person. For example, Girl D at the playground screams and pushes the plate away when given new food such as apple slices. She is over responding to the unfamiliar wet and slimy appearance of the apple slices. Sensory modulation difficulties can affect a person's ability to maintain an appropriate level of alertness, pay attention, and regulate their emotions to participate in activities.

    Common signs:

- Easily distracted by noises
- Overly sensitive to sounds
- Dislikes nail/hair cutting
- Dislikes clothing of certain textures/fits/styles
- Upset about seams in socks
- Reacts defensively to tastes or textures of food
- Easily distracted by visual stimuli

B. *Sensory-based motor disorder*

An individual with sensory-based motor disorder has difficulties with balance, motor coordination, and the performance of skilled, non-habitual and/or habitual motor tasks. This can lead to issues with planning, sequencing and executing unfamiliar actions resulting in awkward and poorly coordinated motor skills. For example, Boy B at the playground does not quite understand where his body is moving as he tries climbing up a ladder. He relies on his vision to move his hands and feet up the ladder, and has a hard time keeping his trunk upright.

    Common signs:

- Problems with daily life tasks like dressing or using utensils
- Eats in a sloppy manner

- Difficulty following multi-step directions
- Strong desire for sameness or routines
- Has an awkward pencil grasp
- Has poor handwriting
- Dislikes or reluctant to participate in sports

C. *Sensory discrimination disorder*

Sensory discrimination disorder refers to a problem in accurately interpreting the similarities or differences of sensory input. Individuals with sensory discrimination difficulties have issues determining the characteristics of what they have seen, heard, felt, tasted, or smelt, and hence cannot perceive and use the sensory information meaningfully. For example, Girl C at the playground appears to be unaware of the sand on her body. She has difficulty using the spades and moulds to build a sandcastle as she uses too much force and knocks the sandcastle down instead. She prefers rolling around the sand with her whole body as that does not require many refined motor skills, and she can feel the sand better so much better. Individuals with poor sensory discrimination may appear awkward in both gross and fine motor tasks and/or inattentive to people and objects in their environment. They may take extra time to process the important aspects of sensory stimuli.

Common signs:

- Jumps a lot on beds
- Bumps or pushes others
- Grasps objects too tightly or uses too much force
- Frequently drops things or knocks things over
- Mouths, licks, chews, or sucks on non-food items
- Craves movement, e.g. likes to spin self around
- Afraid of heights, swings or slides
- Has poor balance

Our sensory systems are highly interconnected with one another, and hence SPD may affect one or more sensory system. Individuals with SPD can also experience difficulties with one or more of the above sensory processing problems.

Who experiences SPD?

Children and adolescents with autism and other developmental disabilities often experience sensory processing challenges. There are many studies that have shown the prevalence of sensory processing challenges in individuals with Autism Spectrum Disorder (ASD). These studies show percentages of up to 90% of autistic children in their research having sensory processing challenges (Leekam *et. al.*, 2007; Marco *et al.*, 2011; Baker *et al.*, 2007). However, sensory processing disorder can also be associated with premature birth, brain injury, learning disorders, and other conditions.

Journeying with sensory processing challenges across the lifespan

A person with sensory processing challenges often experiences emotional, behavioural, social, attentional, or motoric problems. Depending on the person's unique makeup, family and environmental context, as well as life stage, these challenges can take many forms and look different. Individuals with sensory processing challenges may face difficulties engaging in activities meaningful to them at their respective life stage.

At Rainbow Centre, we work with individuals with varying needs including those with ASD, as well as those with developmental, physical and multiple disabilities. We serve individuals across the lifespan of their childhood, namely those in their early years (0–6 years), and children and teenagers (7–18 years).

0–6 years old

Meaningful activities	Possible challenges
• Developing various skills through play • Rest and sleep • Engaging in basic daily living activities • Participating in educational activities	• Difficulties learning to navigate the environment • Difficulties manipulating objects during play • Difficulties with sleep • Difficulties participating in basic daily living activities such as showering, toothbrushing, dressing, diaper changes

(Continued)

Meaningful activities	Possible challenges
	• Difficulties with food and nutrition (fussy eating) • Difficulties attending to instructions in class

7–12 years old

Meaningful activities	Possible challenges
• Engaging in basic daily living activities • Communicate to engage in learning and meet functional needs • Self-regulate and possess the skills and positive attitudes for learning • Cooperate with others and actively participate in group activities • Be aware of personal safety and ways to seek support	• Difficulties with daily living activities such as personal grooming, showering, eating • Difficulties attending to and being successful in school-related tasks such as writing • Difficulties organising self for learning • Difficulties participating in social group games or activities

13–18 years old

Teenagers experience hormonal changes through puberty which affects their emotions. These changes can lead to teenagers having different sensory preferences as compared to when they were younger. They are also presented with new social experiences and expectations from others, which can be difficult for those with sensory processing difficulties. Many teenagers may experience self-esteem issues as they deal with feelings of isolation due to their sensory challenges.

When a sensory challenge affects one's ability to participate in his/her daily lives, that is often when seeking outside intervention and strategies is helpful.

Meaningful activities	Possible challenges
• Engage in basic and instrumental activities of daily living • Recognise strengths, preferences, interests • Explore new activities and experiences • Develop and maintain friendships • Navigating the community • Adapt to changing or challenging personal and community contexts • Access information, resources and services in the community for meaningful engagement and living	• Difficulties participating in instrumental activities of daily living such as shopping, meal preparation, taking care of own space and belongings • Difficulties identifying and engaging in new interests • Difficulties establishing and maintaining relationships with others • Difficulties taking transportation and navigating the community • Difficulties adapting to new experiences and exploring different and unfamiliar places in the community

SUPPORTING CHILDREN WITH SENSORY PROCESSING CHALLENGES

Before the 2010s, intervention approaches which focused on enhancing the central nervous system's ability to process sensory information were used predominantly by occupational therapists in Singapore to treat challenges associated with sensory processing. For example, Ayres Sensory Integration (Ayres, 1972), a technique that is designed to address sensorimotor challenges to enhance a person's function and participation in his/her daily life, influences the practices of many local occupational therapists. Additionally, sensory based interventions like the Wilbarger Therapressure Protocol (Wilbarger & Wilbarger, 2001), various sound based programmes like Therapeutic Listening (Frick & Hacker, 2001), weighted vest and many others were also commonly used. Along with individualised sensorimotor activities, they were directed at sensory modulation, sensory discrimination and sensory based disorders. These intervention approaches tended to be child-focused, targeting the underlying neurological challenges.

However, occupational therapists do not simply treat the client, but also the systems surrounding them. This includes the environment the children and adolescents function in, and their families whom they live with and receive support from. As a result, they do not focus only on the challenges faced by the child but also the impact of these challenges across multiple systems in their lives (Reynolds *et al.*, 2017). Hence, to address the complexity of interactions faced by the children and adolescents and their systems, multiple intervention approaches that target the children and adolescents as well as their various systems had to be considered.

When providing interventions to children and adolescents with sensory processing challenges, occupational therapists working in paediatric settings use three broad types of intervention. They are: (1) child-focused, therapist-led interventions related primarily to skill building or eliciting neurological change; (2) environmental support and adaptations; and (3) caregiver-focused interventions, including parent- and teacher-mediated interventions (Reynolds *et al.*, 2017).

Occupational Therapists in Rainbow Centre employ the following practices, namely, 1) Environmental support and adaptations 2) Empowering caregivers through coaching and 3) Occupation-based interventions. These are practices that have gained much momentum in the last decade, and some even more so during the period of COVID-19, to support our children and adolescents to learn and participate better in class, home and the community.

ENVIRONMENTAL SUPPORT AND ADAPTATIONS

The environment may enable or present as a barrier to learning and participation. Sensory components of the environment may limit participation to those who are over-responsive to certain sensory input and exhibit avoidance or distracting behaviours. On the other hand, children and adolescents who seek sensory input may persevere in them (Piller & Pfeiffer, 2017). Conversely, a lack of a sensory rich environment may result in a lack of interest, thus leading to poor engagement in activities planned. These behaviours can potentially disrupt learning and participation.

In these scenarios, most occupational therapists will consider providing child-focused interventions targeting the underlying neurological challenges resulting in over/under responsiveness. This will enhance the child's abilities to function in different sensory environments, and thus participate in a variety of sensory activities. However, this usually requires some time before changes occur. With recommendations of support and/or adaptations to enhance the specific environment the child has to function in, it may result in improved function immediately, if not quickly. This is an important consideration in intervention planning as it allows the child to increase learning and participation as quickly as possible, while the child-focused interventions continue.

In the planning of environmental support, the child's sensory processing challenges and the activities they need to participate in need to be considered. They may include strategies to reduce or enhance sensory stimulation in the environment to organise their attention thus improving learning and participation (Reynolds *et al.*, 2017). Environmental support to increase sensory input may include different seating options (like ball chairs, air cushions, rocker chairs), sensory rich teaching materials (like brightly coloured/tactile materials), compression clothing, fidget toys, and weighted tools. Likewise, environmental support to reduce sensory stimuli includes the use of headphones, visors, sunglasses, study carrels and light covers.

Adaptations to the physical environment like using warmer, dimmable and non-direct LED lighting, a more neutral colour palette for walls, and acoustic treatments for noise/echo reductions can be helpful for those with visual and/or auditory hypersensitivity. These have been trialled in some classrooms at Rainbow Centre and teachers had reported increased attention and engagement of children and adolescents in activities. These reports are congruent with findings by Kinnealey *et al.* (2012).

An unintended result reported of these adaptations is the calming effects it has on class teachers. Teachers, a key facilitator of learning and participation, are an important component of the system around the child and adolescent. Such lighting adaptations may induce a calmer state not only in the children and adolescents in class, but also teachers who may spend hours in the classrooms. The acoustic treatment also reduces vocal strain during teaching as sounds are absorbed by the acoustic materials, rather than reflected as echoes. All these reduce the fatigue experienced over time, and thus result in greater focus during teaching.

Empowering caregivers through coaching

Children and adolescents with autism experiencing sensory processing challenges often express them as 'problem' behaviours, giving rise to parenting stress (Chiang *et al.*, 2019). Similar to how sensory processing challenges may disrupt learning and participation in school, these challenges affect a child's daily functioning and participation in family routines, leading to increased burden on and stress in parents (Schaaf *et al.*, 2011). Intervention approaches that are home-based and parent-directed may reduce stress by increasing their capabilities in managing these challenges (King *et al.*, 2004).

Many intervention approaches can be carried out to enhance a parent's capabilities in managing these behaviours occurring in daily family routines. For example, occupational therapists can provide training to parents to increase their knowledge in sensory processing challenges and intervention strategies. The parents then need to directly and independently translate the knowledge learnt to manage the sensory processing challenges faced by their child (Miller-Kuhaneck & Watling, 2018). However, the process of applying what was learnt to the unique environment and activities their child needs to participate in is no easy task. In addition, the sensory processing challenges their child has may be manifested differently, and the intervention strategies may need individualisation for them to be successful.

In contrast, coaching is a collaborative process that uses observations, action, reflection, and feedback (Rush & Shelden, 2005) to help parents develop awareness, knowledge, and skill that enable and empower them to design their own solutions to meet their child's needs (King *et al.*, 2017). It is an evidence-based intervention that is family centred and promotes adult learning. Coaching takes into consideration family related settings, and promotes parent-directed goals and solutions. Though coaching may appear similar to parent-mediated interventions, it encourages parents to create their own strategies, and identify their goals in their routines for their unique circumstances (Little *et al.*, 2018). This is unlike parent-mediated interventions in which the parents implement a therapist's recommendation. By identifying their goals and implementing sensory based interventions in family routines, it builds parents' efficacy and confidence to manage the challenges they face daily (Dunn *et al.*, 2012).

During the height of the COVID-19 pandemic in 2020, there were periods when students had to learn from home through virtual means. Such arrangements spanned up to two weeks, with the longest period of home-based learning stretching for up to three months. Occupational therapists at Rainbow Centre, with other Allied Professionals and teachers, had to deliver interventions via telepractice. As many of our children and adolescents were unable to access learning through telepractice, their interventions had to be delivered through their parents. This situation became the catalyst to work even more closely with parents by coaching through telepractice.

For example, one of our occupational therapists met the mother of a student with eating and drinking challenges weekly during home-based learning to support implementation of interventions in a home environment during home-based learning. The mother reported the support had a positive impact on self-efficacy and increased her capabilities to manage the challenges faced at home during mealtimes.

Occupational performance coaching (Graham *et al.*, 2020) is the model we use to guide our coaching with parents. The process is outlined in the figure below, though it is important to note that the process is carried out collaboratively with the parents, and that the environment, tasks to be carried out, and the person(s) involved are considered carefully.

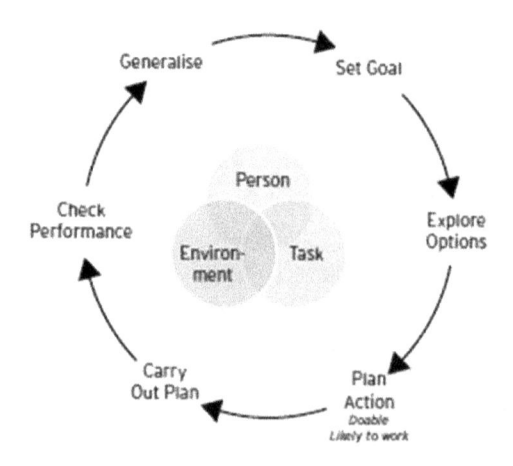

(Graham & Rodger, 2010)

Figure 3.   The structured process of Occupational Performance Coaching

We have found that children and adolescents are able to improve if not achieve the goals set within a shorter time when parents are involved in delivering the interventions. Parent coaching is conducted alongside direct therapy services to the student. This is carried out face to face to face, or through telepractice, for one to two sessions, after the occupational therapist has completed an assessment to understand the student and their families. Many parents who were able to collaborate with the occupational therapist found the process to be helpful in integrating the strategies within their lives as the coaching process considered their environment, routines and challenges.

Intervention through occupations

As occupational therapists, the use of occupations as an intervention and outcome lies at the core of our practice. For clients at Rainbow Centre, occupation is defined as everyday activities that they do as individuals, with their families, and with their communities to learn, occupy time and bring fun and enjoyment to their lives. These are things they need to do, want to do, and are expected to do in their everyday routines and other events in their lives (WFOT, 2012a 2020). Hence, occupation as an intervention involves the use of activities within daily routines, or leisure activities that are a part of their play and hobbies as a means to promote improvements in targeted outcomes.

Occupation-based interventions are founded on the premise that engagement in specific types of daily activities will improve participation, quality of life, and well-being. Self-care, work (including volunteer partic-ipation) and leisure (including play) activities are frequently identified as the goal areas for the children and adolescents (The American Journal of Occupational Therapy, 2020). These activities have been found to enhance the functioning of children and adolescents with sensory processing chal-lenges (Pfeiffer *et al.*, 2018; Laverdure & Beisbier, 2021) when integrated with sensory processing intervention principles.

An advantage of using occupational-based interventions is the pro-vision of important opportunities for development of various skills. As self-care, work and leisure activities are carried out frequently, it allows a higher frequency of intervention outside a school setting. It also serves as an opportunity to build a set of meaningful activities that can be integrated into their lifestyle over time. Such a routine can promote positive and healthy engagement in relevant occupations and social communities, complementing the engagement they have in open/sheltered and day activity centres, if not increasing their level of independence in activities of daily living, and work, while having more leisure activities in which they enjoy and have fun.

CONCLUSION

We perceive and interact with people and the world through our senses. When we have challenges processing this sensory information accurately, we may experience the world in a different way. As a result, it affects how we learn and participate.

While Rainbow Centre serves our children and youths till 18 years old, services to support them and their families are currently limited beyond that. Depending on their strengths and capabilities, they may be in supported employment or day activity centres. However, such opportunities are few, with long waiting lists for day activity centres. (Kok, 2021; Menon, 2022). As a result, as many of them grow up, they face the possibility of a lifestyle without meaningful engagement opportunities, which might give rise to challenging behaviours at home. This is even more so for our adolescents and adults with autism and sensory processing challenges.

At the end of the day, the impact of sensory processing challenges can be limited when we adapt our support systems surrounding the individual. Current practices in Rainbow Centre are moving beyond individual skill-building and towards building caregiver capacities through caregiver coaching and environmental adaptations. By supporting both the individual and the systems around them, we hope to enhance the quality of life of those with sensory processing challenges, and take steps towards a world where persons with disabilities are empowered and thrive in inclusive communities.

RESOURCES

Kid Sense Child Development Corporation Pty Ltd https://childdevelopment.com.au/areas-of-concern/sensory-processing

Lindsey Biel www.sensorysmarts.com

Sensory Process Disorder Network https://sinetwork.org/

Sensory Smart Parent https://www.sensorysmartparent.com/post/2015/07/22/teenagers-and-sensory-issues-special-challenges-for-a-special-time

SPIRAL Foundation https://thespiralfoundation.org/about-spd/#sensory-information

STAR Institute for Sensory Processing www.spdstar.org

https://sensoryhealth.org/basic/understanding-sensory-processing-disorder

TherapyWorks, Inc www.alertprogram.com

REFERENCES

Ayres, A. J. (1972). *Sensory integration and learning disorders.* Los Angeles: Western Psychological Services.

Ayres, A., & Robbins, J. (2005). *Sensory Integration and the Child: Understanding Hidden Sensory Challenges.* Los Angeles: WPS

Chiang, W. C., Tseng, M. H., Fu, C. P., Chuang, I. C., Lu, L., & Shieh, J. Y. (2019). Exploring Sensory Processing Dysfunction, Parenting Stress, and Problem Behaviors in Children With Autism Spectrum Disorder. *American Journal of Occupational Therapy, 73*(1), 7301205130. https://doi.org/10.5014/ajot.2019.027607

Dunn, W., Cox, J., Foster, L., Mische-Lawson, L., & Tanquary, J. (2012). Impact of a Contextual Intervention on Child Participation and Parent Competence Among Children With Autism Spectrum Disorders: A Pretest–Posttest Repeated-Measures Design. *American Journal of Occupational Therapy, 66*(5), 520–528. http://dx.doi.org/10.5014/ajot.2012.004119

Frick, S. M., & Hacker, C. (2001). *Listening with the whole body.* Madison, WI: Vital Links.

Graham, F., Kennedy-Behr, A., & Ziviani, J. (2020). *Occupational Performance Coaching: A Manual for Practitioners and Researchers.* Routledge.

Graham, F., & Rodger, S. (2010). Occupational Performance Coaching: Enabling Parents' and Children's Occupational Performance. In S. Rodger (Ed.). *Occupation Centred Practice with Children: A Practical Guide for Occupational Therapists.* Oxford, England: Wiley-Blackwell.

King, S., Teplicky, R., King, G., & Rosenbaum, P. (2004). Family-Centered Service for Children With Cerebral Palsy and Their Families: A Review of the

Literature. *Seminars in Pediatric Neurology, 11*(1), 78–86. http://dx.doi. org/10.1016/j.spen.2004.01.009

King, G., Williams, L., & Hahn Goldberg, S. (2017). Family oriented services in pediatric rehabilitation: a scoping review and framework to promote parent and family wellness. *Child: Care, Health and Development, 43*(3), 334–347. https://doi.org/10.1111/cch.12435

Kinnealey, M., Pfeiffer, B., Miller, J., Roan, C., Shoener, R., & Ellner, M. L. (2012). Effect of Classroom Modification on Attention and Engagement of Students with Autism or Dyspraxia. *The American Journal of Occupational Therapy, 66*(5), 511–519. http://dx.doi.org/10.5014/ajot.2012.004010

Kok, A. (2021, April 19). Photography exhibition sheds light on challenges faced by persons with autism, caregivers. *The Straits Times.* https://www. straitstimes.com/singapore/photography-and-video-exhibition-sheds-light-on-challenges-faced-by-persons-with-autism

Kranowitz, C. (2007). *The Out-of-Sync Child.* New York: Perigee.

Laverdure, P., & Beisbier, S. (2021). Occupation- and Activity-Based Interventions to Improve Performance Activities of Daily Living, Play, and Leisure for Children and Youth Ages 5 to 21: A Systematic Review. *The American Journal of Occupational Therapy, 75*(1), 7501205050. https://doi.org/10.5014/ajot.2021.039560

Little, L. M., Pope, E., Wallisch, A., & Dunn, W. (2018). Occupation-Based Coaching by Means of Telehealth for Families of Young Children With Autism Spectrum Disorder. *The American Journal of Occupational Therapy, 72*(2), 7202205020. https://doi.org/10.5014/ajot.2018.024786

Menon, M. (2022, April 4). More can be done to support adults with autism, says parent. *The Straits Times.* https://www.straitstimes.com/singapore/more-can-be-done-to-support-adults-with-autism-says-parent

Miller, L.J., Fuller, D.A., & Roetenberg, J. (2014). *Sensational Kids: Hope and Help for Children with Sensory Processing Disorder (SPD).* New York: Penguin.

Miller-Kuhaneck, H., & Watling, R. (2018). Parental or Teacher Education and Coaching to Support Function and Participation of Children and Youth With Sensory Processing and Sensory Integration Challenges: A Systematic Review. *The American Journal of Occupational Therapy, 72*(1), 7201190030. https://doi.org/10.5014/ajot.2018.029017

Pfeiffer, B., Clark, G. F., & Arbesman, M. (2018). Effectiveness of Cognitive and Occupation-Based Interventions for Children With Challenges in Sensory Processing and Integration: A Systematic Review. *The American Journal of Occupational Therapy, 72*(1), 7201190020. https://doi.org/10.5014/ajot.2018.028233

Piller, A., & Pfeiffer, B. (2017). The Impact of the Sensory Environment on Participation of Preschool Children With Autism Spectrum Disorder. *The American Journal of Occupational Therapy, 71*(4_Supplement_1), 7111515252p1. https://doi.org/10.5014/ajot.2017.71S1-PO5091

Reynolds, S., Glennon, T. J., Ausderau, K., Bendixen, R. M., Kuhaneck, H. M., Pfeiffer, B., Watling, R., Wilkinson, K., & Bodison, S. C. (2017). Using a Multifaceted Approach to Working With Children Who Have Differences in Sensory Processing and Integration. *The American Journal of Occupational Therapy, 71*(2). https://doi.org/10.5014/ajot.2017.019281

Rush, D. D., & Shelden, M. L. (2005). Evidence-based definition of coaching practices. CASEinPoint, 1(6), Article 8. Retrieved from https://ttac.gmu.edu/telegram/archives/aprilmay-2012/article-8

Schaaf, R. C., Toth-Cohen, S., Johnson, S. L., Outten, G., & Benevides, T. W. (2011). The everyday routines of families of children with autism: Examining the impact of sensory processing difficulties on the family. *Autism, 15*(3), 373–389. https://doi.org/10.1177/1362361310386505

The American Journal of Occupational Therapy. (2020). Occupational Therapy Practice Framework: Domain and Process — Fourth Edition. *The American Journal of Occupational Therapy, 74*(Supplement_2), 7412410010p1–7412410010p87. https://doi.org/10.5014/ajot.2020.74S2001

Wilbarger, P. L., & Wilbarger, J. L. (2001). *Sensory defensiveness: A comprehensive treatment approach.* Panorama City, CA: Avanti Educational Programs.

Williams, M. S., Shellenberger, S. (1996). *"How does your engine run?®" A leader's guide to The Alert Program for Self-Regulation.* Albuquerque: TherapyWorks Inc.

World Federation of Occupational Therapists. (2012a). About occupational therapy. Retrieved from https://www.wfot.org/about-occupational-therapy

19 Empowering Families Through Behavioural Support at Home

Faridah Ali Chang and Kang Poh Sim

INTRODUCTION

"It was really the realisation that I can actually be a major influence on my child's behaviour that helped me change the way I approach my child. This was my big aha moment."
(Madam Mas, mother of Az, a 7-year-old boy with non-verbal autism spectrum disorder (ASD))

It had not always been so easy for Madam Mas. Initially, she approached her child's behaviour with a lot of trepidation. Imagine being awoken by the startling high-pitched scream of your child in the wee hours of the morning on a daily basis, only to find yourself stressed and not knowing what to do. In that very moment, all you would want would be to find a way to quieten your child before the neighbours think abuse was taking place and call the police on you. This was how life was like for Madam Mas before she sought help from Az's school.

"When you're caught in the throes of the behaviour, it is difficult to think of your next move, much less be able to know how to comfort your child. At that moment, all I want is to stop the behaviour from continuing."
(Madam Mas, former client of Rainbow Centre's Family Empowerment Programme or FEP)

When a child with autism or developmental challenges displays a behaviour that is challenging to the witnesses in the environment, the behaviour may seem to have happened 'out of nowhere' randomly. However, such behaviour is rarely random and more usually purposeful. The effect is often emotional to the caregivers upon seeing their child in great distress. Each time she recounted the experiences with her son, Madam Mas would be very emotional and tear up.

During major meltdowns, most caregivers often report that all they cared about was not further triggering their child's behaviour. Unless one knows the function of a behaviour being displayed as well as the context within which the behaviour occurs, the behaviour will seem challenging to the onlookers. It is not uncommon for others, whether they are teachers, professionals or even caregivers, to feel inadequate and to lose control when confronted with a child displaying such behaviour. To them, these behaviours are hard to change and cause 'problems' for others[1].

> "He hits his head with his fist so hard that we literally hear a thud. If there is a wall nearby, he would go to it as if aiming his head at the wall...seeing this breaks my heart...we are so worried that this will cause brain damage, especially if he continues to hit his head like this. We bought a helmet for him to use whenever he started hitting his head, just to protect his head... He was biting his own hands until there are open wounds... now you see the calluses on his hand...He would hit me if his meltdowns got worse."
> (Mrs Chan, mother of WX, age 12, diagnosed with ASD)

Caregivers like Mrs Chan and Madam Mas, face behaviours by their children that challenge their caregiving on a daily basis. The behaviour might be functional to the child but it is difficult for caregivers to see beyond the inappropriateness of the behaviour. Regardless, it is indicative of the child's needs not being met. In the case of WX, his inability to communicate made it hard for him to express his needs and for others to understand him. His behaviour was the only means by which he could express himself — inappropriate from the perspective of the onlooker but functional for him — to seek for or to escape from, in the moment of need.

Caregivers will do whatever it takes to prevent their child from injuring themself, hitting out at others, or destroying property. They do not want to see their children hurt themselves and in doing so, inevitably develop high levels of anxiety and stress at the expense of their own safety and well-being. For families of children and youths with disabilities who exhibit challenging behaviours that persist over time, effective proactive behaviour support is important for the peace of the family. A high percentage of families resort to reactive or physical measures but physical intervention must be done with proper training[2], without which, unbeknownst to them, can exaggerate their already challenging circumstances. These can in turn negatively impact the physical, emotional and psychological well-being of the caregivers and other family members[3].

A behaviour can be acceptable in a setting, but challenging in another. Besides the screaming behaviour mentioned, Madam Mas' son displayed other concerning behaviours at home such as throwing the phone and other household items out of the window. Even though she lives on the lowest floor of the block, the constant thought of a passer-by getting hurt and complaining about her family was daunting and caused her stress. More often than not, family and friends are unaware of these challenging behaviours, and yet it is important to find out about them and to provide support for the stressed out parents of these children.

This chapter will focus on the support given to these caregivers, from the perspective and experience of the professionals who work in collaboration with caregivers to coach them. Before explaining how caregivers like Madam Mas and Mrs Chan are being supported at home, it is important to appreciate what behaviour support looks like for children at Rainbow Centre.

Behaviour support in the school setting

When a student with autism displays a behaviour that is 'challenging', the staff — special educators and early interventionists — trained in the use of the ABC (Antecedent Behaviour Consequence) model will observe the behaviour to understand the function of the behaviour (see Figure 1), before deciding on the strategies used to prevent or respond to the behaviour. The ABC model is one of the most effective and easy-to-use tools

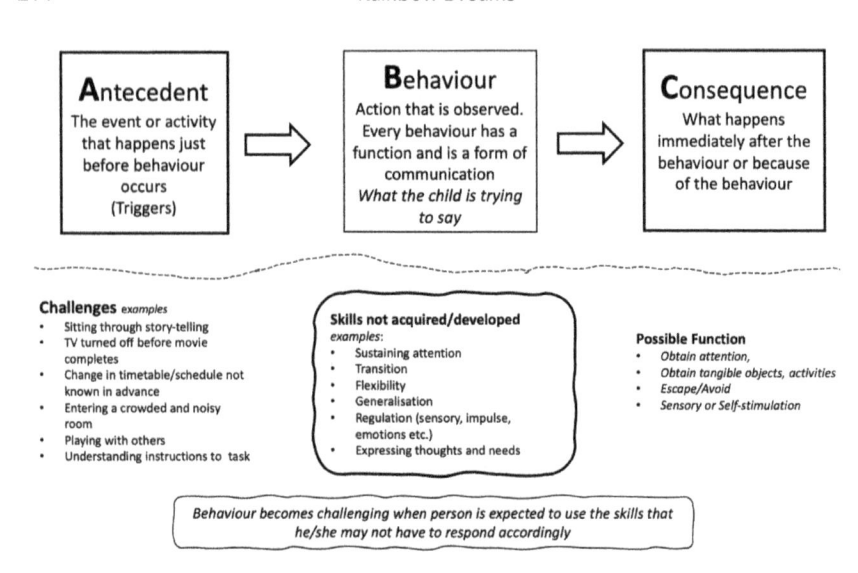

Figure 1.   The ABC model of behaviour and the underlying difficulties

to observe and understand behaviour. Information about the student's behaviour is documented during an event that occurs just before (A) the display behaviour (B) followed by what happens immediately following the occurrence (C). The staff can then share the observations with those who did not witness the behaviour, to easily identify the behaviour of the student being observed. The information documented allows for better awareness and understanding of the student within the context that the behaviour had occurred.

However, it is the understanding of the characteristics of the student's autism and the underlying reasons for his behaviour that are important to be addressed when supporting behaviour that interferes with the student's participation in the school setting. Such understanding can help the staff make adjustments to the antecedent to trigger a positive response from the student. With behaviour support, the time and resources needed will be factored in by the school team to follow through with the behaviour and eventually, allow for improvement on the part of the target student, enhancing the situation for those around the student.

So, what happens when the challenges in the student behaviour occur outside of the school setting or when the student does not pose any challenges in school but is reported to be otherwise at home? How are the caregivers supported?

Facing challenges with a child's behaviour at home

Unlike the training that the staff receive to manage behaviour and the multi-disciplinary team that supports the staff in their work with the students, caregivers do not have the same support when their child's behaviour occurs in the home or in the community.

In 2018, Rainbow Centre started a pilot programme titled Family Empowerment Programme (FEP). Supported by the Koo Foundation, the programme specifically supports caregivers who face great difficulty managing their child at home. It was clear to Rainbow Centre that there was a gap between the support provided by the school team to address the behaviour of the children in school and the transfer of the support provided in school into the home. The caregivers are assigned to a key worker who provides personalised coaching to support the caregivers for about three months to acquire tools to help them support their children's behaviour at home (Appendix A).

Approach to behaviour support for caregivers

The support for caregivers in the FEP programme is urgent and the decision to design appropriate coaching intervention for them will rely on the combination of expert or specialised input from various disciplines. The unavailability of time is a major stressor for the caregivers. The key worker needs to recognise that time as a resource might be limited for the families.[4] Hence, FEP key workers work within the limitations of time.

The following segment will provide the process of the support given to the caregivers through FEP and how they learn to support their child's behaviour at home, from the perspective of FEP key worker.

(a) Building relationships while gathering pertinent information

Right from the start, the key worker must be ready and open with the caregivers to manage their expectations on the type of support they will receive during the programme. The key worker would begin the interaction by being mindful of his/her stance to allow for safe and relaxed conversations with the caregivers. The interaction is intentional, respecting the caregiver's readiness and comfort level with the key worker, the latter always mindful of the caregivers' vulnerability and life challenges.

The key worker pays close attention to the information gathered during conversations with the caregivers about 'a day in their child's life' (Appendix B). The key worker applies clinical judgment in analysing the information gathered to derive the target areas for coaching. These are discussed with the caregivers, who would, frequently, agree with the recommendations of the key workers. At the early part of the FEP coaching, most caregivers may not have clarity as to the direction of the coaching. However, as the caregivers are taught the necessary skills and learn to apply the strategies (e.g. self-regulation / visual schedule) into their daily routines, they gradually come to see the light at the end of the tunnel.

(b) *Understand their child — autism revisited*

The caregivers revisit their understanding of autism and learn to make the connection between their child's behaviour challenge and the possible underlying reasons which usually stem from the characteristics of their child's autism. Even though the caregivers have knowledge of autism, most may not be aware of or have learned to map the autism characteristics to their own child. This tends to occur especially when caregivers focus on the behaviours that are challenging. Most may not be aware or have the clarity in using strategies, known or unknown to them, to address the challenges. The most commonly identified challenges tend to be linked to the challenges their children face in areas relating to communication, sensory issues, rigidity, poor regulation of impulse and emotions, and in transition, among others. These tend to manifest in behaviours that are not easy to manage by the caregivers, such as emotional outbursts, self-injurious behaviours, screaming and shouting, etc.

Impact of stress and emotions

Research has often reported that parenting a child with ASD can be more challenging compared to those whose children do not have ASD, with the former often reporting high levels of anxiety and stress[5]. Stress is also present in parents whose children with autism display inappropriate or unpredictable behaviour[6]. Most of the caregivers do not have strategies to cope with their emotions and stress, much less realising how this can affect their child. One of the most common and important areas of support for the caregivers of FEP is in their regulation; most walk on tiptoe as they fear further triggering their child's sudden behaviour. Some are compelled to respond or do something about their child's behaviour that inadvertently makes their child's behaviour even more challenging to manage.

(a) *Importance of being aware and regulated — mindfulness strategy*

Often, caregivers are more aware of their child's behaviour and emotions than their own, much less how their own behaviour can influence the way they engage with their child. Working with the caregivers on being more aware of their emotions and level of stress, and helping themselves first and foremost, is the most important step before providing them with the strategies to support their child's behaviour.

First, the caregivers are coached to be made aware of and recognise how stress feels like physiologically — quickened heartbeat, sweaty palms, quick paced in speech, higher pitched voice, etc. They are then introduced to deep breathing techniques to calm themselves down, following which the caregivers are usually able to differentiate between the feeling during stress and when they are calm. Finally, they are taught the 4-Step Mindfulness Strategy (Appendix C). The caregivers are also able to choose any other method that they are comfortable with to calm themselves, such as sipping water, physically leaving the stressful situation i.e. go for a walk or even going to the toilet. Embedded within the coaching of mindfulness is the use of the 4S strategies from Hanen© — Say Less, Stress the key words, Go Slow and Show. Caregivers are also advised to use a softer voice when speaking to the children.

Madam Mas had a turning point during the coaching on mindfulness. It was an emotional moment for her, because prior to the coaching, she had not experienced such calmness following a deep breathing exercise. At that point, she understood how she could become a positive influence for her son, Az by beginning to be regulated first in his presence, before engaging him. This has helped her make adjustments to her behaviour, which she noticed also helped her son to respond calmly to her.

(b) *Use of visual support system for organisation and predictability*

Children with ASD respond better to structured routines and visual support. This system of support is commonly used at Rainbow Centre as well as at other special education programmes that support students with ASD. However, for the caregivers in FEP, the visual support system may not be used as consistently and for most, the use of visuals has taken a backseat, whilst trying to manage their child's behaviour, the main focus.

Understanding the child's cognitive rigidity, concrete and literal thinking, with little or no room to change their world which to them is black or white, helps the caregivers to better understand their child's behaviour. This also helps the caregivers appreciate that their child creates their preferred routine (in their mind), and any interference (to their routine) will be met with resistance. At this juncture, most of the caregivers would further understand why strategies like visual schedule not only help them with organisation but whose predictability is appreciated as it provides comfort for their child with autism, regardless of age.

For caregivers who do not usually use visual support in the home, the First-Then approach is introduced, beginning with a familiar routine that the child is already doing at home (Figure 2). This is to help the child transit during routine activities, and also for the child to eventually generalise to the system being used at home, and most importantly, accepting the caregivers' use of it at home. The caregivers will also need to anticipate some discomfort in their child at the start. However, by this time, the caregivers

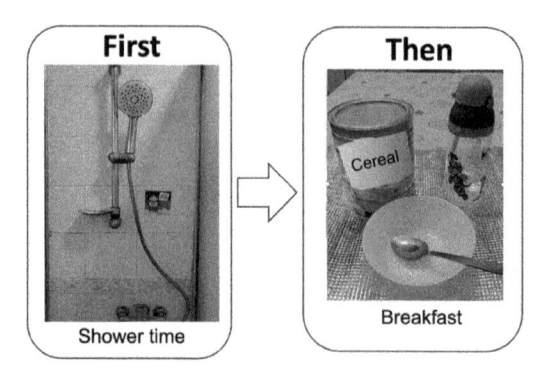

Figure 2. Example of First-Then using pictures contextualised using familiar activity and objects

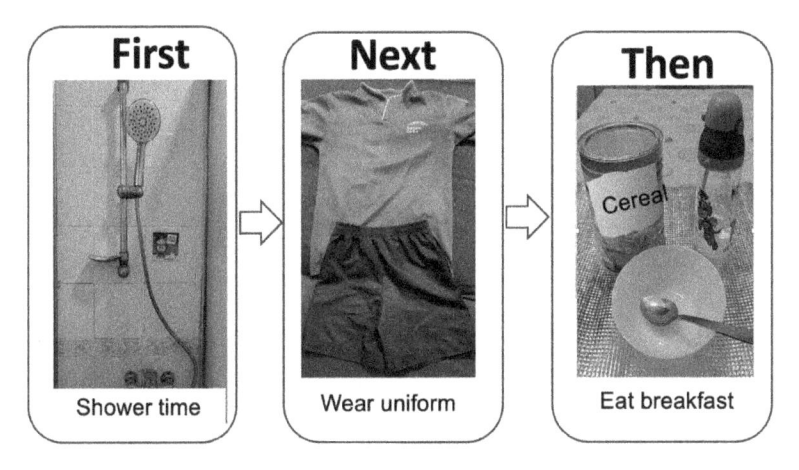

Figure 3.   Example of First-Then gradual expansion to add another routine

Figure 4.   Mrs Chan's proposed schedule for her son WX

would have also learned to apply mindfulness before they apply the strategy with their child. Through consistency in the use of First-Then strategy, the caregivers will gradually add another routine to the visuals (Figure 3).

Once their child is used to the visual system, most caregivers become more confident in planning their child's routine to suit their (the caregivers') day, unlike in the past (Figure 4).

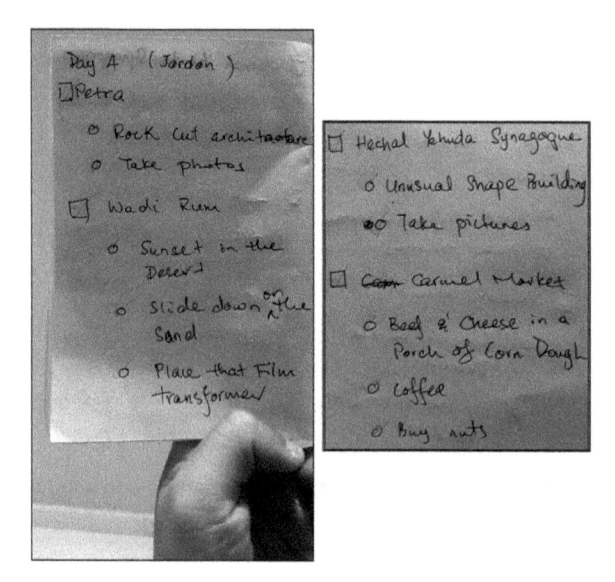

Figure 5.   Sample checklist used by Mdm P for her son during an overseas trip

This strengthens the caregivers' understanding that they need to take over the planning of the home routine via the visuals in the physical environment, so that the child gets used to the new routine that provides him with organisation and predictability. Once the child is used to such visual support in the home, this can be expanded for use beyond the home.

> "I learned to make a visual checklist and planned our holiday routine in advance. I used pictures of the places that we planned to visit each day from the internet and included activities so my son could get involved, e.g. counting the number of statues in the museum, taking photos, or choosing the restaurant for lunch. For the first time, we went as a family instead of having one of us accompany him back to the hotel just because he did not like the places that we went to."
>
> (Mdm P, self-referred to FEP, mother of teenager BP with autism)

(c) Planning functional and meaningful routine at home

Related to the need for structure and routine is the importance of the child with autism to be engaged meaningfully at home. Behavioural issues tend

Betty 帮忙擦五次。擦完五次后，停。
Betty 是个好孩子！

Betty Wipe 5 times. Finish.
Betty is a good girl!

Figure 6. Use of visuals to support functional activity at home, with both Mandarin and English descriptions for the caregiver and Betty respectively

to crop up when the child is not engaged meaningfully. Some would indulge in repetitive behaviours, e.g. repeated watching of videos, obsessive and prolonged wiping of moisture from the air conditioner, etc. Sometimes, to support such behaviours would mean using visuals of the actual behaviour but to structure the activity in such a way that a clear start and finish is indicated, e.g. wiping the air conditioner only five times (instead of 20 in total) (Figure 6).

> "I am so grateful that the pictures and the wordings on them helped to reduce my child's obsessive wiping (minimum 20 minutes) unless I stop her. At least, now I can use the same method to get her to help me in the kitchen, which she is beginning to do."
>
> (Mrs Tan, mother of Betty, 17-year-old girl with ASD)

(d) *Augmenting communication to express thoughts and needs*

> "I asked him 'What? What is it that you want? I don't understand what you need', and the more I asked, the more he screamed

and in the end, his behaviour escalated to throwing things, hitting and pushing me."

(Madam Mas, before learning how to use Augmentative and Alternative Communication (AAC) with Az)

Most caregivers are used to only using verbal communication when engaging with their family members. Augmenting communication means to use or add more than simply speech (such as pictures, objects, and signs/gestures, etc) to make the message clearer to the listener. The role of augmenting communication for caregivers with their child at home is not a natural habit. Yet, this is so important as a bridge to help them communicate effectively — to understand what is being said by the caregivers and to provide an opportunity for both to express themselves effectively.

Augmenting the child's communication is a crucial aspect for caregivers to assist their child in understanding what is being communicated and to provide an opportunity for the child to express their needs. This is especially critical when the child uses their behaviour to express themself. Often, this would have to be second guessed by the caregivers, which triggers the escalation of the behaviour.

Most caregivers in the programme also tend to instruct or speak to their child repeatedly, not realising that their child with autism needs time to process information, especially information received aurally. Hence, the coaching to use OWL (Observe Wait Listen) by Hanen® is included for the caregivers to intentionally allow their child time to respond. This has helped to alleviate their frustration which then leads to a positive outcome of their communication.

The use of visual support has helped the caregivers augment communication with their child, helping them to better understand their child's needs. The caregivers are coached to ensure that the communication board is always made available to the child and if possible, to be placed within reach.

Madam Mas' son, Az was angry but she managed to calm him before her husband returned from work. She related the incident to her husband who then went into his son's room. He saw the communication board and said, "Umi say", as he pointed to a picture and said, "You angry" and paused. Az looked at his communication board, pointed instead to

Figure 7.   Visual support used to augment Az's communication

the picture "upset". His father was very surprised at his non-verbal son's correction of his emotion, to which he acknowledged thereafter. This was the turning point in achieving meaningful communication between parents and Az.

So, for caregivers who have experienced the effectiveness of using visual support to augment communication, they do not leave home without it.

What works for FEP caregivers in supporting their child's behaviour

The caregivers in FEP began their journey with the programme needing help in managing their child with autism, whose behaviour was challenging and stressful to cope with. The caregivers are coached directly by the key workers to acquire skills that support the behaviour of their children at home. Behaviour support for the caregivers in the short programme had to take a different route, one that respected the caregivers' capacity within their daily lives, to commit to and apply the appropriate strategies.

The key areas of support are summed up as follows:

- **The role mindfulness plays in the caregivers' well-being**. For most caregivers, if caring for themselves was not emphasised, they would continue to display their anxiety and stress whenever they engaged with their children. They would also not give themselves permission to make time for themselves which is crucial for self-care and well-being. Hence, being able to calm and intentionally plan 'me time' should be the prerequisite before supporting their child's behaviour.

> *"I realised that my wife did not have much time for herself. I started to spend more time with both my children so that my wife (Mrs Chan) could have 'me time'."*
> *(Mr Chan, WX's father).*

In the process of spending more time with his children, Mr Chan grew closer to his boys, compared to before coaching began. He could also see how much happier his wife had become.

- **The importance of routine and meaningful engagement**. When caregivers create meaningful and sustainable routines in the home that engage the person with autism and the caregivers, this often creates a platform for doing things together. When caregivers realise that they can use functional activities within the home to engage with their children, they are able to plan these within their control and ability, and implement them successfully.
- **The need to apply visual support systems** to develop structure and enhance understanding of the routine. The caregivers appreciate the use of visuals as these help their child to process the information/instruction and follow through with them. Using visuals also enhances the intentional communication of both the caregivers and their child. These help bridge and deepen their relationship.
- **The attitude of openness among all parties**, caregivers, community members and FEP KWs, has been a crucial stepping stone to collaboration and sustained efforts.
- **The expansion of the support network, access to community resources** and weaving of the collaboration throughout the community in terms of support and resources for the families have cemented the continued help for the FEP families, especially when families continue to face ongoing challenges as the programme winds to a close.

> *"I am definitely a lot calmer than I was before I began FEP. I have become clearer and surer of the strategies to use. I understand my child better and can redirect her, not giving her behaviour a chance to escalate. I am also better organised in planning activities for her. Even my husband noticed this about me. My daughter has also become more responsive. I feel that*

I am well supported by all the people working with us. I know we will be ok. We are definitely happier as a family."
(Mdm Faz, mother of Sara, 6-year-old girl with autism, completed FEP in July 2022)

REFERENCES

1. Elven, B. H. (2010). *No Fighting, No Biting, No Screaming: How to Make Behaving Positively Possible for People with Autism and Other Developmental Disabilities*. London: Jessica Kingsley Publishers.
2. Wodehouse, G., & McGill, P. (2009). Support for family carers of children and young people with developmental disabilities and challenging behaviour: what stops it being helpful?. *Journal of Intellectual Disability Research, 53*(7), 644–653.
3. Wolkorte, R., van Houwelingen, I., & Kroezen, M. (2019). Challenging behaviours: Views and preferences of people with intellectual disabilities. *Research in Intellectual Disability, 32*,1421–1427. https://doi.org/10.1111/jar.12631
4. Raver, S. A., & Childress, D. C. (2014). Collaboration and Teamwork with Families and professionals. In S. A. Raver & D. C. Childress (Eds.), *Family-Centered Early Intervention* (pp. 31–52). Baltimore, Maryland: Brookes Publishing. https://archive.brookespublishing.com/documents/collaboration-and-teamwork-with-families.pdf
5. Falk, N. H., Norris, K., & Quinn, M. G. (2014). The factors predicting stress, anxiety and depression in the parents of children with autism. *Journal of Autism and Developmental Disorders, 44*(12), 3185–3203. doi: 10.1007/s10803-014-2189-4
6. Osborne, L. A., & Reed, P. (2009). The Relationship between Parenting Stress and Behavior Problems of Children with Autistic Spectrum Disorders. *Exceptional Children, 76*(1), 54–73. https://doi.org/10.1177/001440290907600103

APPENDIX A

From 2019, the Family Empowerment Programme (FEP) provided services to caregivers of children and youths with autism and included those with other disabilities, extending the age range up to 35 years of age. The caregivers are referred to the programme because they continue to have challenges with their child at home, whether or not their child is being supported in the school or centre.

FEP adopts the Key Worker model where the key worker's role is to empower caregivers by providing them with the tools that support their well-being, teaching them to apply strategies to manage and engage their child meaningfully at home and, offering access to resources, personalised to the needs of the caregivers and/or their family. The FEP team is made up of experienced allied professionals — speech therapists, an occupational therapist and a psychologist — with many years of direct experience in early intervention and special education schools. Each caregiver is assigned to a key worker for a period of two to three months. The work requires sensitivity to and consideration of the caregivers' current capacity to manage their children at home given the challenges they go through in their lives.

APPENDIX B

How the Key Worker builds rapport during interviews

- The process of seeking information about the daily life of the caregivers and their child allowing for a more natural flow of conversation to occur between the caregivers and the key worker is crucial to the support process. The communication style should not be too formal or too professional.
- The language used should match the caregiver's comfort level no matter who they are. Most caregivers would be open to sharing their day which naturally provides information about their child's routine, current skills, and engagement or lack of.
- Questions to elicit information about possible challenges or underlying causes are embedded naturally to help with the conversation flow.

- The ABC model is also embedded in questions and conversations to elicit the caregiver's awareness of triggers and responses that happen with the child during the course of the daily routine.
- Sometimes, added information is gathered through direct observation of the child at home, in the class and/or from video sent to the key workers by the caregivers.

APPENDIX C

Four Steps of Mindfulness strategy introduced to bring about the caregiver's:

(a) self-awareness — being aware of the situation they are in, of themselves and especially of the child in their presence and being aware of the process that goes through their mind and their body
(b) self-reflection — a quick check of their mental and physical state — understanding that these can influence their environment and their child.
(c) self-regulation — remembering to apply deep-breathing to calm down when necessary
(d) conscious choice — making the right decision to say or act (e.g. in response to the child)

20 Music Therapy

Dawn Chik, Grace Low and Calvin Eng

"Music therapy is the scientific use of music interventions within a therapeutic relationship towards observable or measurable functional, educational, rehabilitative or well-being outcomes by a credentialed professional."[1]

Music therapy is an established health profession in which music is used within a therapeutic relationship to address physical, emotional, cognitive, and social needs of individuals. After assessing the strengths and needs of each client, the credentialed music therapist provides an indicated treatment experience which may include creating, recreating, improvising, and/or listening to music. Through musical involvement in the therapeutic context, clients' abilities are strengthened and transferred to other areas of their lives.

Music therapists based in Singapore often pursue further studies in the United States, United Kingdom, Australia, or New Zealand. Upon completion of their music therapy degree, they will be credentialed music therapists accredited by their country of training. Such rigorous training is essential as it not only teaches music therapy techniques but develops the therapist as an individual and his or her clinical sensitivity.

Music therapists are required to maintain their credentials with the respective certification board, by re-certifying and or going through Continuing Education courses. This is to assure continuing competence, accountability of professionals, and to ensure maintenance of professional standards. This is common among healthcare professionals, and music therapists are no exception. Some examples of advanced or specialised training include Neurologic Music Therapy, Austin Vocal Psychotherapy, and Bonny Method Guided Imagery and Music.

As at 2022, music therapy services are offered in at least 28 healthcare institutions, social service agencies and private settings across Singapore.

MUSIC THERAPY IN RAINBOW CENTRE, SINGAPORE

Music therapy at Rainbow Centre began in the early 1990s. Music therapists serve children aged seven to 18 years old with special needs such as those with Autism Spectrum Disorder, Cerebral Palsy, Global Developmental Delay (GDD), and multiple disabilities in the Special Education programme. These therapists work closely with the Individualised Education Plan (IEP) team, which involves physiotherapists, occupational therapists, speech language therapists, psychologists, teachers, social workers, and parents.

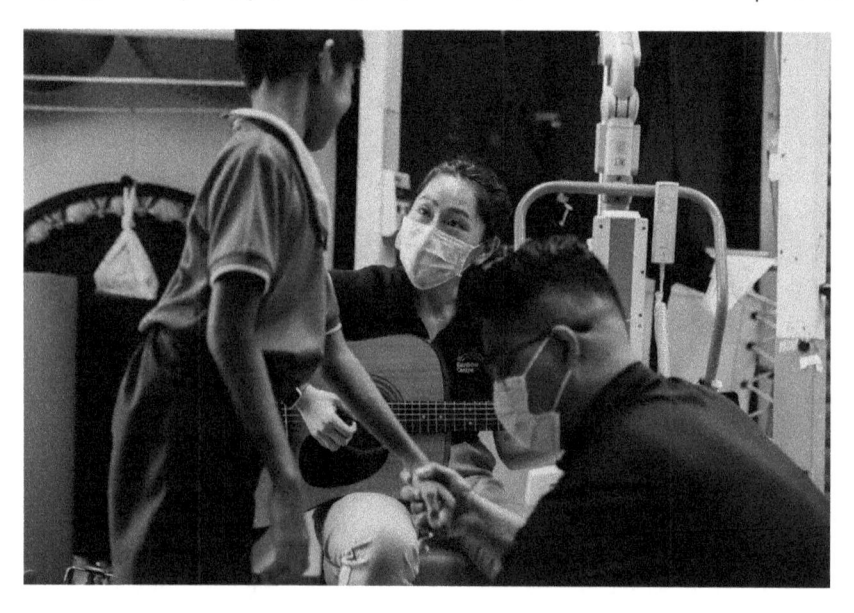

Grace Low, Music Therapist (middle) and Iqbal Kamari, Physiotherapist (right), working with a 9-year-old student (left) who has mobility challenges due to his GDD diagnosis, in a joint Music Therapy-Physiotherapy session

WHY MUSIC?

Music is fun and motivating. It is also generally safe, non-invasive, and non-threatening. However, music might evoke emotions and memories that could be pleasant or painful. Music therapists are trained to be attuned to and support clients in managing these pleasant or unpleasant emotions and memories.

Music is processed throughout the brain, whether one is playing, reading, listening to or creating music; these experiences activate and involve every part of the brain. Music is intrinsically motivating for many of us, offering a multi-sensory experience. Music embeds emotional and social meaning and evokes memories. Music, as a means of communication and creative expression is especially significant for individuals who have communication challenges.

In special education, music therapists use music to address behavioural issues[2], communication skills, emotional regulation[3], social skills[4], sensory-motor skills[5], and/or cognitive goals[6]. Through music therapy, one's overall quality of life and interpersonal relationships are enhanced. Music therapists create and provide a safe environment for individuals with special needs to express in a unique, intentional, and developmentally appropriate manner.

MARTY'S* MUSIC THERAPY JOURNEY

*Name of the student has been changed.

Getting to know Marty

Marty was eight years old when he was referred for music therapy by the educational psychologist on his IEP team. Marty is a spritely individual who is bright-eyed, thin and often wears a tightly-clenched smile on his face accompanied by occasional giggles. Despite his small build, Marty is very strong and agile. Marty enjoys watching videos and listening to a wide genre of music from nursery rhymes to Cantonese pop music from the 1980s. He is a very musical child who often hummed while piecing together a puzzle; he also dances and moves to the beat of the song playing on the radio. Marty was diagnosed with autism at age 3 and since then, had been receiving early intervention support to bridge gaps in his development, especially in the area of social-emotional regulation.

He communicates through gestures and expresses his needs and wants using two- or three-word phrases. When in distress, Marty bites himself, hurts familiar adults and damages furniture in his surroundings. Marty also displays seemingly random and sudden outbursts of cries throughout the day. The triggers may be driven both internally or externally. After observing and interacting with him in and out of therapy sessions, the therapist learnt that his tightly-clenched smiles were not reliably indicative of positive emotions. Instead, they showed when Marty was feeling anxious and fearful.

Marty is the older of two siblings in the family, with a younger sister aged one. Marty's parents are very devoted to him and actively sought out Traditional Chinese Medicine and Complementary and Alternative Medicine to help with Marty's behavioural challenges and frequent temper tantrums. With the birth of his sister, Marty started attending an after school programme after his morning session at Rainbow Centre. Marty started spending longer periods of time away from his mother and at home.

The early sessions

When Marty first entered the music therapy room, he gravitated towards melodic instruments such as the piano, xylophone and guitar. He would become totally absorbed in exploring the keys, oblivious of the people in his surroundings. At times, he would suddenly abandon what he was doing and move to another instrument, with no sense of purpose and achievement. He seemed not to hear when spoken to; he often stared blankly, looking through the therapist rather than at the therapist. Marty rejected fiercely the sharing of a musical instrument and the sharing of a musical experience. Marty had a keen ear and sought to play the melodies of his favourite tunes on the piano, in the respective keys he had heard them in. Some of his favourite tunes were *The Wheels on the Bus* and *Old Macdonald Had a Farm*. He was fiercely resistant to changes in his music and this was also evident in how he made music and interacted with the musical instruments.

The *Wheels on the Bus* had to be played in the key of D major and *Old MacDonald Had a Farm* in the key of G major. All the verses of the songs had to be sung in sequence and in their entirety. Any modification would send him into a full-blown rage and temper tantrum. Every session, he entered the room and plucked only the E-string on the guitar in the same rhythmic pattern for minutes with seemingly no end in mind before abruptly moving to press down on the C-note on the piano. When the therapist attempted to sing or play with him, Marty would move himself away from her, cover her mouth or grab her fingers and 'throw it away' from the instrument. At times when he was feeling frustrated with the music therapist's musical interjections, he would scratch and pinch the therapist.

Collaborating as an IEP team: Therapeutic aim

In spite of Marty's strong liking for music, the therapist realised that his interest in music seemed to further isolate him as he sought to 'hide' himself in music. He also had strong 'rules' for how he took part in these sessions and did not easily allow others to participate and play together with him. After discussing with the IEP team, the music therapist focused on exploring emotional expression, addressing regulation skills and building social relatedness through music and music-based activities.

A shift in therapeutic relationship

Initially, the therapist used client-preferred songs, and recreated familiar musical experiences and expectations with Marty to establish rapport. Subsequently, the therapist attempted to break into his musical world through structured clinical improvisations (based on similar chord progressions of his preferred songs) which challenged Marty's tolerance for changes. These musical changes offered opportunities for Marty to explore and expand his musical expressions in a contained and predictable musical structure. The music therapist intentionally created musical invitations or 'breaks' to encourage Marty to join in and express himself spontaneously through music. Through structured improvisation, Marty had opportunities to learn to relate to, and build his confidence in the therapist as his play partner. The therapeutic aim was to have music become a two-way means of communication between him and others around him. Marty demonstrated awareness of his one-on-one relationship with the therapist and came to accept the sharing process. Because Marty loved and enjoyed music, the process of making music was intrinsically rewarding and satisfying for him. As his class teachers shared, Marty looked forward to seeing 'Music Therapy' on his schedule.

After ten months of weekly therapy sessions, Marty demonstrated more tolerance for changes during sessions, be they structural or musical.

He was observed to be more spontaneous and expressive when communicating with the therapist, using a mix of words and gestures. Marty still had frequent emotional outbursts in class and therapy sessions, and engaged in self-injurious behaviours. However, the intensity of these incidents was reduced overall and he was able to regulate more quickly when the therapist hummed his favourite tune while matching his breathing or squeezing his hands. The music therapist shared these observations with the IEP team members. Collectively, the team decided that it would be appropriate to explore generalising Marty's musical play and his relationship with the therapist into the classroom environment.

Collaborating as an IEP team: Generalisation

The music therapist frequently communicated and shared session updates with Marty's teachers and the educational psychologist on the team. Likewise, his teachers would share and inform the music therapist of any notable changes or significant events relating to Marty's behaviours, mood, home environment, diet and sleep. Over the period of a year, Marty established a safe and reliable one-on-one relationship with the music therapist. At this point, the IEP team members came together to reflect and consider the next steps in Marty's intervention programme.

When a group of individuals come together, it creates opportunities for the development of interpersonal relationships, tolerance and acceptance. Collectively, the team discussed the need for generalisation of relational and interpersonal skills with various people in Marty's life. In the educational context, the relationships with his teachers and his peers were identified. Hence, as part of Marty's education plan, weekly group music therapy was implemented.

Group integration with peers and teachers

With the purpose of supporting him to experience and generalise connecting with others via music and through music-based activities, Marty started weekly group music therapy with four of his classmates. Marty had two sessions of closure and termination with the music therapist individually before the June holidays. When he returned from the school break, group music therapy took place in the classroom with the support of his class teachers.

The music therapist facilitated the group by using songs, rhythm and harmonies that she had used with Marty during his individual sessions. The familiar musical structures and cues brought Marty some comfort and served as an anchor amidst the changes which inevitably evoked fear and uncertainty for him. In the initial group sessions, Marty showed high resistance and poor tolerance for changes in his 'musical soundscape'. He started hiding behind his defences and demonstrated self-injurious behaviours, physical aggression and hostility to his peers and teachers; the music therapist was not exempted as well. Clearly, Marty was struggling to reconcile and make sense of what was happening in music therapy sessions. Having to be in the presence of others' musical space and expression, waiting for his turn to voice out, learning to tolerate and accept the music of others, and so forth, were all new and challenging for Marty.

The music therapist persevered, continuing to be a consistent and reliable musical play partner in the group to Marty and his peers. The therapist focused on structuring predictable musical breaks and turns, facilitating opportunities for all to play together by recreating familiar musical experiences. Through structured improvisation, Marty learned to build, and started building, musical relationships with his new play partners. He developed awareness and acceptance of the musicality of his peers and also anticipated his peers' participation.

After four months of weekly group sessions, Marty grew to share his musical space with others, participating in the same activity (i.e. grooving to the same beat, using the same props and so forth) while maintaining proximity with the group. When Marty and his peers moved together to music, it helped them to build awareness of, and learn to relate to, one another. Meanwhile, the teachers in the group were also learning how to communicate and engage with Marty through music. The teachers were encouraged to participate and share their musicality with the students. The teachers were often invited to sing or play an instrumental solo during the structured improvisations, just like the students. The teachers experienced managing and balancing the dynamics between the students in the group. The music therapist also observed shifts in the interpersonal dynamics between Marty and the teachers. Playfulness and spontaneity were evident in their interaction. During check-ins and IEP team sharing, the teachers reported feeling more comfortable and confident in being one-on-one with Marty during music group sessions and out-of-music contexts.

In conclusion, Marty worked with the music therapist over a period of two years, having experienced both individual and group music therapy sessions in support of his learning in the area of social-emotional skills such as emotional expression, regulation and relating to others. As the therapeutic aims were addressed, the direct support of the music therapist was terminated at the end of the second school year. The IEP team members, with the music therapist as a resource member, continued to work on Marty's education goals in the following school year.

OUR HOPES FOR MUSIC THERAPY IN RAINBOW CENTRE

Music therapy services have been around in Rainbow Centre for 31 years[7], and the music therapy department has grown alongside Rainbow Centre as it expanded from one to three campuses. Constant advocacy is needed to raise awareness of the profession, through modes such as local research studies on the efficacy of music therapy, educating Rainbow Centre employees and stakeholders, and deepening conversations with parents and caregivers.

Rainbow Centre strives to provide the best service experience for our students and families, and we see the value of offering music therapy services.

"Alone we can do so little, together we can do so much"

Helen Keller

REFERENCES

1. Association for Music Therapy (Singapore). What is music therapy. http://musictherapy.org.sg/what-is-music-therapy/
2. Boso, M., Emanuele, E., Minazzi, V., Abbamonte, M., & Politi, P. (2007). Effect of long-term interactive music therapy on behavior profile and musical skills

in young adults with severe autism. *The Journal of Alternative and Complementary Medicine, 13*(7), 709–712. https://doi.org/10.1089/acm.2006.6334

3. Carpente, J. A. (2017). Investigating the effectiveness of a developmental, individual difference relationship-based (DIR) improvisational music therapy program on Social Communication for children with autism spectrum disorder. *Music Therapy Perspectives, 35*(2). 160–174. https://doi.org/10.1093/mtp/miw013

4. Hosseini, M., Fayyaz, I., Arab, S., Naghashian, H., Poudineh, Z., & Ghasemtabar, S. N. (2015). Music therapy: An effective approach in improving social skills of children with autism. *Advanced Biomedical Research, 4*(1), 157. https://doi.org/10.4103/2277-9175.161584

5. Bharathi, G., Jayaramayya, K., Balasubramanian, V., & Vellingiri, B. (2019). The potential role of rhythmic entrainment and music therapy intervention for individuals with autism spectrum disorders. *Journal of Exercise Rehabilitation, 15*(2), 180–186. doi:10.12965/jer.1836578.289

6. Quintin, E. M., Bhatara, A., Poissant, H., Fombonne, E., & Levitin, D. J. (2011). Emotion perception in music in high-functioning adolescents with autism spectrum disorders. *Journal of Autism and Developmental Disorders, 41*(9), 1240–1255. doi: 10.1007/s10803-010-1146-0

7. Ruyters-Lim, A. (1997). Music therapy. In K. Lyen, E. H.Lee, & J. S. Y. Tham-Toh (Eds.), *Rainbow dreams: How to help your child with developmental delay* (pp. 266–284). Singapore: Armour.

4C Partnerships Around the Client

21 Making Work Possible

Nursidah Malik, Kay Huang Shujian, Goh Ting Ying, Bernice Lim Miaoxin and Belinda Chua

INTRODUCTION

As children grow up to become youths, and youths mature to become adults, they go through several life-changing moments in each age stage. The transition into the next age stage or new phase of life can be particularly stressful and difficult for persons with autism and their families. One of the major changes that a person with autism goes through is the transition from youth to adulthood. This is a crucial life-changing period as the person moves from a heavily supported school environment into a space where he or she needs to be independent in many different aspects, from daily living to social interactions and financial ability. The young adult needs to use the skills learned during their school years and apply them in adulthood. One area that is challenging for young adults with autism and other developmental disabilities is to find and sustain employment.

The traditional transition to employment sees persons with disabilities move from a special education school to a workplace in the form of open employment. This process is usually done with support from dedicated employment agencies or employers who are inclusive in their hiring practices. However, this route is typically limited to persons requiring low support, are able to self-regulate, have a good understanding of the work expectations and are able to deliver the work tasks independently. Even so, many of them face significant difficulties in maintaining their employment[1].

For persons requiring moderate to high support, they are unable to access the open employment space.

The COVID-19 pandemic has affirmed that to be meaningfully employed, one is not restricted to merely being physically present in a workplace. The proliferation of home businesses has made it timely for social service agencies to explore opportunities for persons with moderate to high support needs to obtain employment in an environment that is familiar and conducive for them to be engaged.

EMPLOYABILITY SERVICES

Rainbow Centre has been striving to bridge the gaps in meeting our students' needs. As more of our students graduate, we want to see them applying all the skills, knowledge and values that they have learned throughout their school years with us. One area of attention is vocational skills, defined as practical or first-hand skills, that help a person take on a trade or a job. This has led Rainbow Centre to endeavour to create work as a continuum through the establishment of the Employability Services (ES) unit to understand students' vocational needs, maximise their talents and strengths, as well as equip them and their families with skills for future employment opportunities.

ES runs three programmes to meet these needs, prepare students for post-18 life and work with families to kick-start their employment opportunities after graduating from Rainbow Centre. The first programme is Workability. Here, job coaches impart vocational skills in various areas to students, and support them during their internship at external work sites. The second programme is Artability, where art trainers equip students who have exceptional visual art talents with art skills and bring their talents to the next level. Lastly, it runs the Micro Business Academy (MBA), where graduates and their families are assisted to set up and run small home-based businesses customised to their skills and needs.

WORKABILITY

The Workability Programme provides opportunities to students with the potential to work in the open employment space by equipping them with the hard and soft skills needed for work. This two-year programme offers internships at external work sites. Job coaches work with students and their supportive families who are willing to collaborate with the school to achieve a shared employment goal for the student. Job coaches also seek partners who are keen to offer internship opportunities for students. The job coaches work closely with the supervisors and staff to provide a supportive learning experience for the students during internship. RC's allied professionals and teachers also partner job coaches to teach essential soft skills needed in the workplace. Some of the internships have also blossomed into employment for the students, achieving into win-win outcomes for both students and partners.

ARTABILITY

The Artability Programme is a vocational arts programme that develops students with talent in visual arts by exposing them to new art techniques, growing their personal styles and partnering stakeholders to showcase their works to the public. Students learn to use a variety of art media and styles under the guidance of art trainers. Those with a higher level of understanding will progress to conceptualising their own artworks while deepening their use of art techniques. Beyond giving students the right opportunities, the trainers also provide emotional support to strengthen the students' ability to communicate, express themselves confidently as well as develop a stronger sense of self, identity and esteem, all of which are needed for them to grow into young adults. Adding to this, through partnership opportunities, Artability students gain first-hand experience participating in exhibitions and events with their artworks, learning to describe details of the artworks to external parties such as the media and event participants, as well as understanding that these efforts contribute to the sales of their artworks. This experience builds up their confidence and helps them to view their creative talents as a potential source of income when they graduate from RC.

MICRO BUSINESS ACADEMY

Our Micro Business Academy (MBA) works with graduates with moderate to high support needs and their families to ensure that they are meaningfully engaged through a family-driven micro business when they become adults. With person-centric skills coaching, this 24-month programme equips caregivers and students with special needs with family-centric business planning and development skills. MBA is open to Rainbow Centre (RC) and non-RC graduates, with trainers and coaches working with supportive families in exploring suitable business ideas such as home baking, home kueh making, home crafting and running a canteen snack stall.

RC's mission to enable its students to achieve their full potential and support their needs and aspirations are clearly reflected in the three ES programmes. With the guiding principle of looking at employment as a continuum, staff from these three programmes work together to ensure there is a smooth transition for the graduates to head to their next phase of life. Being fairly new programmes of about five years old and less, Workability, Artability, and Micro Business Academy collectively have a number of success stories. Though their journey into young adulthood can be difficult at times, the graduates are able to find meaningful employment opportunities, thanks to the training that the students had in RC and the support from their parents.

OUR STORIES

Shu Hao (Workability)

Shu Hao is a young adult who spends each day meaningfully. Since his graduation, he has been in contact with his peers and teachers. Shu Hao is especially close to three of his peers and they would often go out together or to one another's house for meals. He participates in many outdoor activities and would spend time doing his favourite activity — clay art. He would share photos of his outings and clay art with his mum too, demonstrating his desire to share his favourite activities with others. Shu Hao also enjoys walks with his mum, May, making their bond closer and more special.

Shu Hao was trained under the Workability programme and had internship exposure at a food and beverage company, where he took on duties at the front of house. He learnt to apply the skills required to perform

Figure 1. Shu Hao (right) and his Workability job coach, Ting Ying

his role well at work, including staying on task, requesting for help when needed, managing emotions and behaviour, and adapting to changes at work. This internship opportunity enabled him to transit to SG Enable's School-to-Work programme after graduation, where he secured full-time employment with a food packing company, where he has been working since. His performance is highly appreciated and valued by his supervisor and co-workers. During the days when he might want to speak loudly or throw a tantrum, May would remind him that he is 21 years old and has to be mindful of his young adult image. Such reminders helped him to regulate himself as he understood the image that he needed to portray.

May noted that the training Shu Hao had in school was important in helping him to integrate into the community and provided him with more opportunities to interact with people outside of the school. These experiences were crucial and help him to interact better with his colleagues in his current job.

Like every parent, May's ultimate hope for her son is for Shu Hao to be happy. She hopes that Shu Hao will continue to lead a meaningful and fulfilling life, have a stable job and friends, and can continue doing his favourite crafts. She also wishes that he will be able to work hard and eventually buy his own house. May's advice to parents with a special needs child who is graduating, "Don't be too concerned about the negative remarks or comments that others make about your child. Being too concerned about the remarks would only hurt you and your child. Our patience and love are really important for them. Hence, we need to stay strong and cheer them on."

Noah (Workability and Artability)

Noah graduated from RC as a Valedictorian and was part of the Workability and Artability programmes. He did an internship as a barista. Noah's mother, Rosyniah, has seen Noah's social and communication skills improve throughout the 13 years he was in RC. In particular, she noted how ES programmes developed him into a more patient and confident person who acquired vocational and artistic skills.

Noah's dream is to be a professional artist and he has successfully created a name for himself in the visual arts scene of the special needs community. Noah has worked hard towards his dream, earning him a distinction in NAFA-CLE Certificate in Visual Arts. The Nanyang Academy of Fine Arts (NAFA) established the Centre for Lifelong Education (CLE) in November 2005 to provide opportunities for enthusiasts who are keen to

Figure 2.   Noah at the Goh Chok Tong Enable Award ceremony

further their interests in the arts[2]. Noah's artistic achievements in recent years include having his artworks printed on Uniqlo T-shirts for fundraising, being featured in Dr Janson Yap's book, "Average to Aces" and being commissioned for an artwork by Inclusive Sports Conference for Madam Halimah Yacob, President of the Republic of Singapore. In 2021, Noah was the recipient of the prestigious Goh Chok Tong Enable Award. His artistic successes has opened new doors for him such as being a co-facilitator for ART:DIS Singapore Inclusive Art Making Masterclass at NAFA and receiving more requests for commissioned artworks.

Apart from his dedication to visual arts, he is also Singapore's Special Olympics Singapore (SOSG) Bowling athlete and has won five gold medals in national bowling competitions including the most recent SOSG Bowling competition in April 2022.

Noah's successes do not stop at arts and bowling. He is also passionate in sport stacking ever since he first tried cup stacking in class five years ago. Continuing with his passion, he competed in World Sports Stacking Championship 2022. Noah came in first place for Singapore and third place in the World under the Special Stackers Division.

Rosyniah plays an integral role in Noah's life and his successes. She appreciates the support given by RC throughout Noah's schooling and she continues to help him achieve his dreams, ensuring that he is happy, independent and able to earn a living doing what he loves most. Rosyniah encourages parents to, "Keep believing in them and never give up. Support their dreams and passion. Anything is possible!"

Jarrod (Micro Business Academy)

Jarrod graduated from RC in 2021 and has adapted well to the new change in his life. Jarrod joined Micro Business Academy (MBA) after graduation to ensure that he is able to get work opportunities from home. He sells wire art keychains by hand twisting them into four different words: Home, Hope, Joy and Love. MBA supported Jarrod and his family in starting up the micro business and continuously looks for ways to promote his craft products to ensure that he gets regular orders.

Working life can sometimes be tough, especially for our students. The initial days were harder as Jarrod needed time to understand the work assigned to him. Although Jarrod is on 'one word' per instruction currently,

Figure 3. Jarrod doing his work at home

he is performing well now as he is able to associate with the work meaningfully. However, there are days when he is not in the mood to do work; he will then self-declare a day off by saying, "Jarrod is sleepy". At other times, he will not start work when he is confused.

Jarrod's parents, Miki and Joseph work closely with him. Miki hopes that his handmade craft products will continue to bring meaning to others. Like all mothers, she wants Jarrod to be physically healthy and spiritually well. Miki's message to all parents with a child with special needs is, "Believe that your child has a special gift."

REFERENCES

1. Griffiths, A. J., Giannantonio, C. M., Hurley-Hanson, A. E., & Cardinal, D. (2016). Autism in the Workplace: Assessing the transition needs of young adults with Autism Spectrum Disorder. *Journal of Business and Management, 22*(1), 5–22.
2. Nanyang Academy of Fine Arts. *Centre for Lifelong Education.* https://www.nafa.edu.sg/schools/centre-for-lifelong-education

22 Community Partnership: The Force of Friendship

Jean Loo and Toh Ee Ming

For youths with disabilities, leaving the sheltered confines of a special education school — often compared to standing at the edge of a cliff — brings a myriad of challenges like unemployment and social isolation. Those with higher support needs usually have few options other than day activity centres or home care services.

Social inclusion and participation in authentic communities are critical for a good quality of life for our clients. This has explained why, over the years, we have stepped up efforts to model, partner and train individuals and organisations, because we believe that inclusive practices lead to inclusive communities.

Among the diverse partnerships Rainbow Centre (RC) has cultivated from a strong spirit of co-creation, shared experiences and collaborative relationships, a tiny community which packs a punch — befrienders — has emerged.

Unlike classroom volunteers and donors of corporate partners, befrienders interact with our young adults in purely social settings, driven by shared interests, hobbies and a strong desire to contribute to a more inclusive society.

Since 2018, RC has recruited 110 Good Life Befrienders who play an important role in connecting students to community resources through shared interests and experiences. These befrienders are integral to our young adults being included in the community through shared interests and outings.

Looking back at the genesis of the Good Life Befrienders Programme, which was started to enhance our young adults' network of support so they could achieve their Good Life Plans, we have come to realise that befrienders, too, have emerged from the programme as stronger citizen advocates for persons with disabilities.

Research Assistant Si Ying, 23, is one such befriender. A volunteer with Rainbow Centre since July 2018, she has taken on a myriad of roles. From assisting students and teachers as a classroom support volunteer, she became a Good Life Befriender to a youth with disability in March 2021.

As opposed to being a 'teacher' to students in class, befriending also appealed to her as it allows her to explore a different role of being a friend to them and levelling the relationship. She said, "Volunteering injects meaning into my life. I've had lots of fond memories with many of the people I've worked with in this community who have really inspired me to want to do more for this group of people that I care so much about."

Here are four takeaways from our Good Life Befrienders, on why befriending matters.

"WE HAVE TO BE READY FIRST"

A former Rainbow Centre student is Kai Lee who continues to be contacted by her befriender, Weiyan. The two are so alike that they are often mistaken as sisters. They share the same bubbly, larger-than-life personality and infectious energy — the only difference being that Kai Lee is the "super uninhibited, unfiltered version of myself," jokes Weiyan. Balancing them out is Jiajin, another befriender, whose zen vibes complement the two.

Right from the get-go, they drew up a list of common interests to get a sense of what they could do together — from flying kites, doing art and craft, and cycling to eating good food. The trio have taken part in a treasure hunt at Jurong Lake Gardens, flown kites at Marina Barrage and crafted Christmas trees. As friends, they wanted the friendship to be about everyone, and not merely Kai Lee. This also helped them plan a series of outings and activities to do.

Kai Lee's parents view the befrienders as a great source of support. Confiding their sorrows and worries for their child, they shared that once, when Kai Lee disappeared from home, they fretted for her safety. They found her buying a Ramly burger and other food at the nearby *pasar malam* (pop-up food fair with stalls selling different items). Weiyan and Jiajin even designed an Amazing Race on the MRT (subway system) so she could learn to be public transport-literate.

Jiajin recalled his favourite moment when Kai Lee's mother, a delivery food rider, gifted him with her free limited edition World Cup mug from McDonalds from her collection of treasured possessions. It was a simple gesture, but one that left him moved beyond words.

Weiyan said, "It's super refreshing to learn how to make friends again and to re-evaluate what it means to have a deeper human relationship that is positive and healthy. Isn't friendship one of the things which makes life beautiful?"

One year, in celebration of Halloween, knowing that Kai Lee loves Western culture, they took her out for trick-or-treat. As it was their first outing, they were nervous about whether she would get upset as her trigger was crying children. To prepare for the outing, Weiyan read up as much as she could online and ran through all the worst-case scenarios in her mind. That night, she was on high alert, surveying the scene for additional stressors like scary figures. She also actively planned the route and checked in every five minutes to see if Kai Lee needed a rest amid the chaos.

With his calm demeanour, Jiajin took the lead. It turned out that they had completely underestimated Kai Lee. She was oblivious, gamely sprinting to wacky and scary characters to take photos.

Over an intense supper session, the befrienders reflected on what they had learnt. Said Weiyan, "I realised that I was the one who was disabling Kai Lee. I was a prisoner of my own preconceived fears. We have to be ready first. While we can worry about the right things, we should also know when to step back and let her show the way."

"EVERYONE HAS DREAMS"

The befriending programme has brought together an unlikely pairing between the outgoing Filmer and his somewhat more introverted befrienders Theng Soon and Valerie, who joke that they have been pushed to become more sociable themselves. Filmer, who was born with pilocytic astrocytoma (a rare type of brain tumour), is a friendly, chatty teenager with a chiffon cake business on the side.

Over the last two years, the trio have attended the Purple Parade, soaked up the Mid-Autumn festivities in Chinatown, gone museum hopping in City Hall and hunted for footballs at Decathlon to add to Filmer's growing collection. Good food is a must — they have gone for a *dim sum* date at Swee Choon Tim Sum restaurant, savoured meatballs at Ikea and tried the chicken rice by Singapore's Michelin-starred Hawker Chan.

Professing to be someone who would shy away from meeting new people, engineer Theng Soon quips he is forced to come out of his shell. Likewise, Valerie Chan, a social worker, said that Filmer is probably the most outgoing person whom she has met.

"When we go to the shopping mall, Filmer always says 'hi' to every security guard and shopkeeper. All the neighbours would also stop to say hello. I think almost the whole neighbourhood knows him! We also make new friends through him."

Theng Soon recalled that initially, they were unfamiliar with one another and had many considerations for each outing. He said, "Over time, it has evolved into a kind of friendship. We don't even need a lot of planning to make it work, just a casual dinner. It has become so natural over these two years."

Before both of them joined as befrienders, Valerie and Theng Soon did not think much about youths with special needs having dreams. Shared Valerie, "Since we met Filmer, we're constantly amazed by his passion for baking! I'm pretty sure we've tried all the different flavours of his cakes. Not everyone has that level of aspiration and determination."

Reflecting on advice for new befrienders, the pair shared that it was important to explain. Once, while queuing for food at Ikea, Filmer excitedly asked a COVID-19 safety distancing ambassador what the menu was. His befrienders had to explain patiently why his questions were not directed at the right person, and to be patient as he could see the menu board up close at the front of the queue. Theng Soon said, "If we explain to him in simpler terms, then he will understand why we shouldn't be doing certain things."

As sociable and chatty as Filmer may be, his befrienders also noticed that crowded places caused him to be overwhelmed. For example, in malls, Filmer would tend to walk very fast in order to get out of the place; hence, planning outings in advance to manage his expectations was ideal.

"He has his own preferences, so sometimes we follow, and other times, we insist on our way," said Valerie. "It's about learning to compromise as friends."

But perhaps most importantly, both Theng Soon and Valerie agree that they must remember to help him become more independent. "Sometimes in the rush to help him, we forget the bigger goal is about getting him to be more independent," said Theng Soon. For example, as Filmer's left hand is weaker, both befrienders often offer to help him carry items like food trays. They have since become more sensitive to letting him try first.

"We try to be more conscious with other things like letting him handle money on his own, even if the store owner is standing there and waiting for a very long time," said Valerie. "It's a chance for him to practise interacting with others."

"PLAN, SOURCE. TRUST"

For the longest time, befrienders Ee Ming and Ludi struggled to communicate with Keith, 21, who has autism and is minimally verbal.

The pair, who first met Keith while working on a community theatre arts project on the hopes and dreams of Rainbow Centre's graduating students, didn't know what he was feeling or if he even understood them. Nearly three months into rehearsals, Keith suddenly uttered the words written on his dream board. He spoke haltingly, stumbling over the words but they could hear him clearly for the first time.

"When I grow up, I want to be an artist," he said. They exchanged looks with each other, hardly daring to believe it and secretly screaming inside.

Ee Ming and Ludi's soft spot for Keith cemented the start of an unlikely friendship. Ee Ming is a freelance journalist with a passion for social issues while Ludi is a medical student at Nanyang Technological University. They decided to join as befrienders to build on their friendship and simply have fun.

Over the last year, the trio have gone kite-flying, done a photo walk, chilled out at home and had art jam sessions at Labrador Nature Reserve. One of their favourite memories was exploring the colourful shophouses at Katong as it was full of unplanned surprises — they took a detour to an old-school ice cream distributor, stumbled on a pretty plant boutique store, climbed a vertical playground and taught Keith how to use a camera app.

When asked if all their outings were so eventful, both befrienders shared that they have learnt to plan and prioritise either engaging the body or mind.

"We tend to start off with very ambitious plans and want to cover many activities in one day," said Ee Ming, "but everyone ends up exhausted." She advises staying put at one place, where there is an opportunity for more in-depth interaction or going out where more time is spent travelling.

For each session, they prepare visual schedules and communicate with Keith using an iPad. Visual schedules are a must, and these are sent to parents in advance. Ludi said, "We give Keith a hard copy so it's easier for everyone to refer to it along the way, instead of having to pull out our phone and zoom in."

The pair would use the iPad to ask him questions on what he prefers to do, what food he wants to order and even create portrait sketches of one another. Keith took to communicating via the iPad really quickly, even playing around with the colours and drawing tools. Ee Ming said, "At every stage in our life, we will have to care for and communicate with a minimally verbal being, whether it's a baby or an elderly person. It's okay to learn at any stage."

Sourcing for safe spaces to travel to is also a key area of planning for the pair. They noticed that Keith, who claps his hands and jumps when he's excited or anxious, would jump even more in noisy and overstimulated environments. Ee Ming said, "Even as typically developing people, our energy level gets drained, so it's important to look for quiet and safe spaces so everyone has time to wind down during the outing."

Ludi laughed when she recalled the time they had just started going out together. As Keith has a habit of checking under seats repeatedly before he leaves places like the bus and MRT, both befrienders were at first confused and tended to hurry him off the subway carriage to avoid stares.

Over time, they began to understand that it was his way of being responsible, accountable and aware of his surroundings. Ee Ming said, "We would ask the bus driver to give us more time and say things like, 'Okay Keith. We understand why you're doing this. Checking is good, but only two times, three times okay?' More than once, Keith had helped Ludi rescue items she had left behind!

The pair have realised that they think they are the ones guiding him, but Keith has shown himself to be much more capable and independent than they give him credit for. They credit his amazingly 'chill', loving and supportive family, who has played a huge part in how Keith has become so independent.

To them, Keith is like a younger brother they look out for. "It's the same as getting to know a new person," said Ludi. "Only that the surprise element is amplified but that's part of what makes it so special!"

"ALWAYS CHECK IN"

Whether it is playing frisbee, bowling, kicking a football around or taking a walk in the park, Hongshin, Xinyu and Oliver can always be found doing a sports activity on their outings. They hardly hang out inside a shopping mall, because Oliver feels most comfortable outdoors.

For Hongshin, an illustrator and children's book author, it was his first brush with a youth with special needs. Xinyu, on the other hand, was looking to volunteer while in between jobs and wanted hands-on experience in the social sector space. Before this, she had only had brief encounters with people with autism.

One of their favourite moments was when they played football at the field at Buona Vista before a sudden downpour wrecked their plans and they had to race to the nearby Star Vista mall. Oliver liked to imitate their actions — he would copy how Hongshin ducked under a tree branch and the way he ran. He would even chuckle when Xinyu laughed. "It was very funny and memorable, I think it's a way of saying he's connected with us," said Hongshin.

Over time, Oliver has grown more comfortable with them. Once, while sitting at a quiet staircase at VivoCity, Oliver doodled over Hongshin's portrait of him. "At first, I was a bit stunned. I thought he was trying to erase my drawing, but I realised that maybe he wanted to make it collaborative," said Hongshin.

At another time, they noticed that Oliver was fine with the younger kids joining in their game while at Botanic Gardens. "That's when I saw he really opened up," said Xinyu, a programme coordinator.

From things like communicating with Oliver through a whiteboard, being very observant to non-verbal cues and building trust, the pair said they have learnt a lot from each other and from Oliver as well. For example, they learnt from Oliver's social worker how to use a whiteboard to communicate.

Reflected Hong Shin, "He is very sensitive to the emotions of others around him and internalises them. We realised it happens quite often so we give him a whiteboard to write down what he feels. It's a way to help him relax, so that he can express his feelings without fear of judgement."

Before every outing, the pair will write on the whiteboard what they plan to do for the day, like a word search, play football and then meet his dad. They have also progressed to let Oliver write down the schedule for the next outing, so he gets to choose where he wants to go next. Xinyu said, "It's important that he has the power to make the decision and have some ownership over it."

Hong Shin added that the pair constantly asks him whether he is tired, thirsty or wants to stop, as Oliver does not really express himself using words. Once at Bishan Park, Oliver hovered near the dog run. Knowing that he likes animals, both befrienders walked towards the dog run area and gently asked him, "Oliver, do you want to go?", to which he replied, "Yes."

Said Xinyu, "A lot of the time, as befrienders, we may think that he's interested in something but it's perceived on our side. We need to check in with him."

The pair have also had to adjust their tone and language while speaking to Oliver, so that they talk to him as if he is an adult, not a child. This includes giving Oliver more decision-making opportunities, rather than talk down to him as if he was a child.

"We are a bridge," summed up Hong Shin. "Often, we are quick to avoid someone who looks or behaves differently but these can be opportunities to approach, accommodate, and even engage them."

23 Hopes and Dreams

Kenneth Lyen, Faridah Ali Chang,
Manoj Pathnapuram, Tan Sze Wee
and Kenneth Poon

Singapore has come a long way in the setting up of early intervention, special education as well as other specialised programmes and services to support and care for autistic and developmentally challenged individuals. The Rainbow Centre has played a significant role in these areas since its establishment in 1987. Starting with a special school to serve students with multiple disabilities, it now caters to a wide range of developmental challenges and individuals on the autism spectrum. It has grown to encompass three schools, two early intervention programmes, two special student care centres, a training and consultancy centre. It provides speech therapy, music therapy, physiotherapy, occupational therapy, psychology and social work assistance, and it supports and trains caregivers. Our staff and board members contribute to planning committees of government ministries of Health, Education, Social and Community Development; and National Council of Social Service, as well as providing support in the setting up of other schools for these children and adults locally and across Asia. Here are some of our hopes and dreams for the future:

(a) Towards a Good Life
Our goal is to build good lives, lives that are empowered and thriving. Using the World Health Organization's definition of Quality of Life, we developed our Good Life Framework in 2019. Six domains have been identified, including: being safe, independent, healthy, connected, engaged, as well as being included and heard. Harnessing these principles, our interactions and dialogues with students and families have strengthened as they are better empowered to articulate their worries and aspirations.

(b) Early detection is key

With greater awareness and professionalisation of early intervention services, demand has been increasing grow as the number of children diagnosed with special needs rises. While the sector has made considerable strides over the past decades, we must continue to encourage families to be more open to intervention, so their children receive the help they need at an early stage.

(c) Amplifying the use of assistive technology

With more general awareness about the benefits of assistive technology, we believe that social service professionals, educators and caregivers must have knowledge and practice of how to use these technologies and innovative solutions, so that their children will be able to live more independently and participate more fully in school and outside of school. This means building their own knowledge of using the communication apps and devices, being more empathetic towards their child's speed of building his or her abilities to respond and adapt to new forms of communication, and collaborating with the various professionals working around the child.

(d) Making work possible

One area that has been challenging for young adults with autism and other developmental disabilities is to find and sustain employment. We have to make work possible for those we serve by educating employers on disability awareness, job support and accessibility efforts. More importantly, we must demonstrate the creation of new models of work — like microjobs — which will enable them to contribute meaningfully to society and spend their time productively after graduation. More effort must also be made to develop the talents of those who are inclined in the area of arts, music, sports or other fields of interest, so they can fulfil their potential.

(e) Supporting caregivers' emotional and mental well-being

Caregivers are the ultimate case manager of their child's development. We have to create more opportunities for coaching of families so that they can engage and connect with their developmentally challenged children meaningfully and functionally at home and in the community. Children often behave differently in different settings, and it can be difficult for caregivers to cope with the challenges. One must not forget that looking after them can place considerable stress not only on these individuals but also on other family members. We must create more channels of empowerment for caregivers systematically, enabling them to build resilience for the journey and become advocates, so that they in turn can confidently support others and become a rich resource for professionals.

(f) Advocating for a more inclusive society

Social inclusion and participation in authentic communities are critical to a good quality of life for persons with disabilities. Over the years, we have stepped up efforts to model, partner and train individuals and organisations to influence everyone's understanding of inclusion. At the heart of it, inclusion requires taking action to enable people with disabilities to feel valued and welcome. Inclusivity is a universal philosophy where we do not discriminate anyone according to their ability, gender, race, and beliefs. We are all part of the human family, and we should look after each other to our very best.

SUMMARY

Let us travel through time and look at the evolution and understanding in the way that our society has regarded and treated people with different challenges. We still have a long way to go, but slowly, step by step, we are making progress. Peering into the future, we aspire to see children and youth who have developed a deeper quality of life through meaningful education and community involvement. We watch parents and caregivers being actively involved in their child's development and education, and are encouraged that the general public is becoming more aware and supportive of people with disabilities. We see individuals participating as adults through supported employment, talent development, quality leisure activities and community engagement, at the same time being provided with appropriate forms of lifelong care, so that they can grow old gracefully and with dignity.

We invite all of you to join us on this journey to strive towards a world that is more inclusive and empowering for children and youth with disabilities!

Index

CPSIA information can be obtained
at www.ICGtesting.com
Printed in the USA
JSHW031136271122
33794JS00003B/240